A Kafka Bibliography 1908-1976

Other books on Kafka

edited by Angel Flores

THE KAFKA PROBLEM

FRANZ KAFKA TODAY
[co-editor Homer Swander]

THE PROBLEM OF "THE JUDGMENT"

THE KAFKA DEBATE

all published by Gordian Press, Inc.
85 Tompkins Street
Staten Island, N.Y. 10304

ANGEL FLORES

A *Kafka Bibliography*

1908-1976

New York
GORDIAN PRESS
1976

PUBLISHED BY GORDIAN PRESS, INC.
STATEN ISLAND, NEW YORK 10304

Library of Congress Cataloging In Publication Data

Flores, Angel, 1900—
    A Kafka bibliography, 1908-1976.

      1. Kafka, Franz, 1883-1924--Bibliography.
I. Title.
Z8459.28.F63 [PT2621]   016.833′9′12   76-21333
ISBN 0-87752-206-5

Preface

This bibliography consists of four sections.

Section I lists the few works which Kafka published in the course of his lifetime as well as those salvaged by his friend Max Brod after his death. Three stages in the assembling of his writings into "Collected Works," including letters and diaries, are then detailed; followed by an index to all of Kafka's works available in English, together with dates of composition.

Section II comprises all secondary sources in the major European languages.

Section III is a recapitulation of the entries dealing with biographical and background material, including his social, cultural and geographical milieu.

Section IV recapitulates all interpretative studies and commentaries on specific novels, stories, parables and fragments.

I wish to express my gratitude to Peter U. Beicken, Kate Flores, Richard Sheppard, Walter H. Sokel and the staff of Schocken Books for invaluable help and advice.

Angel Flores

March 1976
Palenville, New York 12463

Contents

I The Works of Kafka

[*Date of composition in brackets*]

[1] Published during his lifetime:

1908 "Betrachtung" [1904-1907]. Eight short pieces: Der Kaufmann, Zerstreutes Hinausschaun, Der Nachhauseweg, Die Vorüberlaufenden, Kleider, Der Fahrgast, Die Abweisung, Die Bäume. In the bi-monthly literary journal *Hyperion* (Munich), I, No. 1 (Jan.-Feb. 1908), 91-94.

1909 "Die Aeroplane in Brescia" [1909]. An account of an airplane flight which took place in Brescia, Italy. In the newspaper *Bohemia* (Prague), LXXXII, No. 269 (Sept. 29, 1909), 1-3.

"Gespräch mit dem Beter" and "Gespräch mit dem Betrunkenen" [1904-1905]. Two dialogues which constituted the opening section of "Beschreibung eines Kampfes." In *Hyperion,* I, No. 8 (Mar.-Apr. 1909), 126-131 and 131-133.

1910 "Betrachtungen" [1907-1910]. Five short pieces: Kleider, Der Fahrgast, Zum Nachdenken für Herrenreiter" and two previously published in *Hyperion* (1908): Zertreutes Hinausschaun (now retitled Am Fenster) and Die Vorüberlaufenden (now retitled In der Nacht). In *Bohemia,* LXXXIII, No. 86 (Mar. 27, 1910,) 39.

1912 "Die erste lange Eisenbahnfahrt." [1912]. Chapter I of "Richard and Samuel," a novel planned, but never completed, with Max Brod. In the monthly magazine *Herderblätter* (Prague), I, No. 3 (May 1912), 15-25.

1913 *BETRACHTUNG* (Meditation) [1904-1912]. Leipzig: Ernst Rowohlt Verlag, 1913 (printed and copyrighted in 1912), 99 pp. Kafka's first book; it contains eighteen pieces, most of which had appeared in *Hyperion* in 1908 and in *Bohemia* in 1910: Kinder auf der Landstrasse (Children on a Country Road), Entlarvung eines Bauernfängers (Unmasking a Confidence Trickster). Der plötzliche Spaziergang (The Sudden Walk). Entschlüsse (Resolutions). Der Ausflug ins Gebirge (Excursion into the Mountains). Das Unglück des Junggesellen (Bachelor's Ill Luck). Der Kaufmann (The Tradesman). Zerstreutes Hinausschaun (Absent-Minded Window-gazing). Der Nachhausweg (The Way Home). Die Vorüberlaufenden (Passers-by). Der Fahrgast (On the Tram). Kleider (Clothes). Die Abweisung (Rejection). Zum Nachdenken für Herrenreiter (Reflections for Gentlemen-Jockeys). Das Gassenfenster (The Street Window). Wunsch, Indianer zu werden (The Wish to Be a Red Indian). Die Bäume (The Trees). Unglücklichsein (Unhappiness).

1913 "Das Urteil" [1912]. In *Arkadia* (1913), a yearbook edited by Max Brod and published by Kurt Wolff in Leipzig, pp. 53-65.

DER HEIZER. EIN FRAGMENT (The Stoker. A Fragment) [1912]. Leipzig: Kurt Wolff Verlag, 1913, 47 pp. (Bücherei "Der jüngste Tag," Band 3).

1915 "Die Verwandlung" [1912]. In the monthly literary journal *Die Weissen Blätter* (Leipzig), II, No. 10 (Oct. 1915), 1177-1230.

DIE VERWANDLUNG (The Metamorphosis) [1912]. Leipzig: Kurt Wolff Verlag, 1915, 73 pp. (Bücherei "Der jüngste Tag," Band 22/23).

BETRACHTUNG (Meditation) [1904-1912]. Leipzig: Kurt Wolff Verlag, 1915, 99 pp., 2nd ed.

"Vor dem Gesetz" [1914]. In the journal *Selbstwehr* (Prague), IX, No. 34 (Sept. 7, 1915), 2.

1916 "Vor dem Gesetz" [1914]. In *Vom jüngsten Tag. Ein Almanach neuer Dichtung.* Leipzig: Kurt Wolff Verlag, 1916 [printed in 1915], 126-128.

DER HEIZER. EIN FRAGMENT (The Stoker. A Fragment) [1912]. Leipzig: Kurt Wolff Verlag, 1916, 47 pp., 2nd ed.

DAS URTEIL. EINE GESCHICHTE (The Judgment. A Story) [1912]. Leipzig: Kurt Wolff Verlag, 1916, 29 pp. (Bücherei "Der jüngste Tag," Band 34).

"Ein Traum" [1914/1915]. In *Das jüdische Prag. Eine Sammelschrift.* Prague: Verlag der "Selbstwehr," 1917 (really 1916), also reprinted in *Der Almanach der neuen Jugend auf das Jahr 1917.* Berlin: Verlag Neue Jugend, [1916], 189, and in *Prager Tagblatt* (Prague), Jan. 6, 1917.

1917   "Ein altes Blatt" [1917], "Der neue Advokat" [1917], and "Ein Brudermord" [1917]. In the bi-monthly publication *Marsyas* (Berlin), No. 1 (July-Aug. 1917, 80-83.

"Zwei Tiergeschichten: 1. Schakale und Araber [1917]. 2. Ein Bericht für eine Akademie [1917]." In *Der Jude* (the monthly journal edited by Martin Buber). (Berlin/Vienna) II, (Oct. 1917), 488-490, and (Nov. 1917), 559-565.

1918   "Ein Landarzt" [1917] and "Der Mord" [1917] (first draft of "Ein Brudermord"). In *Die neue Dichtung. Ein Almanach.* Leipzig: Kurt Wolff Verlag, 1918 (really 1917), 17-26 and 72-76.

DER HEIZER. EIN FRAGMENT (The Stoker. A Fragment) [1912]. Leipzig: Kurt Wolff Verlag, 1917/1918, 47 pp., 3rd ed.

DIE VERWANDLUNG (The Metamorphosis) [1912]. Leipzig: Kurt Wolff Verlag, 1918 (Copyrighted 1917), 75 pp., 2nd ed.

1919   *IN DER STRAFKOLONIE* (In the Penal Colony) [1914]. Leipzig: Kurt Wolff Verlag, 1919, 71 pp.

"Eine kaiserliche Botschaft" [1917]. In the weekly publication *Selbstwehr* (Prague), XIII, No. 38-39 (Sept. 14, 1919), 4.

"Die Sorge des Hausvaters" [1917]. In *Selbstwehr,* XIII, No. 51-52 (Dec. 19, 1919).

EIN LANDARZT. KLEINE ERZAHLUNGEN (A Country Doctor) [1914-1917]. Munich/Leipzig: Kurt Wolff Verlag, 1919, 189 pp. Contains 14 short pieces: Der neue Advokat (The New Advocate). Ein Landarzt (A Country Doctor). Auf der Galerie (Up in the Gallery). Ein altes Blatt (An Old Manuscript). Vor dem Gesetz (Before the Law). Schakale und Araber (Jackals and Arabs). Ein Besuch im Bergwerk (A Visit to a Mine). Das nächste Dorf (The Next Village). Eine kaiserliche Botschaft (An Imperial Message) Die Sorge des Hausvaters (The Cares of a Family man). Elf Söhne (Eleven Sons). Ein Brudermord (A Fratricide). Ein Traum (A Dream). Ein Bericht für eine Akademie (A Report to an Academy)

1920　*DAS URTEIL* (The Judgment) [1912]. Munich: Kurt Wolff Verlag, 1920, 29 pp., 2nd ed.

1921　"Der Kübelreiter" [1917]. In *Prager Presse* (Prague), Jg. 1921, No. 270 (Dec. 25, 1921), 22.

"Erstes Leid" [1921]. In the journal *Genius. Zeitschrift für werdende und alte Kunst* (Munich), III, No. 2 (1921, really 1922), 312 ff.

1922　"Ein Hungerkünstler" [1922]. In the monthly journal *Die neue Rundschau* (Berlin/Leipzig), (Oct. 1922), 983-992.

1924　"Josefine, die Sängerin" [1924]. In *Prager Presse* (Prague), Jg. 1924, No. 110 (Apr. 20, 1924), 4-7.

EIN HUNGERKÜNSTLER. VIER GESCHICHTEN (A Hunger Artist. Four Stories) [1921-1924]. Berlin: Verlag Die Schmiede, 1924, 86 pp. The four stories: Erstes Leid (First Sorrow). Eine kleine Frau (A Little Woman). Ein Hungerkünstler (A Hunger Artist). Josefine, die Sängerin oder Das Volk der Mäuse (Josephine the Singer, or the Mouse Folk).

[2] Posthumous:

Der Prozess (The Trial) [1914]. Berlin: Verlag Die Schmiede, 1925, 411 pp.; Berlin: Schoken, 1935, 286 pp.; N.Y.:

Schocken, 1946, 287 pp.; Frankfurt: Fischer, 1950 and 1953, 328 pp.; Frankfurt: Fischer Bücherei, 1960, N.Y.: Schocken, 1957, 1965; Frankfurt: Fischer Taschenbuch No. 676, 1975 (13th ed).

Das Schloss (The Castle) [1922]. Munich: Kurt Wolff Verlag, 1926; 504 pp.; Berlin: Schocken, 1935, 425 pp.; N.Y.: Schocken, 1946, 429 pp.; Frankfurt: Fischer, 1951, 499 pp.; Frankfurt: Fischer Bücherei, 1968, N.Y.: Schocken, 1965; Frankfurt: Fischer Taschenbuch No. 900, 1975 (9th ed).

Amerika (Amerika) [1912]. Munich: Kurt Wolff Verlag, 1927, 392 pp.; Berlin: Schocken, 1935, 315 pp.; N.Y.: Schocken, 1946, 315 pp.; Frankfurt: Fischer, 1953, 362 pp.; Frankfurt: Fischer Bücherei, 1956, 235 pp.; Berlin: Rütten & Loening, 1967, 317 pp.; Frankfurt: Fischer, 1966.

Beim Bau der chinesischen Mauer (The Great Wall of China) [1917]. Berlin: Gustav Kiepenhauer Verlag, 1931, 266 pp.; Cologne: Kiepenhauer, 1948, 252 pp. The original edition contained twenty-two pieces: Beim Bau der chinesischen Mauer (The Great Wall of China). Zur Frage der Gesetze (The Problem of Our Laws). Das Stadtwappen (The City Coat of Arms). Von den Gleichnissen (On Parables). Die Wahrheit über Sancho Pansa (The Truth about Sancho Panza). Das Schweigen der Sirenen (The Silence of the Sirens). Prometheus (Prometheus). Der Jäger Gracchus (The Hunter Gracchus). Der Schlag ans Hoftor (The Knock at the Manor Gate). Eine Kreuzung (A Sport). Die Brücke (The Bridge). Kleine Fabel (A Little Fable). Eine alltägliche Verwirrung (A Common Confusion). Der Kübelreiter (The Bucket Rider). Das Ehepaar (The Married Couple). Der Nachbar (My Neighbor). Der Bau (The Burrow). Der Riesenmaulwurf (The Giant Mole)—same as Der Dorfschullehrer. Forschungen eines Hundes (Investigations of a Dog). "Er" ("He"). Betrachtungen über Sünde, Leid, Hoffnung und den wahren Weg (Reflections on Sin, Pain, Hope, and the True Way). Nachwort (von M.B. und H.J. Sch.) (Afterword by Max Brod and Hans Joachim Schoeps).

Vor dem Gesetz (Before the Law) [1914-1922]. Berlin: Schocken, 1934, 80 pp. Contains: Von den Gleichnissen (About Parables). Vor dem Gesetz (Before the Law). Beim Bau der chinesischen Mauer (The Great Wall of China). Josefine, die Sängerin, oder das Volk der Mäuse (Josephine the Singer, or the Mouse Folk). Bericht für eine Akademie (A Report to an Academy). Nachwort von H.P. (Afterword by Heinz Politzer).

Erzählungen und kleine Prosa (Short Stories and Short Prose Pieces) [1904-1924]. Berlin: Schocken, 1935, 280 pp.; N.Y.: Schocken, 1946, 287 pp.; Frankfurt: Fischer, 1952, 334 pp. Contains: Gespranïch mit dem Beter (Conversation with the Supplicant). Gespräch mit dem Betrunkenen (Conversation with the Drunken Man). All the pieces of *Betrachtung* (Meditation). Das Urteil (The Judgment). Die Verwandlung (The Metamorphosis). All the stories of *Ein Landarzt* (A Country Doctor). In der Strafkolonie (In the Penal Colony). All the stories of *Ein Hungerkünstler* (A Hunger Artist). Die erste lange Eisenbahnfahrt (The First Long Train Journey).

Beschreibung eines Kampfes. Novellen, Skizzen, Aphorismen aus dem Nachlass (Description of a Struggle) [1904-1917]. Prague: Heinrich Mercy Sohn, 1936, 319 pp.; N.Y.: Schocken, 1946, 336 pp.; Frankfurt: Fischer, 1953, 336 pp. Contains: Beschreibung eines Kampfes (Description of a Struggle). All the stories in *Beim Bau der chinesischen Mauer* (The Great Wall of China). Die Abweisung (The Refusal). Poseidon (Poseidon). Der Geier (The Vulture). Der Aufbruch (The Departure). Gibs auf! (Give It Up!). Nachts (At Night). Der Steuermann (The Helsman). Der Kreisel (The Top). Die Prüfung (The Test). Fürsprecher (Advocates). Heimkehr (Homecoming). Gemeinschaft (Fellowship). Blumfeld, ein älterer Junggeselle (Blumfeld, an Elderly Bachelor), and the short play Der Gruftwächter (The Warden of the Tomb); *Beschreibung eines Kampfes. Die zwei Fassungen Parallelausgabe nach den Handschriften.* Ed. by Ludwig Dietz. Afterword by Max Brod. Frankfurt: S. Fischer, 1969.

Tagebücher und Briefe (Diaries and Letters) [1910-1923]. Prague; Heinrich Mercy Sohn, 1937, 351 pp.; N.Y.: Schocken, 1946, 351 pp. Contains selections from Kafka's diaries and notebooks; travel notebooks; an autobiographical sketch; and Fragment zum "Bericht für eine Akademie" (Fragment of "A Report to an Academy"). Fragment zum "Bau der Chinesischen Mauer" (Fragment of "The Great Wall of China"). Die Truppenaushebung (The Conscription of Troops). Fragment zum "Jäger Gracchus" (Fragment of

"The Hunger Gracchus"). In unserer Synagoge (In our Synagogue). Neue Lampen (New Lamps). Das Schwert (The Sword). Betrachtungen über Sünde, Leid, Hoffnung und den wehren Weg (Reflections on Sin, Pain, Hope, and the True Way). Meditationen (Reflections), and letters to Oskar Pollak. Oscar Baum, Felix Weltsch, Robert Klopstock, Max Brod, and Elsa Brod.

Der Heizer (The Stoker) [1912]. Berlin: Neue Geist, 1947, 48 pp.; Zurich: Verlag der Arche, 1954, 47 pp.

Tagebücher 1910-1923 (Diaries 1910-1923) [1910-1923]. N.Y.: Schocken, 1951, 737 pp.; Frankfurt: Fischer, 1951, 737; Frankfurt: Fischer, 1967, 737 pp.; Frankfurt: Fischer Bücherei, 1973. Diaries and travel journals.

Das Urteil und andere Erzählungen (The Judgment and Other Stories) [1912-1913]. Frankfurt: Fischer Bücherei, 1952, Frankfurt: Fischer Taschenbuch No. 19, 1975 (37th ed).

Briefe an Milena (Letters to Milena [1920-1923]. Ed. by Willy Haas. Frankfurt: Fischer, 1952, 287 pp.; N.Y.: Schocken, 1952, 287 pp.; Frankfurt: Fischer Bücherei, 1966.

Erzählungen (Short Stories) [1904-1924]. Frankfurt: Fischer, 1952, 287 pp.; Frankfurt: Fischer Bücherei, 1966, Frankfurt: Fischer Taschenbuch No. 756, 1974 (7th ed).

Hochzeitsvorbereitungen auf dem Lande und andere Prosa aus dem Nachlass (Wedding Preparations in the Country and Other Posthumous Prose) [1907-1920]. Frankfurt: Fischer, 1953, 456 pp.; N.Y.: Schocken, 1953, 456 pp. Contains: Hochzeitsvorbereitungen auf dem Lande (Wedding Preparations in the Country). Betrachtungen über Sunde, Leid, Hoffnung und den wehren Weg (Reflections on Sin, Pain, Hope and the True Way). Die 8 Oktavhefte (The Eight Octavo Notebooks). Brief an den Vater (Letter to his Father). Fragmente aus Heften und losen Blättern (Fragments from Notebooks and Loose Pages). Paralipomena (Paralipomena). Rede über die jiddische Sprache (Speech on the Yiddish Language).

Die Verwandlung (Metamorphosis) [1912]. Wiesbaden: Insel Bücherei, 1958, 73 pp.

Briefe 1902-1924 (Letters 1902-1924). Ed. by Max Brod.

Frankfurt: Fischer, N.Y.: Schocken, 1958, 531 pp.; Frankfurt: Fischer Taschenbuch, 1975.

Erzählungen und Skizzen (Short Stories and Sketches) [1907-1920]. Ed. by Klaus Wagenbach. Darmstadt: Moderner Buch-Club, 1959, 159 pp.

Die Verwandlung (Metamorphosis) [1912]. Ed. by Majorie L. Hoover. N.Y.: W.W. Norton, 1960, 90 pp.

Brief an den Vater (Letter to his Father) [1919]. Afterword by Wilhelm Emrich. Munich: Piper-Bücherei, 1960, 71 pp.; Frankfurt: Fischer Taschenbuch No. 1629, 1975.

Die kaiserliche Botschaft (The Imperial Message) [1917]. Ed. by J. Mühlberger. Graz/Vienna: Stiasny-Bücherei, 1960, 128 pp.

Die Erzählungen (The Short Stories) [1904-1924]. Ed. by Klaus Wegenbach. Frankfurt: Fischer, 1961.

Die Verwandlung (The Metamorphosis) [1912]. Ed. by C.F. Brookes and C.E. Fraenkel. London: Heinemann Educational Series, 1962.

Er (He) [1917-1919]. Ed. by Martin Walser. Frankfurt: Suhrkamp, 1963, 224 pp. Anthological excerpts: stories, parabels. Brief an den Vater (Letter to his Father). Afterword: "Arbeit am Beispiel" by Martin Walser.

Short Stories [1912-1924]. Ed. by J.M.S. Pasley. Oxford University Press, 1963. Contains: Das Urteil (The Judgment), Vor dem Gesetz (Before the Law). Auf der Galerie (Up in the Gallery). Ein altes Blatt (An Old Page). Eine kaiserliche Botschaft (An Imperial Message). Die Sorge des Hausvaters (The Cares of a Family Man). Ein Berich für eine Akademie (A Report to an Academy). Erstes Leid (First Sorrow). Ein Hungerkünstler (A Hunger Artist). Josefine, die Sängerin, oder Das Volk der Mäuse (Josephine the Singer, or the Mouse Folk).

Erzählungen. Der Prozess. Das Schloss (Short Stories. The Trial. The Castle) [1904-1923]. Afterword by Klaus Hermsdorf. Berlin: Rumtten & Loening, 1965, 820 pp. Contains: Short stories, *The Trial* and *The Castle*.

Sieben Prosastücke (Seven Prose Pieces) [1912-1924]. Ed. and interpreted by Franz Baumer. Munich: Kösel, 1965, 135 pp. Contains: Vor dem Gesetz (Before the Law). Auf der Galerie (Up in the Gallery). Das Urteil (The Judgment). Ein Landarzt (A Country Doctor). Beim Bau der chinesischen Mauer (The Great Wall of China). Der Bau (The Burrow). Ein Hungerkünstler (A Hunger Artist).

Die Romane. Amerika. Der Prozess. Das Schloss. (The Novels: Amerika, The Trial, The Castle). [1912-1922]. Frankfurt: S. Fischer, 1965, 1969, 1974, 816 pp.

Das Kafka-Buch. Eine innere Biographie in Selbstzeugnisses (The Kafka Book). Ed. by Heinz Politzer. Frankfurt: Fischer Bücherei, 1965, 271 pp. Autobiographical excerpts: a kind of Kafka par lui-même; Frankfurt: Fischer Taschenbuch No. 708, 1975 (10th ed.).

Der Heizer, In der Strafkolonie, Der Bau (The Stoker, In the Penal Colony, The Burrow) [1912, 1914, 1923/1924]. Ed. by Malcolm Pasley. Cambridge University Press, 1966, 152 pp.

Briefe an Felice und andere Korrespondenz aus der Verlobungzeit (Letters to Felice [Bauer], [Grete Bloch, and others]) [1912-1917]. Ed. by Erich Heller and Jürgen Born. Frankfurt: Fischer, 1967, 784 pp.; N.Y.: Schocken, 1967, 784 pp.; Frankfurt: Fischer Taschenbuch No. 1697, 1976.

Tagebücher 1910-1923 (Diaries 1910-1923) [1910-1923]. Frankfurt: S. Fischer, 1967 (Die Bücher der neunzehn); Frankfurt: Fischer Bücherei, 1973.

Dichter über ihre Dichtungen: Franz Kafka (Writers on their Art: F.K.) Ed. by Erich Heller and Joachim Beug. Munich: Heimeran, 1969, 186 pp. Kafka's comments on his craft.

Der Prozess. (The Trial) [1914]. Ed. by H.F. Brookes and C.E. Gawne-Cain. London: Heinemann, 1969, 217 pp.

Sämtliche Erzählungen (Collected Short Stories) [1904-1924]. Ed. by Paul Raabe. Frankfurt: Fischer Bücherei, 1970, 406 pp.; Frankfurt: Fischer Taschenbuch, No. 1078, 1975 (10th ed.).

Meistererzählungen (Collected Short Stories) [1904-1924]. Ed. by Paul Raabe. Frankfurt: S. Fischer, 1972, 447 pp.

Der Heizer (The Stoker) [1912]. Ed. by Wolfgang Klimke. Paderborn: Schöningh Verlag, 1972, 46 pp.

Der Prozess (The Trial) [1914]. Ed. by Martin Pfeiffer. Hollfeld/Ofr.: Bange, 1972, 320 pp. (Königs Erl, 209).

Die Verwandlung (Metamorphosis) [1912]. Frankfurt: Bibliothek Suhrkamp, 1973, 91 pp.

Der Heizer (The Stoker) [1912]. Frankfurt: Bibliothek Suhrkamp, 1975, 84 pp.

Briefe an Ottla und die Familie (Letters to Ottla and the Family) [1909-1924]. Ed. by Klaus Wagenbach and Harmut Binder. Frankfurt: S. Fischer, 1975, 248 pp.

In der Strafkolonie (In the Penal Colony). Ed. by Klaus Wagenbach. Berlin: Wagenbachs Taschenbücherei, 1975, 94 pp.

Collected Works

The contents of these volumes have been itemized above.

Gesammlete Schriften (Collected Writings). Ed. by Max Brod with the assistance of Heinz Politzer, 6 vols.: Vol. I-IV published in Berlin by Schocken, 1935 and Vol. V-VI published in Prague by Henry Mercy Sohn, 1936-1937.

    Vol. I   *Erzählungen und kleine Prosa* (Short Stories and Short Prose Pieces)

    Vol. II   *Amerika* (Amerika)

    Vol. III   *Der Prozess* (The Trial)

    Vol. IV   *Das Schloss* (The Castle)

    Vol. V   *Beschreibung eines Kampfes* (Description of a Struggle)

    Vol. VI   *Tagebücher und Briefe* (Diaries and Letters)

Gesammelte Schriften (Collected Writings). Ed. by Max Brod. N.Y.: Schocken, 1946, 5 vols.

    Vol. I   *Erzählungen und kleine Prosa* (Short Stories and Short Prose Pieces).

    Vol. II   *Amerika* (Amerika)

Vol. III   *Der Prozess* (The Trial)
Vol. IV   *Das Schloss* (The Castle)
Vol. V   *Beschreibung eines Kampfes* (Description of a Struggle)

Gesammelte Werke (Collected Works). Ed. by Max Brod and Others. N.Y.: Schocken, 1950-; Frankfurt: Fischer, 1950-

Vol. I   *Der Prozess* (The Trial)
Vol. II   *Das Schloss* (The Castle)
Vol. III   *Tagebücher 1910-1923* (Diaries 1910-1923)
Vol. IV   *Briefe an Milena* (Letters to Milena)
Vol. V   *Erzählungen* (Short Stories)
Vol. VI   *Amerika* (Amerika)
Vol. VII   *Hochzeitsvorbereitungen auf dem Lande und andere Prosa* (Wedding Preparations in the Country and Other Prose Pieces)
Vol. VIII *Beschreibung eines Kampfes* (Description of a Struggle)
Vol. IX   *Briefe 1901-1924* (Letters 1901-1924)
Vol. X   *Briefe an Felice und andere Korrespondenz aus der Verlobung* (Letters to Felice)
Vol. XI   *Briefe an Ottla und die Familie* (Letters to Ottla and the Family)

[3] *In English translation:*

Abraham (Abraham). P, 40-45.

Absent-minded Window-gazing (Zerstreutes Hinausschaun) [1907]. PC, 33; CS, 387. Also tr. by Muriel Kittel as "Fleeting Glimpse," QRL, 174-175.

The Advocates (Fürsprecher) [Feb. 1922]. DS, 210-214; CS, 449-450; SW1, 145-147.

The Aeroplanes at Brescia (Die Aeroplane in Brescia) [Sept. 1909]. GW, 299-311; PC, 299-311. Also tr. by G. Humphreys Roberts, in Max Brod: *F.K. A Biography.* N.Y.: Schocken, 1947, 221-230.

Alexander the Great (Alexander der Grosse). P, 94-95.

Amerika (Amerika) [Oct.-Nov. 1912]. Tr. by Willa and Edwin
Muir. Preface by Klaus Mann. Afterword by Max Brod.
London: Routledge & Kegan Paul, 1938, 317 pp.; London:
Secker, 1946, 1949, 312 pp.; N.Y.: New Directions, 1940, 299
pp., 1946, 277 pp.; N.Y.: Anchor Books, 1955, 301 pp.
[paperback]; London: Secker & Warburg, 1949 (definitive
ed); 1961, and Penguin Books, 1967; N.Y.: Schocken 1962
[paperback].

The Angel (Ein Engel). [1914]. D 2, 62-64.

The Animal in the Synagogue [Das Tier in der Synagoge]. P,
48-59.

At Night (Nachts) [1920]. DS, 202; CS, 436; SW 1, 125.

Autobiographical Sketch (Skizze einer Selbstbiographie). Tr
by Sophie Prombaum. FKM, 51-54. Cf. "Resumé" in Max
Brod: *F.K. A Biography,* 248-249.

Bachelor's Ill Luck (Das Unglück des Junggesellen) [1911]. PC,
30; CS, 394.

Bauz the Director (Bauz, der Direktor) [1914]. D2, 73-75.

Before the Law (Vor dem Gesetz) [Dec. 1914]. P, 60-79, PC, 30;
CS 3. Also tr. by Philip Horton, in Horace Gregory (ed.):
New Letters in America. N.Y.: Norton, 1947, 145-150.

Blumfeld, an Elderly Bachelor (Blumfeld, ein älterer Junggeselle) [1915]. DS, 97-145, CS, 183-205, SW1, 19-39. Also tr.
by Philip Horton. *Partisan Review,* VI, No. 1 (Fall 1938), 54-
65, and VI, No. 2 (Winter 1939), 96-102.

The Bridge (Die Brücke) [Dec. 1916]. GW. 231-232, CS, 411,
SW1, 50-51.

Bruder, a City Official (Der Magistratsbeamte Bruder) [1914].
D2, 44-46.

The Bucket Rider (Der Kübelreiter) [Feb. 1917]. GW, 233-237,
PC, 184-187, CS, 412-413. Also tr. by G. Humphreys
Roberts as "The Scuttle-Rider." *Life and Letters* (London),
(Dec. 1938), 49.

The Building of a City (Der Bau einer Stadt), P, 100-105.

The Building of the Temple (Der Tempelbau), P, 42-47.

The Burrow (Der Bau) [Nov.-Dec. 1923]. GW, 79-147; SS, 256-304, CS, 325-359, M, 129-166, SW1, 192-225.

The Cares of a Family Man (Der Sorge des Hausvaters) [1917]. PC, 160-161, CS, 427-428.

The Castle (Das Schloss) [Jan.-Sept. 1922]. Tr. by Willa and Edwin Muir. London: Secker & Warburg, 1930, 450 pp.; 1939, 1942, 1947, 1953; N.Y.: Knopf, 1930, 340 pp.; 1941 (with an Introduction by Thomas Mann); 1946, 1949, 1951; 1958; N.Y.: Modern Library, 1969; Penguin Books, 1957, 1961, 1962, 1963, 1964, 1966, 1968, 1970, 1974, 304 pp.; N.Y.: Schocken Books, 1974 (paperback).

The Cell (Die Zelle), P, 116-117.

Children on a Country Road (Kinder auf der Landstrasse) [1904/1905]. PC, 21-25; CS, 379-381. Also tr. by Muriel Kittel as "Children on the Highway." QRL, 175-177.

A Chinese Puzzle (Ein Gedulspiel), P, 176-179.

The City Coat of Arms (Das Stadtwappen) [1920]. GW, 245-247; P, 36-39; CS, 433; SW1, 120-121.

Clothes (Kleider), [1904/1905]. PC, 36, CS, 382.

The Collected Aphorisms, same as Reflections on Sin, Pain, Hope and the True Way.

The Coming of the Messiah (Das Kommen des Messias), P, 80-81.

A Comment (Ein Kommentar) [Dec. 1922]. SW1, 190, same as Give it up! (Gibs auf!)

A Common Confusion (Eine alltägliche Verwirrung) [Oct. 1917]. GW, 229-230; SS, 157-158; CS, 429. Tr. as An Everyday Occurrence, SW1, 103-104.

The Complete Stories. Ed. by N.N. Glatzer. N.Y.: Schocken, 1971, 486 pp.

The Conscription of Troops (Die Truppenaushebung) [1920]. DS, 229-233; CS, 439-440. SW1, 134-136. Tr. by Olga Marx as The Conscription. QRL, 209-210.

Conversation with the Supplicant (Gespräch mit dem Beter) [1904/1905]. PC, 9-17.

A Country Doctor (Ein Landarzt) [1917]. PC, 136-143, SS, 148-156, CS, 220-225. Also tr. by M.B. QRL, 183-188.

Couriers (Kuriere), P, 174-175.

A Crossbreed (Eine Kreuzung) [Spring 1917]. CS, 426; SW1, 80-81. Tr. also as A Sport.

The Dancer Eduardova (Die Tänzerin Eduardowa) [1910]. D1, 9-10.

Dearest Father. Stories and Other Writings. Tr. by Ernst Kaiser and Eithne Wilkins. N.Y.: Schocken Books, 1954, 409 pp. [Contains Wedding Preparations in the Country; Reflections on Sin, Suffering, Hope, and the True Way; The Eight Octavo Notebooks; Letter to his Father; Fragments from Notebooks and Loose Pages; Paralipomena. Published in England as *Wedding Preparations in the Country*. London: Secker & Warburg, 1954, 409 pp.

The Departure (Der Aufbruch) [Feb. 1922]. DS, 200; CS, 449; SW1, 144.

Description of a Struggle. Tr. by Tania and James Stern. N.Y.: Schocken Books, 1958, 241 pp. [Contains Description of a Struggle; Blumfeld, an Elderly Bachelor; The Warden of the Tomb; The Refusal; and 15 short pieces; *Description of a Struggle and the Great Wall of China.* London: Secker & Warburg, 1960, 345 pp.

Description of a Struggle (Beschreibung eines Kampfes) [1904/1905], DS, 9-96, CS, 9-51.

Diaries (Tagebücher). Vol. I. 1910-1913. Tr. by Joseph Kresh. N.Y.: Schocken, 1948, London: Secker & Warburg, 1948. 345 pp.

Vol. II. 1914-1923. Tr. by Martin Greenberg, with the co-operation of Hannah Arendt, N.Y.: Schocken, 1949; London: Secker & Warburg, 1949 343 pp.; and selections from Vol. I and II, as *The Diaries of F.K. 1910-1923.* Penguin Books, 1964, 519 pp.; 1972.

Diogenes (Diogenes), P, 94-95.

A Dream (Ein Traum) [1914]. PC, 170-172, CS, 399-400.

The Eight Octavo Notebooks (Die Acht Oktarhefte), DF, 50-135.

Eleven Sons (Elf Söhne) [1917]. PC, 161-167, CS 419-423.

The Emperor (Der Kaiser), P, 108-109.

Ernst Liman (Ernst Liman) [1913]. D1, 280-284.

An Everyday Occurrence, same as A Common Confusion.

Everything Theater (Lautes Theater) [1911]. D1, 142-144.

Excursion into the Mountains (Der Ausflug ins Gebirge). [1904/1905]. PC 29-30, CS, 383.

Fellowship (Gemeinschaft) [1920]. DS, 217-218; CS, 435; SW1, 124.

The First Long Train Journey (Die erste lange Eisenbahnfahrt) [1911]. first chapter of the unfinished novel "Richard and Samuel," written in collaboration with Max Brod. PC, 281-298.

First Sorrow (Erstes Leid) [1921/1922]. PC, 231-234, CS, 446-448. Also tr. by Lillian F. Turner as "First Grief". *Life and Letters* (London), (Summer 1937), 57-59.

Fragments from Notebooks and Loose Papers (Fragmente aus Heften und losen Blättern). DF. 198-376.

A Fratricide (Ein Brudermord) [1917]. PC, 167-170; SS, 165-167; CS, 402-403.

The Giant Mole (Der Riesenmaulwurf—original title Der Dorfschullehrer) [Dec. 1914-Jan. 1915]. GW, 174-201; M, 203-218; tr. as The Village Schoolmaster, CS, 168-182; SW1, 5-18.

Give it up! (Gibs auf!) [Dec. 1922]. DS, 201; CS. 456; Same as A Comment (Ein Kommentar), SW1, 190.

The Great Wall of China and Other Pieces. Tr. by Willa and Edwin Muir. London: Martin Secker, 1933, 286 pp.; as *The Great Wall of China. Stories and Reflections.* London: Secker & Warburg, 1946 and N.Y.: Schocken, 1946

[Contains "Investigations of a Dog," "The Burrow," "The Great Wall of China," "The Giant Mole," 15 short stories, and Aphorisms: "He" and "Reflections on Sin, Pain, Hope, and the True Way."], 1948 and 1970, 307 pp.

The Great Wall of China (Beim Bau der chinesischen Mauer) [1917]. GW, 148-173; SS, 129-147; CS, 235-247; M, 67-81; SW1, 63-75.

The Great Wall of China, Fragment (Fragment zum Bau der chinesischen Mauer). DS, 226-228; CS, 248-249.

The Green Dragon (Der grüne Drache), P, 150-151.

Gustav Blenkelt (Gustav Blenkelt) [1912]. D1, 276-277.

Hans and Amalia (Hans und Amalia) [1916]. D2, 148-152.

He (Er) [Jan.-Feb. 1920]. GW, 263-277; SW1, 109-119.

The Helmsman (Der Steuermann) [Nov. 1920]. DS, 203-204; CS, 443; SW1, 140.

Homecoming (Heimkehr) [Aug. 1920]. DS, 215-216; CS, 445; SW1, 143.

A Hunger Artist (Ein Hungerkünstler) [1922]. PC, 243-256; SS, 188-201; CS, 268-277. Also tr. by H. Steinhauer, in H. Steinhauer and Helen Jessiman (eds): *Modern German Short Stories.* Oxford University Press, 1938, 203-217; and by M.L. Nielson. *Rocky Mountain Review,* (Winter 1946), 80-89.

The Hunter Gracchus (Der Jäger Gracchus) [Dec. 1916/Apr. 1917]. P, 122-135; GW, 205-214; SS, 181-187; CS, 226-230; SW1, 52-60.

The Hunter Gracchus, A Fragment (Der Jäger Gracchus, Ein Fragment) [Apr. 1917]. P, 136-141; D2, 170; DS, 234-241; CS, 231-234.

The Hunter Strike (Die Unersätttlichsten), P, 186-187.

Hyperion (Hyperion). GW, 315-317.

I Am a Memory Come Alive (Autobiographical Writings). Ed. by Nahum N. Glatzer. N.Y.: Schocken, 1974, 264 pp.

"I walked through a long row of houses" (Ich ging durch eine lange Häuserreihe) [1911]. D1, 88-90.

The Imperial Colonel (Der kaiserliche Oberst) P, 106-109.

An Imperial Message (Eine kaiserliche Botschaft) [1917]. P, 12-15; PC, 158-159; CS, 4.

In the Caravansary (In der Karawanserei). P. 110-115.

In the Penal Colony (In der Strafkolonie) [Oct. 1914]. PC, 191-227; SS, 90-128; CS, 140-167; and as "In the Penal Settlement," M, 169-199. Also tr. by Eugene Jolas. *Partisan Review* (N.Y.), (Mar. 1941), 98-107 and (Apr. 1941), 146-158; and *Horizon* (London), (Mar. 1942), 158-183.

In the Penal Colony, Fragments (In der Strafkolonie, Fragmente) [1917]. D2, 178-181.

In the Penal Settlement. Tales and Short Prose Works. London: Secker & Warburg, 1949 and 1972, 298 pp.

In the Theater (Im Theater) [1911]. D1, 153-156.

An Introductory Talk on the Yiddish Language [Feb. 18, 1912]. (Notes taken by Mrs. Elsa Brod). DF, 381-386.

The Invention of the Devil (Die Erfindung eines Teufels) [July 1912]. P, 118-119; D1, 264-265.

Investigations of a Dog (Forschungen eines Hundes) [Jul. 1922]. GW, 3-78; SS, 202-255; CS, 278-316; M, 85-126; SW1, 148-184.

Jackals and Arabs (Schakale und Araber) [1917]. PC, 150-154; CS, 407-410. Also tr. by Mimi Bartel. *New Directions Yearbook*. N.Y.: New Directions, 1942, 408-412.

Joseph the Coachman (Der Kutscher Josef. [1914]. D2, 31-33.

Josephine the Singer, or the Mouse Folk (Josefine, die Sängerin, oder Das Volk der Mäuse) [Mar. 1924]. PC, 256-277; SS, 305-328; CS, 360-378. Also tr. by Clement Greenberg as "Josephine the Songstress." *Partisan Review* (N.Y.) (May/Jun. 1942), 213-228.

The Judgment (Das Urteil) [Sept. 1912]. PC, 49-63; SS, 3-18; CS, 77-88. Also tr. by Rosa M. Beuscher and Kate Flores as "The Sentence." QRL, 189-198.

The Knock at the Manor Gate (Der Schlag ans Hoftor) [1917]. GW, 242-244; CS, 418; SW1, 76-77.

The Landlady (Die Nermieterin) [May 1914], D2, 36-37.

Leopards in the Temple (Leoparden in Tempel). P, 92-93.

Letters to Felice (Briefe an Felice und andere Korrespondez aus
der Verlobungszeit) [Sept. 20, 1912-Oct. 16, 1917]. Ed. by
Erich Heller and Jürgen Born; tr. by James Stern and
Elizabeth Duckworth. N.Y.: Schocken, 1973, London:
Secker & Warburg, 1974, 592 pp.

Letter to his Father (Brief an den Vater) [Nov. 1919]., bilingual
ed., tr. by Ernst Kaiser and Eithne Wilkins. N.Y.: Schocken,
1966, 3rd ed. 1970, 127 pp.; DF, 138-196.

Letters to Milena (Briefe an Milena) [1920-1923]. Ed. by Willy
Haas. Tr. by Tania and James Stern. N.Y.: Schocken, 1953;
London: Secker & Warburg, 1953, 238 pp. Also in paper-
back.

A Little Fable (Kleine Fabel) [Nov.-Dec. 1920]. GW, 260; CS,
445; SW1, 142.

A Little Woman (Eine kleine Frau) [Oct. 1923]. PC, 234-243;
CS, 317-324. Also tr. by Francis C. Golffing. *Accent*
(Urbana, Ill.), (Summer 1943), 223-227.

The Married Couple (Das Ehepaar) [1922]. GW, 215-224; CS,
451-455; SW1, 185-189.

Memoirs of the Kalda Railroad (Erinnerung an die Kaldabahn)
[1914]. D2, 79-91.

The Merchant Messner (Der Kaufmann Messner) [1913]. D1,
312-314.

The Metamorphosis (Die Verwandlung) [Nov. 1912]. PC, 67-
132; SS, 19-89; M, 9-63; CS, 89-139. Also tr. by Eugene Jolas.
Transition (Paris), No. 25 (Fall 1936), 27-38, No. 26 (Winter
1937), 53-72 and No. 27 (Apr.-May 1938), 79-103. Also tr. by
A.L. Loyd as *The Metamorphosis*. London: The Parton
Press, 1937, 74 pp., and as *Metamorphosis,* N.Y.: The
Vanguard Press, 1946, 98 pp.; *Metamorphosis and Other
Stories*. Penguin Books, 1961, 1963, 1964, 1965, etc.;
bilingual ed., tr. by Willa and Edwin Muir. N.Y.: Schocken,
1968, also in paperback; *The Metamorphosis. A Critical
Edition,* ed. and tr. by Stanley Corngold. N.Y.: Bantam
Books, 1972, 202 pp.

Mount Sinai (Der Berg Sinai), P, 44.

My Destination (Das Ziel), P, 188-189.

My education has done me great harm (Meine Erziehung in mancher Richtung sehr geschadet hat) [1910]. D1, 14-22.

My Neighbour (Der Nachbar) [Spring 1914]. GW, 225-228; D2, 37-38; CS, 424-425; SW1, 78-79.

My Visit to Dr. Steiner (Mein Besuch bei Dr. Steiner) [1911]. D1, 57-59.

The New Advocate (Der neue Advokat) [1917]. PC, 135-136; SS, 159-160; CS, 414. Also tr. by Clement Greenberg as "The New Attorney," P, 96-99.

New Lamps (Neue Lampen) [1917]. SW1, 82-83. Also tr. by Olga Marx. QRL, 207-208.

The News of the Building of the Wall, A Fragment (Die Nachricht vom Mauerbau, Ein Fragment). P, 96-99.

The Next Village (Das nächste Dorf) [Winter 1916-1917]. PC, 158; CS, 404.

An Old Manuscript (Ein altes Blatt) [1917]. PC, 145-147; SS, 161-164; CS, 415-417. Also tr. by Sophie Prombaum as "An Old Page." FKM, 67-69.

On Kleist's "Anecdotes" (Über Kleists Anekdoten) [1911]. GW, 314-315.

On Parables (Von den Gleichnissen) [1922/1923]. GW, 258-259; CS, 457; P, 10-11; SW1, 191.

On the Tram (Der Fahrgast) [1907]. PC, 35-36; CS, 388.

Parables (Parabolen). German and English text. Tr. by Willa and Edwin Muir, and Clement Greenberg. N.Y.: Schocken, 1947; enlarged bilingual ed. retitled *Parables and Paradoxes,* ed. by Nahum N. Glatzer. N.Y.: Schocken, 1961 (7th printing, 1970), also paperback.

Paradise (Das Paradies). P, 28-33.

Paralipomena (Paralipomena). DF, 378-393.

Passers-by (Die Vorüberlaufenden) [1907]. PC, 34-35; CS, 388. Tr. also by Muriel Kittel as "The Runners." *QRL,* 182.

The Penal Colony. Stories and Short Pieces. Tr. by Willa and Edwin Muir. N.Y.: Schocken, 1948, 1949 (also paperback) 320 pp.; with the title *In the Penal Settlement.* Tr. by Ernst Kaiser and Eithne Wilkins. London: Secker & Warburg, 1949, 1973, 298 pp.

The Pit of Babel (Das Schact von Babel), P, 34-35.

Poseidon (Poseidon) [1920]. P, 84-87; DS, 195-197; CS, 434; SW1, 122-123. Also tr. by Joseph Kresh. *New Directions Yearbook, No. 9.* N.Y.: New Directions, 1946, 140-141.

The Problem of Our Laws (Zur Frage des Gesetze) [1920]. GW, 254-257; CS, 437-438; P, 154-159; SW1, 131-133.

The Proclamation [Dec. 1916]. SW1, 61-62.

Prometheus (Prometheus) [Jan. 1918]. GW, 251-252; CS, 432; SW1, 108.

Reflections for Gentlemen-Jockeys (Zum Nachdenken für Herrenreiter) [1909/1910]. PC, 37-38; CS, 388.

Reflections on Sin, Pain, Hope, and the True Way (Betrachtungen über Sünde, Leid, Hoffnung und den wahren Weg— so titled by Max Brod) [1917/1918]. GW, 278-307; DF, 34-48; tr. as The Collected Aphorisms, SW1, 84-102.

Rejection (Die Abweisung) [Oct. 1920] CS. 263-267; DS, 179-191. Tr. as "The Refusal", P. 160-175; SW1, 126-130.

A Report to an Academy (Ein Bericht für eine Akademie) [May-Jun. 1917]. PC, 173-187; SS, 168-180; CS, 250-258. Also tr. by William A. Drake as "A Report for an Academy." *The Literary World* (N.Y.), (July 1934), 4-5; and by Rosa M. Beuscher and Kate Flores. QRL, 199-206.

A Report to an Academy, Fragments (Ein Bericht für eine Akademie, Fragmente). DS, 219-225; CS, 259-262.

Resolutions (Entschlüsse) [1912]. PC, 28-29; CS, 398; D1, 229-230.

Robinson Crusoe (Robinson Crusoe). P, 184-185.

The Savages (Die Wilden). P, 120-121.

Selected Short Stories. Tr. by Willa and Edwin Muir. N.Y.: The Modern Library, 1952, 328 pp. [Contains 15 short stories].

Shorter Works. Vol. I. Tr. and ed. by Malcolm Pasley. London: Secker & Warburg, 1974, 225 pp. [Contains 37 pieces].

The Silence of the Sirens (Das Schweigen der Sirenen) [Oct. 1917]. P, 88-91; GW, 248-250; CS, 430-432; SW1, 106-107.

A Singular Judicial Procedure (Sonderbarer Gerichsgebrauch) [1916] D2, 162-163.

The Sirens (Die Sirenen). P, 92-93.

A Sport (Eine Kreuzung) [May-June 1917]. GW, 238-241; tr. as "A Crossbreed", CS, 426; WS 80-81.

The Spring (Die Quelle). P, 184-185.

The Street Window (Das Gassenfenster) [1906/1909]. PC, 39; CS, 384.

The Sudden Walk (Der plötzliche Spaziergang) [Jan. 1912]. PC, 27-28; CS, 397; D1, 214.

The Sword (Das Schwert) [1915]. D2, 109-110. Also tr. by Olga Marx. QRL, 208.

Temptation in the Village (Verlockung im Dorf) [1914]. D2, 48-58.

The Test (Die Prüfung) [1920]. DS, 207-209; CS, 441; P, 180-183; SW1, 137-138.

The Thief (Dieb!) [1914]. D2, 71-72.

The Tiger (Der Tiger). P, 152-153.

The Top (Der Kreisel) [Nov. 1920]. DS, 205-206; CS, 444; SW1, 141.

The Tower of Babel (Der Turm zu Babel). P, 34-35.

The Tradesman (Der Kaufmann) [1907 ?]. PC, 31-33; CS, 385.

The Trees (Die Bäume) [1904/1905]. PC, 39-40; CS, 382. Also tr. by Muriel Kittel, QRL, 181.

The Trial (Der Prozess) [Jul.-Dec. 1914]. Tr. by Willa and Edwin Muir. London: Victor Gollancz, 1937, 285 pp.; N.Y.: Knopf, 1937, 296 pp.; 1944; 1945; 1947; 1948; 1950; 1951; 1955; 1957 definitive ed. with additional material tr. by E.M. Butler: "Unfinished Chapters," "Passages Deleted by the

Author" and "Postscripts" by Max Brod; London: Secker &
Warburg, 1945, 199 pp.; 1947; 1950; 1956 definitive ed.;
Penguin Books, 1953, 1955, 1960, 1962, 1963, 1965, 1966,
1969, 1970; N.Y.: Schocken: 1968 [paperback]. N.Y.:
Modern Library, 1964; Geneva: Edito-Service, distributed in
London by Heron Books, 1968, 281 pp.; N.Y.: Vintage Books,
1969.

The Tricycle and the Automobile (Das Tricycle und die
Automobile) [1911]. D2, 283-287.

Trip to Friedland and Reichenberg (Reise Friedland und
Reichenberg) [1911]. D2, 237-243.

Trip to Switzerland, Italy, Paris, and Erlenbach (Reise
Lugano-Paris-Erlenbach) [1911]. D2, 244-283.

Trip to Weimar and Jungborn (Reise Weimar-Jungborn)
[1912]. D2, 287-315.

The Truth about Sancho Panza (Die Wahrheit über Sancho
Pansa) [Oct. 1917]. P, 178-179; GW, 253; CS, 430; SW1, 105.

Unhappiness (Unglücklichsein) [1910]. PC, 40-45; CS, 390-393.
Also tr. by Muriel Kittel as "Being Unhappy." QRL, 178-181.

Unmasking a Confidence Trickster (Entlarvung eines Bauernfängers) [1911/1912]. PC, 25-27; CS, 395-396.

Up in the Gallery (Auf der Galerie) [Winter 1916/1917]. PC,
144-145; CS, 401.

The Urban World (Die städtische Welt) [Feb. 1911]. D1, 47-54.

The Village Schoolmaster, same as The Giant Mole, CS, 168-
182; SW1, 5-18.

A Visit to a Mine (Ein Besuch im Bergwerk) [Jan./Feb. 1917].
PC, 155-158; CS, 404-406.

The Vulture (Der Geier) [Nov. 1920]. DS, 198-199; CS, 443; P,
148-149; SW1, 139. Also tr. by G. Humphreys Roberts.
Twice a Year (N.Y.), No. 1 (Fall-Winter 1938), 129-131; and
by Joseph Kresh. *New Directions Yearbook No. 9.* N.Y.:
New Directions, 1946, 140.

The Warden of the Tomb (Der Gruftwächter) [Dec. 1916]. DS,
147-178; CS, 206-219; SW1, 40-49.

The Watchman (Der Wächter). P, 80-81.

The Way Home (Der Nachhausweg) [1907]. PC, 34. Also tr. by Muriel Kittel. QRL, 182.

Wedding Preparations in the Country and Other Posthumous Prose Writings. (Hochzeitsvorbereitungen auf dem Lande). Tr. by Ernst Kaiser & Eithne Wilkins. London: Secker & Warburg, 1954, 446 pp., rep. 1973. Contains Wedding Preparations in the Country; The 8 Octavo Notebooks; Letter to his Father; Fragments from Notebooks and Loose Papers; Paralipomena.

Wedding Preparations in the Country (Hochzeitsvorbereitungen auf dem Lande) [1907]. DF, 2-31; CS, 52-76.

The White Horse (Das weisse Pferd) [May 1914]. D2, 34-35.

Wilhelm Menz, a Bookkeeper (Wilhelm Menz, ein junger Buchhalter), [1914] D1, 306-307.

The Wish to Be a Red Indian (Wunsch, Indianer zu weredn) [1909/1910]. PC, 39; CS, 390. Also tr. by Muriel Kittel as "A Wish to Be an Indian." QRL, 174.

"You," I said, and gave him a little shove with my knee ("Du," sagte ich und gab ihm einen kleinen Stoss mit den Knie) [1910]. D1, 22-29.

II About Kafka

A

Ackermann, Paul K.: "A History of Critical Writing on F.K."
GQ, XXIII (Mar. 1950), 105-113.

Adams, Robert M.: "Swift and Kafka," in his *Strains of
Discord. Studies in Literary Openness.* Cornell University
Press, 1958, 168-179.

Adeane, Louis: "The Hero Myth in Kafka's Writing." *Fo,* 48-
56.

Adolf, Helen: "From *Everyman* and *Elckerlijc* to Hofmannsthal and Kafka." *CL,* IX (1957), 204-214.

Adorno, Theodor W.: "Aufzeichnungen zu Kafka." *NR,*
LXIV, No. 4 (July-Sept. 1953), 325-353, rep. in his
Prismen. Frankfurt: Suhrkamp, 1955, 325-353; 1967 and
1969 eds. 302-342; tr. by Samuel Munchen and Shierry
Weber as "Notes on Kafka," in *Prisms.* London:
Spearman, Neville, 1967, 245-272.

Albach, Horst: "Zum Bild des Kaufmanns bei Kafke." *DU,*
XX, No. 5 (1968), 52-60.

Alberès, R.M. and Pierre de Boisdeffre: *F.K.* Paris: Editions
Universitaires, 1960, 126 pp., tr. by Wade Baskin as *Kafka:
The Torment of Man.* London: Vision, 1968, 105 pp.,
N.Y.: Citadel, 1968 (paperback), 105 pp.

Albrecht, Erich A.: "Zur Entstehungsgeschichte von Kafkas
'Landartz'." *Monatshefte,* XLVI, No. 4 (Apr.-May 1954),
207-212; "Kafka's *Metamorphosis*-Realiter," in *Homage
to Charles Blaise Qualia.* Lubbock, Texas: Texas Tech
Press, 1962, 55-64.

Allemann, Beda: "Kafka: *Der Prozess,*" in Benno von Wiese (ed).: *Der deutsche Roman von Barock bis zur Gegenwart.* Düsseldorf: Bagel, 1963, 2 vols., Vol. II, 234-290; "Kafka: 'Von den Gleichnissen'." *ZDP,* LXXXIII (Oct. 1963), 97-106; "Kafka et l'histoire," in *L'endurance de la pensée, pour saluer Jean Beaufret.* Paris, 1968, 75-89.

Allen, Walter: "A Note on F.K." *Fo,* 30-33.

Almasy, Miklos: "Diskussion in Kafkas Schloss," in Bela Kopeczi and Peter Juhasz (eds): *Littérature et realité.* Budapest: Akademiai K, 1966, 204-215.

Altenhöner, Friedrich: *Der Traum und die Traumstruktur im Werk F.Ks.* Münster University, 1962 (typ dis).

Alves, Jorge Ruy: *Interpretaçao de Kafka.* Sao Paulo: Oren, 1968, 269 pp.

Amann, Jürg J.: *Das Symbol K. Eine Studie über den Künstler.* Bern/Munich: Francke, 1974, 173 pp.

Anceschi, Luciano: "Intorno a un modo di leggere Kafka," in his *Poetica americana e altri studi contemporanei di poetica.* Pisa: Nistri-Lischi, 1954, 111-122.

Anders, Gunther: "F.K.: Ritual without Religion." *Commentary,* VIII (Dec. 1949), 560-569. *Kafka Pro und Contra.* Munich: C.H. Beck, 1951, 109 pp., 1963, 1969, 1972; tr. by A. Steer and A.K. Thorlby as *Franz Kafka.* London: Bowes & Bowes, 1960, and N.Y.: Hillary House, 1960, 104 pp.; "Reflections on my Book *Kafka Pro und Contra.*" *Mosaic,* II, No. 4 (Summer 1970), 59-72.

Anderson, Barbara: "F.K.'s *The Trial.*" *Bard Review,* I (Summer 1946), 24-30.

Angel, Pierre: "L'Obsession bureaucratique chez Kafka." *EG,* XVII, No. 1 (1962). 1-13.

Angress, R.K.: "Kafka and Sacher-Masoch: A Note on *The Metamorphosis.*" *MLN,* LXXXV, No. 5 (Oct. 1970), 745-746.

Angus, Douglas: "Kafka's *Metamorphosis* and *The Beauty and the Beast* Tale." *JEGP,* LII, No. 1 (Jan. 1954), 69-71; "The Existentialist and the Diabolical Machine." *Criticism,* VI (1964), 134-143.

Aranguren, José Luis: "F.K." *Arbor* (Madrid), XX, No. 71 (1951), 222-233.

Arbeitskreist: *Interpretation zu F.K.* Munich: Oldenbourg Verlag, 1969 (Interpretationen zum Deutschunterricht).

Arcoleo, Sandro: "Presenza di F.K." *Idea* (Rome), XXII (1966), 211-213.

Aréga, Leon: "L'Arpenteur." *Roman* (St. Paul-de-Vence), 10 (1953), 782-789.

Arendt, Hannah: "The Jew as Pariah: A Hidden Tradition." *Jewish Social Studies* (N.Y.), VI (Apr. 1944), 99-122; "F.K.: A Revaluation." *Part,* XI (Fall 1944), 412-422, tr. as "F.K., von neuem gewürdigt." *Wand,* 1, No. 12 (Dec. 1946), 1050-1062, and rep. in her *Sechs Essays.* Heidelberg: L. Schneider, 1948, 128-149.

Arntzen, Helmut: "F.K.: *Der Prozess,"* in his *Der moderne deutsche Roman.* Heidelberg: W. Rothe, 1962, 76-100; "F.K.: 'Von den Gleichnissen'." *ZDP,* LXXXIII (Oct. 1963), 106-112.

Aschka, Friedrich: "Vergleich mit Kafkas *Prozess,"* in his *Die Zeit und die Erscheinung des Menschen im dichterischen Weltentwurf.* Erlangen University, 1959 (typ dis), 118-126.

Asher, J.A.: "The Abuse of F.K." *JAU,* No. 4 (1956), 10-14; "Turning Points in Kafka's Stories." *MLR,* LVII, No. 1 (Jan. 1962), 47-52.

Auden, W.H.: "The Wandering Jew." *The Nation* (N.Y.), (Feb. 10, 1941), 185-186; "K's Quest." *KP,* 47-52; "The I without a Self." *H,* 39-44.

Avery, George C.: "Die Darstellung des Künstlers bei F.K.," in Eduard Goldstücker (ed): *Weltfreunde: Konferenz über die Prager deutsche Literatur.* Berlin: Luchterhand, 1967, 229-239.

Azancot, Leopoldo: "Borges y Kafka." *Indice* (Madrid), XVII, No. 170 (1963), 6.

B

Babler, O.F.: "Frühe tschechische Kafka-Publikationen." *SR*, LIX (Oct. 1959). 369-373.

Backenköhler, Gerd: "Neues zum 'Sorgenkind, *Odradek'*." *ZDP*, LXXXIX, No. 2 (1970), 269-273.

Bahr, Erhard: "Kafka and the Prague Spring." *Mosaic*, III, No. 4 (Summer 1970), 15-29; "Kafka und der Prager Frühling." *PFK*, 516-538.

Baioni, Giuliano: *Kafka. Romanzo e parabola.* Milan: Feltrinelli, 1962, 299 pp.; "Introduzione" to *Opere di Franz Kafka.* Milan: Bompiani, 1974, ix-xiv.

Baker, James R.: *"The Castle:* A Problem in Structure." *TCL,* III (Jul. 1957), 74-77.

Balascheff, Pierre: "Contemporary Figures: F.K." *Colosseum* (London) V (Apr.-Jun. 1939), 139-142.

Bangerter, Lowell A.: "'Der Bau.' Frankz Kafka's Final Punishment." *RS*, 42 (1974), 11-19.

Bansberg, Dietger: "Durch Lüge zur Wahrheit." *ZDP*, 93 (1974), 257-269.

Bänziger, Hans: "'Der Bau'." *Merkur*, XI, No. 107 (1957), 38-49.

Bar-David, Yoram: "Kafka, le célibataire tsaddik (juste). *Reevue de l'Allemagne*, 5(1973), 767-684.

Barnes, Hazel: "Myth and Human Experience." *Classical Journal*, LI (Dec. 1955), 121-127.

Barrault, Jean-Louis: "Cas de conscience devant Kafka." *CCMR*, L (1965), 71-82.

Barthes, Roland: *Essais critiques.* Paris: Editions du Seuil, 1964, 138-142, tr. by R. Howard as *Critical Essays.* University of Illinois Press, 1972, 133-137, and in *H*, 140-143.

Basil, Otto: "Umriss von F.K." *Wort und Tat* (Innsbruck/Vienna), I, No. 2 (Sept. 1946), 98-104.

Bataille, Georges: "F.K. devant la critique communiste."

Critique (Paris), VI, No. 41 (Oct. 1950), 22-36; *La Littérature et le mal.* Paris: Gallimard, 1957, 159-182.

Batt, Kurt: "Neue Literatur zum Werk F.Ks." *NDL*, X, No. 12 (1962), 29-35.

Baudy, Nicolas: "Entretiens avec Dora Dymant." *Evidences* (Paris), No. 8 (Feb. 1950), 21-25.

Bauer, Gerhard: "Nochmals: historisch-materialistische Literatur-wissenschaft, mit Kafka als Zeugen für den Klassenkampf." *Alternative*, XV, No. 84-85 (1972), 102-111; "Literatur als Teil Klassenkampfes in Historizitat." *Sprache & Literatur*, (1974), 209-218.

Bauer, Johann: *Kafka und Prag*, with photographs by Isidor Pollak. Stuttgart: Belser, 1971, 190 pp., tr. by P.S. Falla as *Kafka and Prague.* London: Pall Mall Press, 1971 and N.Y.: Praeger, 1971, 191 pp.

Bauer, Roger: "Kafka a la lumière de la religiosité juive." *Dieu Vivant* (Paris), IX (1947), 105-120.

Baum, Oskar: "F.K." *Der Jude* (Vienna/Berlin), VIII (1924), 482-483; "Erinnerungen an F.K." *Witiko* (Kassel-Wilhelmshöhe), II (1929), 126-128; "Recollections," *KP,* 25-31.

Baumer, Franz: *F.K.* Berlin: Colloquium Verlag, 1960, 96 pp., tr. by Abraham Farbstein as *F.K.,* N.Y.: Ungar, 1971, 122 pp.; *Sieben Prosastücke.* Munich: Kosel, 1965 [Texts of 'Vor dem Gesetz,' 'Auf der Galerie,' 'Das Urteil,' 'Ein Landarzt,' 'Beim Bau der chinesischen Mauer,' 'Der Bau,' and 'Ein Hungerkünstler,' with interpretations].

Baumgaertel, Gertrud: "F.K.: Transformation for Clarity." *RLV*, XXVI (1960), 266-283.

Baumgartner, Walter: "Kafkas Strindberglektüre." *Scandinavica*, VI (1967), 95-107; "Kafka und Strindberg." *Nerthus: Nordisch-deutsche Beiträge,* (Dusseldorf), II (1969), 9-51.

Baxandall, Lee: "Kafka and Radical Perspective." *Mosaic,* III, No. 4 (Summer 1970), 73-79; "The Radical Perspective," *KD.*

Beck, Evelyn T.: *Kafka and the Yiddish Theater: Its Impact on his Work.* University of Wisconsin Press, 1971, 248 pp.

Bedwell, Carol B.: "The Forces of Destruction in Kafka's 'Ein altes Blatt'." *Monatshefte,* LVIII, No. 1 (1966), 43-48.

Beebe, Maurice: *Literary Symbolism.* San Francisco, 1960, 130-142 [On "A Country Doctor"]; (and Naomi Christensen): "Criticism of F.K.: A Selected Checklist." *MFS,* VIII, No. 1 (Spring 1962), 80-100.

Beharriell, Frederick J.: "Kafka, Freud und 'Das Urteil'," in Manfred Durzak and others (eds.): *Texte und Kontexte.* Festschrift für Norbert Fürst. Bern: Francke, 1973, 27-47.

Beicken, Peter U.: *Perspektive und Sehweise.* Stanford University, 1971, (typ dis, 535 pp.); *F.K. Eine kritische Einführung in die Forschung.* Frankfurt: Athenaion, 1974, 453, and as a paperback: Frankfurt: Athenäum Fischer Taschenbuch Verlag, 1974, 453 pp.; "Kafka's Narrative Rhetoric," *KD.*

Beissner, Friedrich: *Der Erzähler F.K.* Stuttgart: W. Kohlhammer, 1952, 51 pp., (4th ed, 1961); *Kafka der Dichter.* Stuttgart: W. Kohlhammer, 1958, 44 pp. (2nd ed., 1961), tr. in part as "Kafka the Artist," *GK,* 15-31; *Der Schacht von Babel: Aus Kafkas Tagebüchern.* Stuttgart: W. Kohlhammer, 1963; *Kafkas Darstellung des "traumhaften innern Lebens".* Bebenhausen: 1972, 43 pp.

Belgion, Montgomery: "The Measure of Kafka." *Criterion* (London), XVIII (Oct. 1938), 13-28.

Benjamin, Walter: *Gesammelte Schriften.* Frankfurt: Suhrkamp, 1955, 2 vols., Vol. II, 196-228; "F.K.: Zur zehnten Wiederkehr seines Todestages," and "F.K.: 'Beim Bau der chinesischen Mauer'," and "Brief an Gershon'," in his *Über Literatur.* Frankfurt: Suhrkamp, 1969, 154-185, 186-193, and 194-202, tr. by Harry Zohn as "F.K.: On the Tenth Anniversary of his Death," and "Some Reflections on Kafka," in Walter Benjamin: *Illuminations.* N.Y.: Harcourt, Brace & World, 1968 and N.Y.: Schocken (paperback), 1968, 111-140 and 141-148; "Le théatre en plein air d'Oklahoma." *CCMR,* 31-41; "F.K.", *PFK,* 143-158.

Bense, Max: *Die Theorie Kafkas.* Cologne: Kiepenheuer & Witsch, 1952, 117 pp.

Benson, Ann T.: *The American Criticism of F.K., 1930-1948.* University of Tennessee, 1958 (typ dis); "F.K.: An American Bibliography." *Bulletin of Bibliography* (Boston), XXII (Jan.-Apr. 1958), 112-114.

Berence, Fred: "Prague de Kafka." *Evidences* (Paris). V, No. 36 (Dec. 1953), 42-45.

Berendsohn, Walter A.: "August Strindberg und Franz Kafka." *DV,* XXXV (1961), 630-633.

Bergel, Lienhard: "Blumfeld, an Elderly Bachelor," *KP,* 172-178; "The Burrow," *KP,* 199-206; "Max Brod and Herbert Tauber," *KP,* 179-180; *Amerika:* Its Meaning," *FKT,* 117-125.

Berger, Hans: "Franz Kafka und die Lebensqual" in *Untergang und Aufgang.* Karlsruhe: Der Karlsruhe Bote, 1968, 65-107 and 142-143.

Bergmann, Samuel Hugo: "Erinnerungen an F.K." *Univ,* XXVII (1972), 739-750.

Bernheimer, Charles: "The Text as Suspension: Reflexive Structures in *The Castle.*" *KD.*

Berté, Antonio: *Commento a Kafka.* Naples: Società Editrice Napoletana, 1975.

Best, Otto E.: "Zweimal Schule der Körperbeherrschung und drei Schriftseller." *MLN,* LXXXV, No. 5 (1970), 134-137.

Beutner, Barbara: *Die Bildsprache Franz Kafkas.* Munich: W. Fink, 1973, 328 pp.

Bezzel, Christoph: *Natur bei Kafka. Studien zur Ästhetik des poetischen Zeichens.* Nuremberg: Hans Carl, 1964, 132 pp.; *Kafka-Chronik. Daten zu Leben und Werk.* Munich: Carl Hanser Verlag, 1975, 217 pp. *Die Freude Kafkas beim Bügeln. Die Freude Mozarts beim Kegeln. Die Freude Bismarcks beim Stricken. Ein Trilogie.* Munich: Hanser, 1972, 192 pp.

Biegel, Daniel: *"Faut-il bruler Kafka?"* *Action* (Paris), No. 99 (Jul. 26, 1946).

Biemel, Walter: *Philosophische Analysen zur Kunst der Gegenwart.* The Hague: Nijhoff, 1968, 263 pp. [On "In der Strafkolonie, 1-37; "Ein Hungerkünstler," 38-65; "Der Bau," 66-140].

Biesel, Herbert: "F.K.: Von Sündenfall und Krankheit der Erlösenden," in his *Dichtung und Prophetie.*, 1972, 109-135.

Billeter, Fritz: *Das Dichterische bei Kafka und Kierkegaard.*

Ein typologischer Vergleich. Winterthur: Keller, 1965, 206 pp.

Binder, Hartmut: *Motiv und Gestaltung bei Franz Kafka.* Bonn: Bouvier, 1966, 406 pp.; "Franz Kafka und die Wochenschrift *Selbstwehr." DV,* XLI (1967), 283-305; "Franz Kafka and the Weekly Paper *Selbstwehr." Publications of the Leo Beck Institute, Yearbook XII* (1967), 134-148; "Kafkas literarische Urteil: Ein Beitrag zu seiner Typologie und Ästhetik." *ZDP,* LXXXVI, No. 2 (1967), 211-249; "Kafkas Hebräischstudien." *JDSG,* XI (1967), 527-556; "Kafka und *Die Neue Rundschau." JDSG,* XII (1968), 94-111; "Kafka und seine Schwester Ottla." *JDSG,* XII (1968), 403-456; "Kafkas Briefscherze: Sein Verhältnis zu Joseph David." *JDSG,* XIII (1969), 536-559; "Kafka und die Skulpturen." *JDSG,* XVI (1972), 623-647; *Kafka Kommentar zu sämtlichen Erzählungen.* Munich: Winkler, 1975, 346 pp.; "'Der Jäger Gracchus': Zu Kafkas Schaffensweise und poetischer Topographie." *JDSG,* XV (1971), 375-440: "Kafka und Napoleon." *Festschrift für Friedrich Beissner.* Bebenhausen: Rotsch, 1974, 38-66; "The Judgment," *PJ.*

Binion, Rudolph: "What the Metamorphosis Means." *Sym,* XV (Fall 1961), 214-220.

Birch, Joan: "Aspects of Narrative Prose Sentence Style in Kafka's *Das Schloss* and Mann's *Doktor Faustus,"* in Ralph W. Baldner (ed.): *Proceedings: Pacific Northwest Conference on Foreign Literature,* (Victoria) Vol. XXI (1970), 190-202; *Dimension of Narrative Prose Sentence Style in Kafka's "Das Schloss" and Mann's "Doctor Faust." DAI,* 30 (1970) 5428 A (Texas, Austin).

Blanchot, Maurice: "La lecture de Kafka." *L'Arche* (Paris), No. 11 (Nov. 1945), 107-116; "Kafka et la littérature." *Les Cahiers de la Pléiade* (Paris), (Spring 1949), 93-105, both of these essays rep in his *La part du feu.* Paris: Gallimard, 1949, 345 pp., 9-19 and 20-34 (also contains "Le langage de la fiction" [On *The Castle*], 80-91) "Kafka et la exigence de l'oeuvre." *Critique,* VIII, No. 58 (Mar. 1952), 195-221, rep in his *L'Espace littéraire.* Paris: Gallimard, 1955, 52-81, tr. as *"The Diaries:* The Exigency of the Work of Art." *FKT,* 195-200; "Le dehors, la nuit." *La Nouvelle NRF,* No. 11 (1953), 877-885 [On "The Burrow"]; "Kafka et Brod." *La*

Nouvelle NRF, No. 22 (1954), 695-707, rep. in his *L'Amitié.* Paris: Gallimard, 1971, 272-325; "Franz Kafka et le 'procès' de la littérature," in F.K.: *Oeuvres complètes.* Paris: Cercle du Livre Précieux, 1963-1965, 8 vols., Vol. VIII, 219-256; *L'Entretien Infini.* Paris: Gallimard: 1969, contains "La fin de héros," 540-555; "La voix narrative," 556-567, and "Le pont de bois," 568-582; "Reading Kafka," *JRT.*

Blei, Franz: "F.K." in his *Zeitgenössische Bildnisse.* Amsterdam: Allert de Lange, 1940, 328-339.

Blengio Brito, Raúl: *Aproximación a Kafka.* Montevideo: Editorial Letras, 1969, 141 pp.

Blumenberg, Hans: "Der absolute Vater." *Hoch* XLV, No. 3 (1953), 282-284.

Bo, Carlo: *Rifflessioni critiche.* Florence: Sansone, 1953, 149-169.

Bödeker, Karl B.: *Frau und Familie im erzählerischen Werk Franz Kafkas.* Bern/Frankfurt: Lang, 1974, 177 pp.

Boden, Gérard: *Franz Kafka. Aspects de son oeuvre.* Algiers: Librairie Chaix, 1947, 55 pp.

Boeschenstein, Hermann: "Emil Utitz, der Philosoph aus dem Prager Kreis." *Rice University Studies* (Houston, Texas), LVII, No. 4 (1971), 19-32.

Boisdeffre, Pierre de: "Kierkegaard et Kafka." *Revue de Paris,* LXII (July 1955), 138-142; "La tragédie de la solitude chez Kierkegaard et chez Kafka." *Civitas* (Immensee), XI (Mar.-Apr. 1956), 341-346; "Kafka, face au mariage." *TR,* No. 150 (Jun. 1960), 65-73; *Les écrivains de la nuit.* Paris Plon, 1973, 101-151.

Bondanella, Peter E.: "F.K. and Italo Svevo." *PCLS,* 17-34.

Bonnet, Gerard: "Le Procès ou la métamorphose." *TM,* No. 201 (1963), 1513-1523.

Borchardt, Alfred: *Kafkas zweites Gesicht/Der Unbekannte/Das grosse Theater von Oklahoma.* Nuremberg: Glock & Lutz, 1960, 203 pp.

Borges, Jorge Luis: "Prefacio" to his translation of F.K.: *La Metamorfosis.* Buenos Aires; Editorial Losada, 1938, 7-11; "Kafka y sus precursores," *La Nación* (Buenos Aires), (Aug. 7, 1951), rep. in his *Otras inquisiciones, 1937-1952.*

Buenos Aires: Sur, 1952, 126-128; tr. as "Kafka and his Precursors," in his *Labyrinths*. N.Y.: New Directions, 1962, and *H*, 18-20; also as "View Points: Origins of *"The Castle,"* in his *Other Inquisitions, 1937-1952*. University of Texas Press, 1964, 101-102.

Borgese, G.A.: "In Amerika con Kafka," in his *Da Dante a Thomas Mann*. Milan, 1958, 253-259.

Born, Jürgen: "Max Brod's Kafka." *BA*, XXXIII (Autumn 1959), 389-396; [and Others]: *Kafka-Symposium*. Berlin: Wagenbach, 1965; "Franz Kafka und Felice Bauer: Ihre Beziehung im Spiegel des Briefwechsels 1912-1917." *ZDP*, 86 (1967), 176-186; "Vom 'Urteil' zum *Prozess:* Zu Kafkas Leben und Schaffen in den Jahren 1912-1914." *ZDP*, 86 (1967), 186-196; "Das Feuer zusammenhängender Stunden: Zu Kafkas Metaphorie des dichterischen Schaffens" in Wolfgang Paulsen (ed.): *Das Nachleben der Romantik*. Heidelberg: Stiehm, 1969, 177-191; "Kafka's Parable 'Before the Law'." *Mosaic* III, No. 4 (Summer 1970), 153-162; "Franz Kafka und seine Kritiker (1912-1924)" *KS*, 127-159; "Kafkas unermüdliche Rechner." *Euphorion*, 64 (1970), 404-413; "Thomas Mann's Homage to Franz Kafka." *OGS*, VII (1973), 109-118. "Kafka," in Helmut Olles (ed.): *Literaturlexikon 20. Jahrhundert*. Reinbek / Hamburg: Rowohlt Taschenbuch, 1971, Vol. II, 420-425; Review of Klaus Ramm: *Reduktion als Erzählprinzip bei Kafka. Monatshefte*, LXVI (1974), 440-443.

Bornmann, Bianca Maria: "Le 'Lettere a Felice' di Kafka." *RLMC*, XXI (1968), 245-290; "Un esempio di ironia in Kafka." *SG*, VII, No. 1 (1969), 93-96 [On *Betrachtung*]; "Momenti classici nell'opera di Kafka." *AION-SG*, XVI, No. 2 (1973), 7-24.

Bradley, Brigitte L.: "Analysis of a Fragment by Kafka / Reflections on the Theme of the Barrier." *GR*, XLIV (1969), 259-272.

Brandstetter, Alois: "Zum Gleichnisreden der Dichter: Hermeneutik einer kafkaschen Parabel." *Zeitschrift für Studierende* (Vienna), XXI (1966), 107-118.

Braun, Günther: "Franz Kafkas Aphorismen: Humoristische Meditation der Existenz." *DU*, XVIII, No. 3 (1966), 107-118.

Braybrooke, Neville. "Celestial Castles: An Approach to Saint Teresa and Franz Kafka," *Dublin Review*, CCXXIX No. 470 (1955), 427-445; "The Geography of the Soul: Saint Teresa and Kafka," *Dalhousie Review* (Halifax, N.S.), XXXVIII (1958), 324-330; "Within the Soul: Teresa of Avila and Franz Kafka." *Renascence* XIII (1960), 26-32.

Breton, André: "Kafka" in *Anthologie de l'humour noir*. Paris: J.J. Pauvert, 1966, 439-460.

Brewer, Mary L.: "The Chaotic Worlds of Apuleius and Kafka." *PCLS*, 35-49.

Bridgwater, Patrick: *Kafka and Nietzsche*. Bonn: Bouvier, 1974, 166 pp.

Brinkmann, Karl: *Erläuterungen zu Franz Kafkas: Das Urteil, Die Verwandlung, Ein Landarzt, Vor dem Gesetz, Auf der Galerie, Eine kaiserliche Botschaft, Ein Hungerkünstler*. Hollfeld/Obfr.: C. Bange, 1961, 72 pp.

Bröckerhoff, Bernhard: *Seinserfahrung und Weltverstädnis des Dichters Franz Kafka*. Bonn University, 1957, (typ dis).

Brod, Max: "The Homeless Stranger" [On *The Castle*]. *KP*, 179-180; *Franz Kafkas Glauben und Lehre*. Winterthur: Mondial Verlag, 1948, 195 pp.; *Franz Kafka, eine Biographie*. Berlin: S. Fischer, 1954, 360 pp.; English translation, N.Y.: Schocken, 1960 (2nd. ed.), 270 pp.; *"The Castle:* Its Genesis," *FKT*, 161-164; *Verzweiflung und Erlösung im Werk Franz Kafkas*. Frankfurt: S. Fischer, 1959, 88 pp.; *Franz Kafka als wegweisende Gestalt*. St. Gallen: Tschudy, 1951; "Bemerkungen zur Lebensgeschichte Franz Kafkas" *NR*, LXIV, No. 2 (1953), 232-244; "Neue Züge zum Bilde Franz Kafkas." *Merkur*, VII, No. 6 (1953), 518-530; "Leben mit Franz Kafka" in his *Streitbares Leben*. Munich: Herbig, 1960, 228-290; (2nd. ed. 1969); "Zusammenarbeit mit Franz Kafka." *Herder-Blätter*, XLIV (1962), 7-9; "Aus Kafkas Freundeskreis." *WZ*, X, No. 6 (1964), 4-6; "Humanistischer Zionismus," in Manfred Schlösser (ed.): *Auf gespaltenem Pfad*. Darmstadt: Erato, 1964, 278-300; "Kierkegaard, Heidegger, Kafka," in his *Das Unzerstörbare*. Stuttgart: Kohlhammer, 1968, 144-150; "The Jewishness of Franz Kafka." *Jewish Frontier* (N.Y.), No. 13 (1964), 27-29; *F. Ks.*

Glauben und Lehre. Winterthur: Mondial Verlag: 1948, 195 pp. [Contains: "Kafka und Tolstoi," and Felix Weltsch's "Religiöser Humor bei F.K."]; *Der Prager Kreis.* Stuttgart, 1966; *Über F.K.* Frankfurt: Fischer Bücherei, 1966, 416 pp. [Contains: *F.K. Eine Biographie; F.Ks. Glauben und Lehre;* and *Verzweiflung und Erlosung im Werk F.Ks.*]; "Sur Kierkegaard, Heidegger et Kafka." *L'Arche* (Paris), III, No. 21 (Nov. 1946), 44-54; "Some Remarks on *The Castle*" in his *F.K. A Biography.* N.Y.: Schoken, 1960, 250-254; "Freuden und Leiden eines Herausgebers." *Neue Zürcher Zeitung* (Zurich), CLXXIX, No. 130 (Jan. 16, 1958) 1-2; "Zur Eröffnung der Prager Kafka-Ausstellung."*Jahrbuch, Freie Akademie der Künste* (Hamburg, 1964), 49-50; "Kafka: Father and Son" in H.M. Ruitenbeek (ed.): *The Literary Imagination.* Chicago: Quadrangle Books, 1965, 81-96; "Zusammenarbeit mit Franz Kafka," in Günter Schultz (ed.): *Transparente Welt.* Bern: Huber. 1965, 321-323

Brück. Max von: "Das Labyrinth." *Wand,* II, No. 4 (May 1947), 295-309; "Versuch über Kafka." *Die Gegenwart* (Freiburg), III, No. 7-8 (Apr. 1948), 25-29, rep. in his *Die Sphinx ist nicht tot.* Cologne/Berlin: Kiepenheuer & Witsch, 1956, 117-135.

Bryant, Jerry H.: "The Delusion of Hope: F.K.'s *The Trial.*" *Sym,* XXIII (1969), 116-128.

Buber, Martin: *Zwei Glaubensweisen.* Zurich: Manesse, 1950, 167-172, tr. *Two Types of Faith.* London & N.Y.: Macmillan, 1951, 162-169; "Schuld und Schuldgefühle." *Merkur,* VIII (1957), 704-729, rep. in his *Schuld und Schuldgefühle.* Heidelberg: L. Schneider, 1957, 50-68; "Kafka and Judaism." *GK,* 157-162; *Briefwechsel aus sieben Jahrzehnten.* Heidelberg: L. Schneider, 1972, (Vol. I, 1897-1918).

Buber-Neumann, Margarete: *Kafkas Freundin Milena.* Munich: G. Müller, 1963, 316 pp., and Berlin/Darmstadt: Deutsche Buch-Gemeinschaft, 1966, 315 pp., tr. as *Mistress to Kafka: The Life and Death of Milena.* London: Secker & Warburg; 1966, 235 pp.

Buch, Hans Christoph: *Ut Pictura Poesis. Die Beschreibungsliteratur und ihre Kritiker von Lessing bis Lukács.* Munich, 1972, 190-169.

Büchler, Franz: *Wasserscheide zweier Zeitalter: Essais.* Heidelberg: Stiehm, 1970, 102-121.

Bullaty, Sonja and Angelo Lomeo: "Kafka's Prague." *Horizon* (London), IX, (Winter 1967), 88-99.

Burgum, Edwin B.: "The Bankruptcy of Faith." *KP,* 298-318; "Freud and Fantasy in Contemporary Fiction." *Science & Society* (N.Y.), (Spring 1965), 224-233.

Burlamqui Kopke, Carlos: *Fronteiras estranhas.* Sao Paulo: Livraria Martins, 1946, 105 pp.

Burnham, James: "Observations on Kafka." *Part.* XIV, (Mar.-Apr. 1947), 186-195.

Burns, Wayne: "Kafka and Alex Comfort: The Penal Colony Revisited." *Arizona Quarterly* (University of Arizona), VIII (Summer 1952), 101-120; "In the Penal Colony: Variations on a Theme by Octave Mirbeau." *Accent* (Urbana, Ill.), XVII (Winter 1957), 45-51.

Busacca, Basil: "'A Country Doctor'." *FKT,* 45-57.

Butler, E.M.: "The Element of Time in Goethe's *Werther* and Kafka's *Prozess." GLL,* XII (1959), 248-258; "Translator's Note," to F.K.: *The Trial.* N.Y.: Knopf, 1957 (definitive ed.), 339-341.

Butor, Michel: [On M. Carrouges' *Kafka*]. *Paru* (Paris), No. 57 (1950), 69-71.

C

Cáceres, J.A.: *Panoramas del hombre y del estilo.* Bogotá: Editorial Espiral, 1949, 31-35.

Caeiro, Oscar: "Kafka en la brevedad." *Revista de Humanidades* (Córdoba, Argentina), VIII, No. 13-14 (1971), 45-70.

Calin, E.: "From Ellipsis into Silence," from his *Expression, Communication and Experience in Literature and Language.* Leeds, 1973, 259-262.

Camus, Albert: "L'espoir et l'absurde dans l'oeuvre de Kafka," in his *Le Mythe de Sisyphe.* Paris: Gallimard, 1948, 169-189, tr. by Justin O'Brien as "Hope and the Absurd in the Work of F.K." in *The Myth of Sisyphus.* N.Y.: Knopf, 1955, 124-138; 1959 Vintage ed., 92-102; "Hope and Absurdity," *KP,* 251-261.

Canetti, Elias: *Der andere Prozess. Kafkas Briefe an Felice.* Munich: Hanser, 1969, 127 pp. tr. by Christopher Middleton as *Kafka's Other Trial. The Letters to Felice.* N.Y.: Schocken, 1974, 121 pp.

Cantoni, Remo: *La coscienza inquieta.* Milan: Mondadori, 1949, 129-169 [On *The Castle*]. *Che cosa ha veramente detto Kafka.* Rome: Ubaldini, 1970, 205 pp.; "Prefazione" to F.K.: *Il Castello.* Milan: Mondadori, 1948, 1949, 1950, 1955, 1972, 9-29.

Caputo-Mayr, Maria Luise and Julius M. Herze: *F.K. Eine kommentierte Bibliographie (1956-1975).* Bern/Munich: Francke, 1976. [Voraussicht Erscheinungsdatum 1976].

Carrive, Jean: "Préface" to F.K.: *La Muraille de Chine et autres récits.* Paris: Seghers, 1948, 273-278 (11th ed. 1950); [on "Ein kleine Frau"], *Le Cheval de Troie* (Paris), No. 6 (1948), 808-809; "La Muraille de Chine." *Paru* (Paris), No. 63 (1950), 74-76; "Dans le rire et les larmes de la vie." *CCMR,* 17-22.

Carrouges, Michel: *F.K.* Paris: Labergerie, 1948, 162 pp.; *Les Machines célibataires.* Paris: Arcanes, 1954, 245 pp.;

Kafka contre Kafka. Paris: Plon, 1962, 182 pp., tr. by Emmet Parker as *Kafka versus Kafka.* University of Alabama Press, 1968. 144 pp.; "Kafka l'Accusateur." *Obliques* (Paris), No. 3 (2nd trimestre, 1973), 30-34; "The Struggle against the Father." *H,* 27-38.

Carvalhal, Tania Franco [and Others]: *A realidade em Kafka.* Porto Alegre: Editora Movimento, 1973, 135 pp.

Caspel, J. van: "Josefine und Jeremias. Versuch einer Deutung einer Erzählung F.Ks." *Neophilologus,* XXXVII, No. 4 (1953), 241-245; "Totemismus bei Kafka." *Neophilologus,* XXXVIII, No. 2 (1954), 120-127.

Castelli, Ferdinando: "Le tre vertigini di F.K." *Civiltà Cattolica,* CXIII, No. 3 (1962), 27-40, rep. in his *Letteratura dell'inquietudine.* Milan, 1963, 140-163.

Cavallo, Luigi: "F.K.: L'amore negativo." *Fenarete,* XVI, No. 2 (1964), 13-16.

Cermák, Josef: "F.Ks. Ironie." *PP,* VII, No. 4 (1965), 391-400; "Ein Bericht über unbekannte Kafka-Dokumente." *PR,* 261-265; "Die tschechische Kultur und F.K.: Die Kafka-Rezeption in Böhmen 1920-1948." *Monatshefte,* LXI, 4 (1969), 361-375; "F.K.: La acogida de Kafka en Bohemia entre 1920 y 1948." *Revista de Occidente* (Madrid), XXIV (1969), 160-181; "L'incartamento 'Kafka' presso la polizia di Praga." *Paragone* (Florence), XX, No. 238 (1969), 62-86.

Cervani, Idole Laurenti: *Considerazioni sulla "Verwandlung" di Kafka.* Trieste: Istituto di Filologia Germanica, 1962, 22 pp.

Chaix-Ruy, Jules: *Kafka: La peur de l'absurde.* Paris: Editions du Centurion, 1968, 213 pp.

Chanda, A.K.: "Post-Conversion: Tolstoy and Kafka." *Jadavpur Journal of Comparative Literature,* X, No. 2 (1973), 21-44.

Chastel, André: "Trois romans." *CdS,* No. 26-27 (Mar. 1940), 193-198 [On *The Castle*].

Chauffeteau, J.G.: "Kafka et le théatre." *CCMR,* No. 20 (1957), 23-29.

Chaves, Fernando: *Obscuridad y extrañeza. A Propósito de F.K.* Quito: Casa de la Cultura Ecuatoriana, 1956, 109 pp.

Chiusano, Itala A.: "Kafka umorista e altre noterelle private" in Paolo Chiarini (ed.): *Miscellanea di studi in onore di Bonaventura Tecchi*. Rome: Edizioni dell'Ateneo, 1969, 557-573.

Church, Margaret. "Time and Reality in Kafka's *The Trial* and *The Castle*," *TCL*, II (Jul. 1956), 62-69; "Kafka and Proust: A Contrast in Time," *Bucknell Review*, VII, No. 2, 1957, 107-112; "Kafka's 'A Country Doctor'." *The Explicator* XVI (May 1958), Item 45; *Time and Reality*. University of North Carolina Press, 1963; "Dostoevsky's *Crime and Punishment* and Kafka's *The Trial*." *Literature and Psychology* (University of Hartford), XIX, No. 3-4 (1969) 47-55; [with Ronald Cummings and Charles Whitaker]: "Five Modern German Novelists: A Bibliography 1960-1970." *MFS*, XVII, No. 1 (Spring 1971), [On Kafka, 143-149].

Claes, Paul: "Voor de Wet: Een structurele Kafka-lecturer." *Strevan* (Amsterdam), 26 (1973), 671-680.

Claudel, Paul: "Le Procès de Kafka ou Le drame de la justice." *CCMR*, No. 50 (1965), 13-16.

Clive, Geoffrey: "The Breakdown of Romantic Enlightenment: Kafka and Dehumanization," in his *The Romantic Enlightenment*. N.Y.: Meridian, 1960, 170-184.

Cohen, Sandy: "Kafka's K. and Joseph K.: A Confusion Eliminated." *GN*, 2 (1971), 45.

Cohn, Dorrit: "Kafka's Eternal Present: Narrative Tense in 'Ein Landarzt' and Other First Person Stories." *PMLA*, LXXXIII (1968), 144-150; "Kafka Enters the Castle. On the Change of Person in Kafka's Manuscript." *Euphorion*, LXII (1968), 28-45; "Erlebte Rede im Ich-Roman." *GRM*, XIX (1969), 305-313; "Castles and Anti-Castles or Kafka and Robbe-Grillet." *Novel*, V (1971), 19-31.

Cohn, Ruby: *"Watt* in the light of *The Castle." CL*, XII, No. 2 (1961), 154-166.

Collignon, Jean: "Kafka's Humor." *YFS*, No. 16 (Winter 1955-1956), 53-62.

Collins, R.G.: "Kafka's Special Methods of Thinking." *Mosaic*, III, No. 4 (Summer 1970), 43-57.

Cook, Albert S.: "Romance as Allegory: Melville and Kafka,"

in his *The Meaning of Fiction*. Wayne State University Press, 1960, 242-259.

Cooperman, Stanley: "Kafka's 'A Country Doctor'." *University of Kansas City Review*, XXIV (Oct. 1957), 75-80.

Corngold, Stanley: "Kafka's *Die Verwandlung:* Metamorphosis of the Metaphor." *Mosaic*, III, No. 4 (Summer 1970), 91-106; "Introduction" to F.K.: *The Metamorphosis*, tr. & ed. by S.G. N.Y.: Bantam Books, 1972, xi-xxii; *The Commentators' Despair: The Intrepretation of Kafka's "Metamorphosis"*. Port Washington, N.Y.: Kennikat Press, 1973, 267 pp.; "'You,' I said." *European Judaism* (London), VIII, No. 2 (1974), 16-22; "Perspective, Interaction, Imagery and Autobiography: Recent Approaches to Kafka's Fiction." *Mosaic*, VIII, No. 2 (Winter 1975), 149-166; "The Question of Law, the Question of Writing." [On *The Trial*], *JRT;* "The Judgment," *PJ.*

Cox, Harvey: "Kafka East, Kafka West." *Commonweal* (N.Y.), LXXX (Sept. 4, 1964), 596-600.

Crawford, Deborah: *Franz Kafka: Man Out of Step*. N.Y.: Crown, 1973, 183 pp.

Currie, Robert: "Kafka and the Defeat of Genius," in his *Genius: An Ideology of Literature*. N.Y.: Schocken Books, 1974, 143-170.

Currie, William J.: *Metaphors of Alienation: The Fiction of Abe, Beckett and Kafka*. University of Michigan (typ dis) DA 35 (74/75), 1094A.

Cusatelli, Giorgio: *Critica e storia: Studi offerti a Mario Fubini*. Padua: Liviana, 1970, 2 vols., Vol. I, 317-328 [On "The Bucket Rider"].

Czermak, Herberth: *"The Metamorphosis" and Other Stories*. Lincoln, Nebraska: Cliff's Notes Inc., 1973, 98 pp.

D

Daemmrich, Horst S.: "The Internal Fairy Tale: Inversion of Archetypal Motifs in Modern European Literature." *Mosaic*, V, No. 3 (1971-1972), 85-95 [On "The Metamorphosis"].

Dahl, John A.: *Das Problem der Verständigung im Werk von F.K.* University of Utah, 1972 (typ dis) DAI 33: (1972/73) 1164A (Utah).

Dalmau, Castañón, W.: "El caso clínico en *La Metamorfosis.*" *CuH*, 27 (Mar. 1952), 385-388.

Daniel-Rops [pseudonym of J.C.H. Pétiot]: "Le Chateau." *NRF*, No. 306 (Mar. 1939), 526-529; "L'univers désesperé de F.K." *CdS*, XVI (Mar. 1937), 161-176; "A French Catholic Looks at Kafka." *Th*, XXIII (Sept. 1948), 401-404; *Où passent des anges*. Paris. Plon, 1957, 156-185; "The Castle of Despair," *KP*, 184-191.

Daniells, Roy: "In the Labyrinth: A Note on F.K." *Manitoba Arts Review*, III (Spring 1942), 3-13.

Darzins, J.: "Transparence in Camus and Kafka." *YFS*, No. 25 (Spring 1960), 98-103.

Dauvin, René: "*Le Procès* de Kafka." *EG*, III (1948), 49-63; "*The Trial:* Its Meaning." *FKT*, 145-160.

David, Claude: "Kafka aujourd'hui." *EF*, XVI (1961), 33-45; "Zu Franz Kafka Erzählung 'Elf Söhne'," in P.F. Ganz (ed.): *The Discontinuous Tradition*. Oxford; Clarendon Press, 1971; 247-259; "L'Amérique de Franz Kafka," in Rainer Schönhaar (ed.): *Dialog*. Berlin: E. Schmidt, 1973, 194-204.

De Angelis, E.: *Arte e ideologia grande borghese. Mann, Musil, Kafka, Brecht*. Turin: Einaudi, 1971.

Deinert, Herbert: "Franz Kafka: 'Ein Hungerkünstler'." *WW*, XII (1963), 78-87; "Kafka's Parable 'Before the Law'." *GR*, XXXIX (1964), 192-200.

Delesalle, Jacques: *Cet étrange secret*. Paris: Desclée de Brouwer, 1957, 60-97.

Deleuze, Gilles and Félix Guattari: *Kafka. Pour une Littérature Mineure*. Paris: Minuit, 1975, 159 pp.

Dell'Agli, Ana Maria: "Problemi Kafkiani nella critica dell'ultimo decennio." *AION-SG*, (1958), 77-105; "Kafka a Berlino: Raconto di un contresso." *SG*, V, No. 1 (1967), 73-84; "Breve volo intorno a Kafka." *SG*, VI, No. 2 (1968), 135-148.

Demetz, Peter: "Franz Kafka a cesky národ," in *Franz Kafka a Praha*, Prague: V. Zikes, 1947, 43-53; "Franz Kafka a Herman Melville," *Casopis pro Moderni Filologii* (Prague), XXXI (1947/1948), 183-185, 267-271; "Zur Interpretation Franz Kafkas," *Plan* (Vienna), II (1948), 370-378; "Kafka in England," *GLL*, IV, No. 1, (Oct. 1950), 21-30; "Kafka, Freud, Husserl: Probleme einer Generation," *ZRG*, VII (1955), 59-69; "Ein Band Kafka gegen ein Moped." *Die Zeit* (Hamburg), (May 8, 1964); "Korrigierte Kafka-Kritik." *Merkur*, XX, No. 3 (1966), 900-902.

Demmer, Jürgen: *Franz Kafka, der Dichter der Selbstreflexion. Ein Neuansatz zum Verstehen der Dichtung Kafkas, dargestellt an der Erzählung "Das Urteil"*. Munich: W. Fink, 1973, 203 pp.

Dentan, Michel: *Humour et création littéraire dans l'oeuvre de Kafka*. Geneva: Droz, 1961, 195 pp.

Dev, Amiya: "Joseph K. and Jean-Baptiste Clamence. A Note on the Ambiguity of Guilt." *Judavpur Journal of Comparative Literature*, X (1972), 124-132 [On *The Trial* and Camus: *The Fall*].

Devitis, A.A.: "Rex Warner and the Cult of Power." *TCL*, VI (1960), 107-116.

D'Haen, Ch.: "Franz Kafka." *Nieuw Vlaams Tijdschrift* (Antwerp), XII (1953), 1260-1291.

Dietz, Ludwig: "Kurt Wolffs Bücherei *Der Jungste Tag*." *Philobiblon*, VII, No. 2 (1963), 96-118; "Franz Kafka: Drucke zu seinen Lebzeiten." *JDSG*, VII (1963), 416-457; "Franz Kafka und die Zweimonatsschrift *Hyperion*." *DV*, XXXVII, No. 3 (1963), 463-473; "Drucke Franz Kafkas bis 1924." *KS*. 85-125; "Die autorisierten Dichtungen Kafkas: Textkritische Anmerkungen." *ZDP*, LXXXVI (1967), 301-317; "Zwei frühe Handschriften Kafkas." *Philobiblon*, XIII (1969), 209-220; "Kafkas Randstriche in

Manuskript B der "Beschreibung eines Kampfes' und ihre Deutung: Eine Ergänzung zur Edition der zweiten Fassung." *JDSG,* XVI (1972), 648-658; "Max Brods Hand in Kafka's Manuskripten der 'Beschreibung eines Kampfes'." *GRM,* XXIII (1973), 187-197; "Editionsprobleme bei Kafka." *JDSG,* 18 (1974), 549-558; "Kafkas letzte Publikation." *Philobiblon,* 18 (1974), 119-128. *Kafka Bibliographie.* Bd. I Die Veröffentlichungen Kafkas zu seinen Lebenzeiten (1908-bis 1924); Lebenzeiten von Kafkas Schriften nach seinen Tode (1924 bis 1974). Eine Bibliographie zur Textgestalt, Druck- und Wirkingeschichte. Heidelberg: Stiehm, 1975.

Diller, Edward: "'Heteronomy' versus 'Autonomy': A Retrial of *The Trial* by Franz Kafka." *CLAJ,* XII (1969), 214-222; "'Theonomous' Homiletics. 'Vor dem Gesetz': Franz Kafka and Paul Tillich." *RLV,* XXXVI (1970), 289-294.

Dittkrist, Jörg: *Vergleichende Untersuchungen zu Heinrich von Kleist und Franz Kafka.* Cologne, 1971 (typ dis).

Döblin, Alfred: "Die Romane von F.K.", in his *Ausgewählte Werke,* ed. by Walter Muschg. Olten/Freiburg, 1963, 283-286 [originally pub. in *Die Literarische Welt* (Berlin) (Mar. 4, 1927); "De simples faits." *CCMR,* L (1965), 66-70.

Donovan, Josephine C.: *Gnosticism in Modern Literature. A Study of Selected Works by Camus, Sartre, Hesse and Kafka.* University of Wisconsin, 1971 (typ dis).

Doppler, Alfred: 'Entfremdung und Familienstruktur. Zu F.Ks. Erzählungen 'Das Urteil' und 'Die Verwandlung'," in his *Zeit- und Gesellschaftskritik in der osterreichischen Literatur des 19. und 20. Jahrhunderts.* Vienna, 1973, 75-91.

Doss, Kurt: "Ist Kafka eine geeignete Lektüre im Deutschunterricht der Oberstufe?" *PPr,* 7-8 (1951), 358-364; "Die Gestalt des Toren in Grimmelhausens *Simplicissimus* und Kafkas *Amerika." PPr,* (1959), 319-330.

Dresler, Jaroslav: "Die Verwirrung der Zungen. F.K. im Spiegel kommunistischer Kritik." *Osteuropa,* X, No. 7-8 (1960), 473-481; tr. as "Kafka and the Communists." *Survey* (N.Y.), No. 36 (1961), 27-32; "Der 'Spätheimkehrer' F.K." *Osteuropa,* XIII (1963), 646-647.

Drews, Richard: "Die grosse Kafka-Mode." *Die Weltbühne* (Berlin), III, No. 21 (1948), 589-591.

Dumont, F.: "Kafka und das Théatre Noir." *Die Quelle* (Konstanz/Leipzig), II, No. 5 (1948), 33-36.

Durant, W.A.: "Kafka" in his *Interpretations of Life.* N.Y.: Simon & Schuster, 1970, 257-268.

Dutour, Jean: "Un auteur tragi-comique." *Nouvelle NRF,* No. 36 (1955), 1081-1090; "Préface" to F.K.: *La métamorphose.* Paris: Imprimerie Nationale, André Sauret, 1955, 13-23.

Dymant, Dora: "Ich habe F.K. geliebt." *Die Neue Zeitung,* (Aug. 18, 1948), and in J.P. Hodin: "Erinnerungen an F.K." *DM,* No. 8-9 (Jun. 1949), 89-96. See also D. Dymant's interviews with Nicolas Baudy and Marthe Robert, and in English, *Horizon* (London), No. 97 (1948), 26-45.

Dyson, A.E.: "Trial by Enigma, Kafka and Lewis Carroll." *TC,* CLX, No. 953 (1956), 49-64, rep. in his *Between Two Worlds.* N.Y.: St. Martin's Press, 1972, 114-134.

E

Eberle, Oskar: "Kafka, der gottsuchende Existentialist." *SR*, LIII, No. 10 (1954), 597-598.

Ebner, Jennie: "Ich bitte Sie, dem Franz manches zu Gute halten" *LuK*, No. 36-37 (1969), 429-436; "Mysterium und Realität." *LuK*, (1974), 392-402.

Eckert, Willehad Paul: "Kunst zu Kafka." *Emuna*, IX (1974), 274-278.

Edel, E.: "F.K.: 'Die Verwandlung': Eine Auslegung." *WW*, VIII, No. 4 (1957-1958), 217-226; "F.K.: 'Das Urteil'." *WW*, IX, No. 4 (1959), 216-225; "Zum Problem des Künstlers bei F.K." *DU*, XV, No. 3 (1963), 9-31.

Edfelt, Johannes: "F.K." in A. Lundkvist (ed.): *Europas Litteraturhistoria.* Stockholm, 1946, 557-563.

Edwards, Brian F.: *The Extent and Development of Autobiographical Material in the Works of F.K.* University of Edinburgh, 1964 (typ dis); "Kafka and Kierkegaard: A Reassessment." GLL, XX, No. 3 (1967), 218-224.

Ehrenstein, Albert: "F.K." *Der Aufbau* (N.Y.), (Jul. 2, 1943), 10, and (Jul. 9, 1943), 16-17.

Eichner, Hans: *Four German Writers.* Toronto: Canadian Broadcasting Corp., 1964, 91 pp.

Eisner, Pavel: "F.K. and Prague." *BA*, XXI (1947), 264-270; *Franz Kafka and Prague.* tr. by Lowry Nelson & René Wellek. N.Y.: Arts, Inc., 1950 (Golden Griffin Books), 100 pp.; "Analyse de Kafka." *La Nouvelle Critique* (Paris), No. 92 (1958), 92-109 and No. 93 (1958), 66-82; "F.Ks. *Prozess* und Prag." *GLL*, XIV, No. 1-2 (Oct. 1960-Jan. 1961), 16-25.

Eisnerová, Dagmar: "Bemerkungen zur ethischen Problematik in Kafkas Romanen und über den Prager Hintergrund im *Prozess.*" *PR*, 131-140.

Ellis, J. [and Others]: "Franz Kafka Bibliography: 1960-1970." *RS*, XL, No. 2 (Jun. 1972), 140-162 and XL, No. 3 (Sept. 1972), 222-238.

Ellis, John M.: "Kafka: 'Das Urteil," in his *Narration in the German Novelle.* Cambridge: University Press, 1974, 188-211; "The Judgment," *PJ.*

Emmel, Hildegard: *Das Gericht in der deutschen Literatur des 20. Jahrhunderts.* Bern: Francke, 1963, 7-21.

Emrich, Wilhelm: *Franz Kafka.* Bonn: Athenäum, 1957, 445 pp., 6th ed. 1970, tr. by Sheema Zeben Buehne as *Franz Kafka. A Critical Study.* N.Y.: Frederick Ungar Publishing Co., 1968, 561 pp.; *Protest und Verheissung.* Frankfurt: Athenäum, 1960, 233-263, 3rd ed. 1968; *Geist und Widergeist.* Frankfurt: Athenäum, 1965, 187-317; *Polemik.* Frankfurt: Athenäum, 1968, 95-127 [On "Die Sorge des Hausvaters," 112-120]; *Genius der Deutschen.* Berlin: Propyläen, 1968, 426-440; "'Der Bau' und das Selbst des Menschen." *Almanach für Literatur und Theologie,* VIII (1974), 170-173.

Engelberg, Edward: *The Unknown Distance: From Consciousness to Conscience. Goethe to Camus.* Harvard University Press, 1972.

Engelsing, Rolf: "Kafka Ausstellung in Berlin." *Börsenblatt für den Deutschen Buchhandel* (Frankfurt), XXII (1966), 264-267.

Engerth, Ruediger: "Kafka in der Begegnung mit Menschen." *WZ,* X, No. 6 (1964), 11-21; [and Others]: "Ein Flug um die Lampe herum—ein unbekanntes Werk von Kafka?" *LuK,* I (1966), No. 6, 48-55; No. 8, 56-60; No. 9, 9-10 and 105-107; *Im Schatten des Hradschin: Kafka und sein Kreis.* Vienna: Stiasny, 1965.

Erlich, Victor: "Gogol and Kafka: Note on 'Realism' and 'Surrealism'," in Morris Halle (ed.): *For Roman Jakobson. Essays on the Occasion of his Sixtieth Birthday.* The Hague: Mouton, 1956, 100-108.

Essner-Schaknys, Günther: *Die epische Wirklichkeit und die Raumstruktur des modernen Romans Dargestellt Thomas Mann, Franz Kafka und Hermann Hesse.* University of Marburg, 1957 (typ dis).

F

Falk, Walter: *Leid und Verwandlung: Rilke, Kafka, Trakl und der Epochenstil des Impressionismus und Expressionismus.* Salzburg: Müller, 1961, 464 pp.

Falke, Rita: "Biographisch-literarische Hintergründe von Kafkas 'Urteil'." *GRM,* X (1960), 164-180.

Fargues, Alfred M.: "Wirkungsgeschichte oder Übereinkunft: Am Nullpunkt der Literatur? *GRM,* XXII (1972), 23-38. [On "Ein Landarzt"].

Fast, Howard: *Literature and Reality.* N.Y.: International Publishers, 1950, 9-12 [On "Metamorphosis"].

Fastout, Jacqueline: "Kafka, solitaire ou solidaire?" *Europe* No. 511-512 (1971), 133-141.

Fauchery, Pierre: "Faut-il bruler Kafka?" followed by replies from 29 writers. *Action* (Paris). Nos. 90 and 93 to 100 (May 24 and Jun. 14 to Aug. 2, 1946).

Fehse, Willi: "Über Kafka" in his *Von Goethe bis Grass.* Bielefeld: Gieseking, 1963, 123-126.

Felheim, Marvin: "'The Judgment'," in M. Felheim, F.B. Newman, and W.R. Steinhoff (eds.): *Study Aids for Teachers, for "Modern Short Stories".* N.Y.: Oxford University Press, 1951, 36-39.

Feigl, Friedrich: "Erinnerungen an F.K." in J.P. Hodin: "Erinnerungen." *DM,* No. 8-9 (Jun. 1949), 89-96.

Ferdière, Gaston: "Cette maladie qui delivra Kafka." *Le Figaro Littéraire* (Paris), (Dec. 22, 1962), 7.

Ferrater, Gabriel: Preface to F.K.: *El procés.* Barcelona: Edicions Proa, 1966, 5-25.

Ferreira, Vergílio: "Kafka: Uma estética do sonho." *Colóquio,* I (1971), 14-19.

Fertonani, R: Introduction to F.K.: *Il Castello.* Milan: Mondadori, 1973, 13-37.

Feuerlicht, Ignace: "Kafka's Chaplain." *GQ,* XXXIX, No. 2 (1966), 208-220; "Kafka's Joseph K.: A Man with Qualities." *Seminar,* III, No. 2 (1967), 103-116; "Omissions and Contradictions in Kafka's *Trial."* *GQ,* XL, No. 3 (1967), 339-350.

Fickert, Kurt J.: "Kafka's 'In the Penal Colony'." *Explicator,* XXIV (1965), Item 11; "The Window Metaphor in Kafka's *Trial."* *Monatshefte,* LVIII, No. 4 (1966), 339-350; "A Literal Interpretation of 'In the Penal Colony." *MFS,* XVII (1971), 31-36; "Fatal Knowledge: Kafka's 'Ein Landarzt'." *Monatshefte,* LXVI (1974), 381-386.

Fiedler, Leslie A.: "Kafka and the Myth of the Jew," in his *No! in Thunder.* Boston: Beacon Press, 1960, 98-101.

Fietz, Lothar: "Möglichkeiten und Grenzen einer Deutung von Kafkas *Schloss*-Roman." *DV,* XXXVII No. 1 (1963), 71-77.

Fingerhut, Karl-Heinz: *Die Funktion der Tierfiguren im Werke Franz Kafkas: Offene Erzählgerüste und Figuren-spiele.* Bonn: Bouvier, 1969, 325 pp.

Fischer, Ernst: "Franz Kafka." *SuF,* XIV (1962), 497-553, rep. in his *Von Grillparzer zu Kafka: Sechs Essays.* Vienna: Globus, 1962, 279-328; "Kafka Konferenz." *PR,* 157-168; and *PFK,* 365-377; "Symposium on the Question of Decadence." *Streets* (May-Jun. 1965), rep. in Lee Baxandall (ed.): *Radical Perspectives in the Arts.* Harmondsworth: Pelican Books, 1972, 225-239; *Kunst und Koexistenz.* Reinbeck: Rowohlt, 1966; *Karl Kraus, Robert Musil, Franz Kafka.* Florence: La Nuova Italia, 1972.

Fischer, Uve Christian: "Il rapporto fra protagonista e antagonista come elemento di struttura in due racconti kafkiani." *Siculorum Gymnasium,* XV (1962), 228-236.

Flach, Brigitte: *Die Erzählungen der kafkaschen Erzählsamm-lungen.* Bad Homburg, 1966; *Kafkas Erzählungen, Strukturanalyse und Interpretation.* Bonn: Bouvier, 1967, 171 pp.; (2nd. ed. 1972, 180 pp.).

Flam, Leopold: *De krisis van der burgerlijke moraal.* Antwerp, 1956, 121-131; *Van Plato tot Sartre.* Antwerp, 1957, 137-178.

Fleischmann, Ivo: "Auf dem Weg zum Schloss." *PR,* 209-214.

Flores, Angel: "Homage to Kafka." *The Literary World* (N.Y.) (Jul. 1934), 1-4; *"The Castle."* *BA,* (Autumn 1941), 480; "Franz Kafka," in Stanley J. Kunitz and Howard Haycraft (eds.): *Twentieth Century Authors.* N.Y.: H.W. Wilson, 1942, 740-741; *Franz Kafka: A Chronology and Bibliography.* Houlton, Maine: Bern Porter, 1944; *The Kafka Problem.* N.Y.: New Directions, 1946, 468 pp.; N.Y.: Octagon Books, 1963, 477 pp.; Staten Island, N.Y.: Gordian Press, 1976; "Light on the Hideous." *New York Herald Tribune,* (Aug. 10, 1947), Section VII, 4; "The Art of Kafka." *Yale Review,* (Winter 1949), 365-367; (& H. Swander), eds.: *Franz Kafka Today.* University of Wis. Press, 1958, 290 pp., [paperback, 1959]; (ed.): *The Problem of "The Judgment."* N.Y.: Gordian Press, 1976. (ed.): *The Kafka Debate.* N.Y.: Gordian Press, 1976.

Flores, Kate: "F.K.: A Biographical Note." *KP,* 1-19; "'The Judgment'." *QRL,* III, No. 4 (1947), 382-405, and revised and enlarged in *FKT,* 5-24; "'La Condena'." *Etcaetera* (Guadalajara, Mexico), V, No. 19 (Sept. 1956), 133-151; "The Nameless Guilt," *PJ.*

Flügel, Heinz: "F.K.: Anwärter der Gnade," in his *Herausforderung durch das Wort.* Stuttgart: Kreuz-Verlag, 1962, 12-24.

Focke, Alfred: "Kafka und Trakl." *EG,* XVII, No. 4 (1962), 411-431.

Fondane, Benjamin: "Kafka et la rationalité absolue." *Deucalion* (Paris), No. 2 (1947), 125-140.

Fort, Keith: "The Function of Style in Franz Kafka's *The Trial." Sewanee Review,* LXXII (1964), 643-651.

Fortini, F.: "Gli uomini di Kafka e la critica delle cose." *Rassegna d'Italia* (Milan), IV (1949), 148-154; rep. in his *Verifica dei poteri.* Milan: Il Saggiatore, 1965; "Die Menschen bei Kafka und die Kritik an den Dingen," in his *Die Vollmacht.* Vienna: Europa-Verlag, 1968, 209-216.

Foti, Francesco: "Kafka e altri amori epistolari." *Narrativa,* X (1965), 33-37.

Foulkes, A. Peter: "Investigations of a Dog," *KD;* "An Interpretation of Kafka's 'Das Schweigen der Sirenen'." *JEGP,* LXIV, No. 1 (1965), 98-104; "Dream Pictures in Kafka's Writings." *GR,* XLI, No. 1 (1965), 17-30; "'Auf der Galerie': Some Remarks Concerning Kafka's Concept and Portrayal of Reality." *Seminar,* II, No. 2 (1966), 34-42; "Kafka's Cage Image." *MLN,* LXXXII No. 4 (1967), 462-

471; *The Reluctant Pessimist: A Study of Franz Kafka.* The Hague: Mouton, 1967, 176 pp.; "Franz Kafka: Dichtungstheorie und Romanpraxis" in Reinhold Grimm (ed.): *Deutsche Romantheorien: Beiträge zu einer historischen Poetik des Romans in Deutschland.* Frankfurt: Athenäum, 1968, 321-346.

Fowler, Albert: "Keats, Kafka and the Critic." *Approach,* XIV (Winter 1954), 3-8.

Fowles, John: "My Recollections of Kafka." *Mosaic,* III, No. 4 (1970), 31-41.

Fraiberg, Selma: "Kafka and the Dream." *Part,* XXIII, No. 1 (Winter 1956), 47-69; rep. in W. Phillips (ed.): *Art and Psychoanalysis.* N.Y.: Criterion Books, 1957, 21-53.

Fraigneux, Maurice: "Kafka Suppliant." *Civitas* (Immensee), VI, No. 10 (1951), 598-605.

Franco Carvalhal, Tanie (ed.): *A realidade em Kafka.* Porto Alegre: Editora Movimento, 1973, 135 pp.

Frank, André: "Feydeau, Kafka, Adamov." *CCMR,* No. 10 (1955), 126-127; "Il y a dix ans." *CCMR,* No. 20 (1957), 30-37.

Frank, Waldo: "Homage to Kafka." *The Literary World* (N.Y.), No. 3 (Jul. 1934), 2.

Frantzke, Willi: "Der Liebespfeil in den Schläfen. Über die Beziehungen von F.K. zu Milena Jesenska." *SR,* LXX (1971), 209-214.

Franzen, Erich: "Die Briefe F.Ks.", in his *Aufklärungen. Essays.* Frankfurt: Suhrkamp, 1964, 85-90.

Frasson, Alberto: "Kafka e la critica marxista." *Osservatore Politico Letterario,* XIII (Jan. 1967), 25-41.

Freedman, Ralph: "Kafka's Obscurity: The Illusion of Logic in Narrative." *MFS,* VIII, No. 1 (1962), 61-74.

Freemantle, Anne: "Franz Kafka." *Commonweal* (N.Y.), XLV (Dec. 6, 1946), 184-188.

Frey, Eberhard: *Franz Kafkas Erzählstil: Eine Demostration neuer stilanalystischer Methoden in Kafkas Erzählung 'Ein Hungerkünstler.'* Bern: Herbert Lang, 1970, 372 pp., (2nd ed., 1974, 374 pp.)

Frey, Gesine: *Der Raum und die Figuren in Franz Kafkas*

Roman "Der Prozess." Marburg: Elwert, 1965 (2nd. ed., 1969), 215 pp.

Frey, Hermann: "Rudolf Steiner und Franz Kafka." *Blätter für Anthroposophie,* VI (1972), 123-129.

Fried, István: "Franz Kafka und die Ungarn." *Arbeiten zur deutschen Philologie* (Dornach), III, No. 12 (1951), 432-440.

Friederich, Reinhard H.: "The Dream Transference in Kafka's 'Ein Landarzt'." *PLL,* IX (1973), 28-34; "K's 'bitteres Kraut' und Exodus." *GQ,* XLVIII, No. 3 (May 1975), 355-357.

Friedman, Maurice: "The Modern Job: On Melville, Dostoievsky, and Kafka." *Judaism* (N.Y.), XII (1963), 436-455; *Problematic Rebel: Melville, Dostoievsky, Kafka, Camus.* N.Y.: Random House, 1963; University of Chicago Press, 1970 (rev. ed.), 512 pp., 285-410.

Friedman, Norman; "Kafka's *Metamorphosis:* A Literal Reading." *Approach,* XLIX (Fall 1963), 26-34; "The Struggle of Vermin: Parasitism and Family Love in Kafka's *Metamorphosis." Ball State University Forum,* IX, No. 1 (1968), 23-32.

Friedmann, R.: "An Analytical Note on the Allegory." *Fo,* 45-47.

Friedrich, Heinz: "Heinrich von Kleist und Franz Kafka." *Berliner Hefte für geistiges Leben* (Berlin), IV, No. 11 (Nov. 1949), 440-448.

Friedrich, Hugo: "Franz Kafka." *NSR,* XXIII (Apr. 1930), 265-269.

Fromm, Erich: *Man for Himself: An Inquiry into the Psychology of Ethics.* N.Y.: Rinehart, 1947, 167-171; *"The Trial"* in his *The Forgotten Language.* London: Gollancz, 1952, 213-224; N.Y.: Rinehart, 1957, 249-263; N.Y.: Grove Press, 1957, 249-263.

Frort, Pavel: "Franz Kafka und das Prager Deutsch." *GP,* (1964), 29-37.

Fryd, Norbert: "Warum gerade Kafka?" *PR,* 215-219.

Frynta, Emmanuel and Jan Lukas: *Franz Kafka lebte in Prag.* Prague: Artia, 1960, 146 pp.; tr. by John Layton as *Kafka and Prague.* London: Batchworth Press, 1960, 146 pp.; *Kafka et Prague.* Paris: Hachette, 1964, 146 pp.

Fuchs, Rudolf: "Social Awareness." *KP,* 247-250; "Reminiscences of F.K." in Max Brod: *Franz Kafka: A Biography.* N.Y.: Schocken, 1960, 255-258.

Fülleborn, Ulrich: "Zum Verhältnis von Perspektivismus und Parabolik in der dichtung Franz Kafkas," in Renate von Heydebrand and Klaus G. Just (eds.): *Wissenschaft als Dialog: Studien zur Literatur und Kunst seit der Jahrundertwende.* Stuttgart: Metzler, 1969, 289-313, 509-513.

Furst, Lilian R.: "Kafka and the Romantic Imagination." *Mosaic,* III, No. 4 (1970), 81-89.

Fürst, Norbert: *Die offenen Geheimtüren Franz Kafkas. Fünf Allegorie.* Heidelberg: W. Rothe, 1956, 86 pp. [On "Investigations of a Dog," 9-15; *The Castle,* 16-35; *The Trial,* 36-52; *Amerika,* 53-71; "Josephine the Singer," 73-74; "A Hunger Artist," 74-76; "A Little Woman," 76-77; "First Sorrow," 77-80, etc.].

G

Gabel, Joseph: "Kafka, romancier de l'aliénation." *Critique,* IX, No. 78 (Nov. 1953), 949-960.

Gaier, Ulrich: "'Chorus of Lies': On Interpreting Kafka." *GLL,* XXII (1969), 283-296; "'Vor dem Gesetz'. Überlegungen zur Exegese einer 'einfachen geschichte'." *Festschrift für Friedrich Beissner.* Bebenhausen, 1974, 103-120.

Gaillard, J.M.: "Une Mythologie du désespoir: *Le Metamorphose* de F.K." *Helvetia* (Bern), (Jun. 1961), 151-158.

Galinsky, Hans: *Deutsches Schrifttum der Gegenwart in der englischen Kritik der Nachkriegzeit (1919-1935).* Munich: Max Hueber, 1938, 450-453 and 467-469.

Gándara, Carmen R.L. de: *Kafka o El pájaro y la jaula.* Buenos Aires: Ateneo, 1943, 133 pp.

Garaudy, Roger: "On Stalin, Picasso and Kafka." *East Europe* (N.Y.), XII, No. 12 (Dec. 1963), 23-25; *D'un réalisme sans rivages: Picasso, Saint-John Perse, Kafka.* Paris: Plon, 1964, 251 pp.; "Kafka, die moderne Kunst und wir." *PR,* 199-207.

Garavito, Julián: "Kafka et quelques écrivains de langue espagnole." *Europe,* No. 511-512 (1971), 179-184.

Gardner, Leo K.: *Organizational Theory as Drawn from Selected Novels of Orwell, Huxley, Camus and Kafka.* Mich. State University, 1971 (typ dis).

Gauthier, Guy: "Wells et Kafka sur la corde raide." *Europe,* No. 511-512 (1971), 184-192.

Gemzoe, Anker: "Processen i Kafkas anti-digtning." *Poetik,* V (1972), 25-57.

Genovés, Antonio: "Kafka y Diáspora." *CuH,* No. 65 (1966), 120-128; "Gustav Janouch." *CuH,* No. 253-253 (1971), 227-243.

Gentile, Francesco Silvio: *Kafka: Processo alla giustizie. Guida alla lettura di "Der Prozess."* Salerno: *ELCAM,* 1970, 130 pp.

Gerhardt, Marlis: *Die Sprache Kafkas. Eine semiotische Untersuchung.* Stuttgart University, 1968 (typ dis).

Geritt, Dora: "Brief Memories of F.K.", in Max Brod: *F.K. A Biography.* N.Y.: Schocken, 1960, 259-260.

Gerlach, Kurt: "Die Mangelhaltung des modernen Menschen in Kafkas Werk." *PPr,* No. 3 (1956), 117-128.

Gianni, Eugenio Viola: "Delle costanti in Kafka." *Nuova Antologia* (Rome), No. 505 (1972), 76-90.

Gibian, George: "Dichtung und Wahrheit: Three Versions of Reality in F.K." *GQ,* XXX (Jan. 1957), 20-31 [On "Letter to Father," "The Judgment," and "Metamorphosis"]; "Karel Capek's Apocrypha and F.K.'s Parables." *American Slavic and East European Review* (N.Y.), XVIII, No. 2 (1959), 238-248.

Giesekus, Woltrand: *Franz Kafka's "Tagebücher".* University of Bonn, 1954 (typ dis, 227 pp.).

Gilman, Sander L.: "A View of Kafka's Treatment of Actuality in *Die Verwandlung." GN,* II, No. 4 (1971), 26-30.

Girard, Alain: "Kafka et le problème du *Journal Intime." Critique,* I, No. 1 (1946), 23-32.

Girard, René: "F.K. et ses critiques." *Sym,* VII (May 1953), 34-44.

Gisselbrecht, André: "Que faire de Kafka?" *La Nouvelle Critique* (Paris), No. 43 (Mar. 1963), 73-81.

Glaser, Frederick B.: "The Case of F.K." *PsR,* LI, No. 1 (1964), 99-121.

Glaser, Hermann: "F.K.: 'Auf der Galerie'," in *Interpretationen Moderner Prosa,* ed. by Fachgruppe Deutsch-Geschichte im Bayerischen Philologenverband. Frankfurt: Verlag Moritz Diesterweg, 1956 (4th ed.), 40-48, (1968, 5th ed.).

Glaser, Martha: "Dichtung am Rande des Christentums." *Die Zeitwende* (Berlin/Munich/Hamburg), XXIII (Feb. 15, 1952), 528-537.

Glatzer, Nahum N.: "F.K. and the Tree of Knowledge," in *Between East and West.* N.Y.: East & West Library, 1958, 48-58, and in A. Cohen (ed.): *Arguments and Doctrines.* N.Y., 1970; (ed.): *I am a Memory Come Alive. Autobiographical Writings by F.K.* N.Y.: Schocken, 1974, 264 pp.

Glicksohn, Jean-Michel: *"Le Procès: Kafka. Analyse critique.* Paris: Hatier, 1971, 80 pp. *

Glinz, Hans: "Methoden zu Objektivierung des Verstehens von Texten, gezeigt an Kafka's 'Kinder auf der Landstrasse'." *Jahrbuch für Internationale Germanistik* (Berlin/Zurich), I, No. 1 (1969), 75-107.

Globus, Gordon G. and Richard C. Pilliard: "Tausk's *Influencing Machine* and Kafka 'In the Penal Colony'." *AI,* XXIII (1966), 191-207.

Gluscevic, Zoran: *Studija o Francu Kafki.* Belgrade: Vuk Karadzic, 1972, 203 pp.

Göhler, Hulda: "Franz Kafkas *Prozess* in der Sicht seiner Selbstaussagen." *Theologische Zeitschrift* (Basel), XXII No. 6 (1966), 415-439.

Gold, Hugo (ed.): *Max Brod. Ein Gedenkbuch. 1884-1968.* Tel Aviv, Olamenu, 1969.

Goldschmidt, H.L.: "Key to Kafka." *Commentary,* VIII (Aug. 1949), 129-138.

Goldstein, Bluma: "A Study of the Wound in Stories by Franz Kafka." *GR,* XLI No. 4 (May 1966), 202-217; "Franz Kafka's 'Ein Landarzt': A Study in Failure." *DV,* XLII (1968), 745-759; *Key Motifs in F.K's "Der Prozess" and "Das Schloss"* Radcliffe College, 1962 (typ dis).

Goldstücker, Eduard: "The Problem of Franz Kafka." *East Europe* (N.Y.), XII, No. 4 (Apr. 1963), 29-30; "Franz Kafka." *Czechoslovak Life* (Prague), (Sept. 1963), 21-24; "Kafkas 'Der Heizer'." *GP,* III (1964), 49-64; (and K. Wagenbach): "Wer hat Angst von F.K.? *Bremer Beiträge,* 7 (1965), 70-85; "Symposium in Prague on the Question of Decadence." *Streets,* (May-Jun. 1965), 46-55 [With J.P. Sartre, Milan Kundera and Ernst Fischer]; *Franz Kafka aus Prager Sicht 1963.* Prague: Verlag der Tschechoslowakischen Akademie der Wissenschaften, 1965; 305 pp.; "Über Franz Kafka aus der Prager Perspektive." *PR,* 23-43; "Zusammenfassung der Diskussion." *PR,* 277-288; "Die Aufnahme F.Ks. in der Tschechoslowakei." *Akz,* XIII, No. 4 (1966), 320-321; "Grenzland zwischen Einsamkeit und Gemeinschaft: Bemerkungen zu Kafkas *Schloss,"* in Wilhelm R. Beyer (ed.): *Homo Homini*

Homo. Festschrift J.E. Drexel. Munich: Beck, 1966, 65-73; (ed.): *Weltfreunde. Konferenz über die Prager deutsche Literatur.* Prague: Akademia, 1967; "10 Years after the Kafka Symposium of Liblice." *European Judaism* (London), VIII, No. 2 (1974), 22-27.

Gómez, Carlos A.: "El hombre Kafka." *Sur,* No. 227 (Apr. 1954), 23-30.

González Paredes, Ramón: "El mundo de F.K." *Revista Nacional de Cultura* (Caracas), XVI, No. 104 (May-Jun. 1954), 75-89.

Gooden, Christian: "Two Quests for Surety. A Comparative Interpretation of Stifter's *Abdias* and Kafka's 'Der Bau'." *Journal of European Studies,* V, No. 4 (Dec. 1975), 341-361; "'The Great Wall of China: The Elaboration of an Intellectual Dilemma." *TBL;* "The Prospect of a Positive Existential Alternative," *KD.*

Goodman, Paul: "Preface" to F.K.: *The Metamorphosis.* N.Y.: Vanguard Press, 1946, 5-8; *Kafka's Prayer.* N.Y.: Vanguard Press, 1947, 265 pp.; "Plot Structure of *The Castle,"* in his *The Structure of Literature.* University of Chicago Press, 1962, 173-183.

Gordon, Caroline: "Notes on Hemingway and Kafka." *Sewanee Review,* LVII, No. 2 (Spring 1949), 215-226, rep. in C. Gordon and Allen Tate (eds.): *The House of Fiction.* N.Y.: Scribner's, 1950, 286-296, and in *GK,* 75-83.

Goth, Maja: *Franz Kafka et les lettres françaises (1928-1955).* Paris: Corti, 1957, 288 pp.; "Der Surrealismus und F.K." *PFK,* 226-266; "Existentialism and Franz Kafka: Jean-Paul Sartre, Albert Camus, and Their Relationship to Kafka." *PCLS,* 51-69.

Grandin, John M.: *Existential Situations in the Narrative Prose of Franz Kafka and Heinrich von Kleist.* University of Michigan (dissertation), *DAI,* 31/6607 A (Mich.), 1971; "Kafka's 'Der plötzliche Spaziergang'." *MLN,* LXXXIX (1974), 866-872.

Grangier, Edouard: "Abraham, oder Kierkegaard, wie Kafka und Sartre ihn sehen." *Zeitschrift für Philosophische Forschung* (Meisenheim/Glan.), IV, No. 3 (1949), 412-421.

Grant, Vernon W.: *Great Abnormals: The Pathological Genius of Kafka, Van Gogh, Strindberg, and Poe.* N.Y.: Hawthorn Books, 1968, 6-71.

Gräser, Albert: *Das literarische Tagebüch: Studien über Elemente des Tagebüches als Kunstform.* University of Saarbrücken, 1955 (typ dis), 63-77.

Gravier, Maurice: "Strindberg et Kafka." *EG,* VIII, No. 2-3 (1953), 118-140; rep. in part in *Obliques* (Paris), No. 3 (2nd. trimestre 1973), 51-58.

Gray, Ronald: *Kafka's Castle.* Cambridge University Press, 1956, 147 pp.; "The Structure of Kafka's Works: A Reply to Professor Uyttersprot." *GLL,* XIII (Oct. 1959), 1-17; (ed.): *Kafka: A Collection of Critical Essays.* Englewood Cliffs, N.J.: Prentice-Hall, 1962, 182 pp., which contains one of his essays: "Kafka the Writer," 61-73; *Franz Kafka.* Cambridge University Press, 1973, 220 pp.; "The Judgment" *PJ;* "But Kafka Wrote in German." *KD.*

Greenberg, Clement: "At the Building of the Great Wall of China." *FKT,* 77-81; "The Jewishness of F.K." *Commentary* (N.Y.), XIX (Apr. 1955), 320-324; rep. in his *Art and Culture.* Boston: Beacon Press, 1961, 266-273.

Greenberg, Martin: "The Literature of Truth: Kafka's 'Judgment'." *Salmagundi* (Flushing, N.Y.), I, No. 1 (1965), 4-22; "It's a Kafkaesque World." *N.Y. Times Magazine,* (May 29, 1966), 12-13, 30-31 and 41-43; "Kafka's *Amerika.*" *Salmagundi,* I, No. 3 (1966), 74-84; "Kafka's *Metamorphosis* and Modern Spirituality." *TriQ,* No. 6 (1966), 5-20 and in *H,* 50-64; *The Terror of Art: Kafka and Modern Literature.* N.Y.: Basic Books, 1968, 241 pp.; London: Deutsch, 1971.

Grenzmann, Wilhelm: "F.Ks. Werk und geistige Welt." *Univ,* VIII (1953), 797-803; "Von Kafka bis Musil: Wege und Ziele der neuen deutschen Romandichtung im Rahmen der modernen europäischen Literatur." *Univ,* XIX (1963), 233-244; "Franz Kafka: Auf der Grenze zwischen Nichtsein und Sein," in his *Dichtung und Glaube.* Frankfurt: Athenäum, 1967, 149-182.

Grieser, Dietmar: "Im Schloss für soziale Wohlfahrt. Landvermessung in einem Kafka-Dorf," in his *Vom Schloss Gripsholm zum River Kwai.* Frankfurt, 1973, 17-22.

Grillet, Frans: *Franz Kafka.* Brugge/Utrecht: Desclée de Brouwer, 1966, 69 pp.

Grmela, Jan: "Ecrit en 1924." *Europe,* No. 511-512 (1971), 4-5.

Groethuysen, Bernard: "A propos de Kafka." *NRF,* XXI, No. 235 (1933), 588-606; *Mythes et Portraits.* Paris: Gallimard, 1947; "The Endless Labyrinth." *KP,* 376-390; *Unter den Brücken der Metaphysik.* Stuttgart: Klett, 1968, 87-104 and 105-115.

Grossman, Jan: "Kafka et Prague." *CCMR,* LXI (1967), 49-51.

Grossvogel, David I.: "Kafka: *The Trial"* in his *Limits of the Novel: Evolutions of a Form from Chaucer to Robbe-Grillet.* Cornell University Press, 1968, 160-188.

Grünter, Rainer: Beitrag zur Kafka-Deutung." *Merkur,* IV, No. 3 (1950), 278-287; "Kafka in der englischen und amerikanischen Kritik." *Das literarische Deutschland* (Heidelberg), II, No. 12 (1951), 6-7.

Guadagnino, L.M.: "La giustizia di Kafka." *Letterature Moderne* (Milan), V, (1954), 626-630.

Guardini, Romano: "Zum Geleit" introduction to Robert Rochefort's *Kafka oder Die unzerstörbare Hoffnung.* Vienna and Munich, 1955, 9-20.

Gugelberger, Georg M.: [review of Klaus Ramm: *Reduktion als Erzählprinzip bei Kafka.*]. *MAL,* VII, No. 1-2 (1974), 242-245.

Guignard, R.: "Les romans de Kafka." *Revue de Cours et Conférences* (Paris), XXXIV, No. 6 (Feb. 28, 1933), 563-576.

Guglielmi, Joseph: "Exile and the Law (Kafka and Jabes)." *European Judaism.* (London), VIII, No. 2 (1974), 38-40.

Gullason, Thomas A. and Leonard Casper (eds.): *World of Short Fiction.* N.Y.: Harper, 1971 (2nd ed.), 658 pp.

Gump, Margaret: "From Ape to Man and from Man to Ape." *KFLQ,* IV, No. 4 (1957), 177-185.

Günther, Joachim: "Der Bote des Königs: Bemerkungen zum Bilde Kafkas." *NDH,* VIII, No. 83 (1961), 65-70; "Kafkas Briefe an Felice." *NDH,* XV, No. 3 (1968), 127-137.

Gunvaldsen, Kaare: "Franz Kafka and Psychoanalysis." *University of Toronto Quarterly,* XXXII (1963), 266-281;

"The Plot of Kafka's *Trial.*" *Monatshefte,* LVI, No. 1 (1964), 1-14.

Gürster, Eugen: "Das Weltbild Franz Kafkas." *Hoch,* XLIV, No. 4 (Apr. 1952), 326-337.

Guth, Hans P.: "Symbol and Contextual Restraint: Kafka's 'Country Doctor'." *PMLA,* LXXX, No. 4 (Sept. 1965), 427-431.

Gütling, Alois: "Erinnerungen an Franz Kafka." *Prager Nachrichten* (Gräfelfing/Munich), No. 10 (Oct. 1, 1951), 3-5.

Gutmann, Anna: "Der Mistkäfer." *Modern Austrian Literature* (SUNY at Binghamton, N.Y.), III, No. 1 (1970), 51-52.

H

Haas, Erika: "Differenzierende Interpretation auf der Oberstufe, dargestelt an Aichinger 'Spiegelgeschichte', Musil 'Die Amsel', Kafka 'Das Urteil'." *DU,* XXI, No. 2 (1969), 64-78.

Haas, Willy: "Kafkas letztes Werk." *Das Tagebuch* (Berlin), No. 13 (1925) 460-463; "Meine Meinung." *Die Literarische Welt* (Berlin), No. 23 (1926), 1-12; "Franz Kafkas Glaube." *Das Tagebuch* (Berlin), No. 24 (1929), 994-995; *Gestalten der Zeit.* Berlin: G. Kiepenheuer Verlag, 1930, 172-199 (new ed. 1962, 208-228); "Auslegung eines Aktes der Freundschaft" in *Dichter. Denker. Helfer. Max Brod zum 50. Geburtstag.* Mährisch-Ostrau: Julius Kittels Nachf., Keller & Co., 1934, 67-73; "Prague in 1912." *Virginia Quarterly Review,* XXIV (Summer 1948), 409-417; "Preface" and "Editor's Note" to F.K.: *Letters to Milena.* N.Y.: Schocken, 1953, 7-13 and 14-16; "Der Klassizist Franz Kafka." *Forum* (Vienna), No. 6 (1954), 20-21; "Ricordo di Franz Kafka." *Paragone* (Florence), No. 64 (1955), 41-52; *Die Literarische Welt. Erinnerungen.* Munich: P. List, 1957, 315 pp. (new ed., 1960); "Franz Kafka" in Hans Jürgen Schultz (ed.): *Juden, Christen, Deutsche.* Stuttgart, Kreuz, 1961, 376-379; "Das Unvergessene." *WZ,* X (1964), 8-10; "Um 1910 in Prag." *Forum* (Vienna), IV, No. 42 (1957), 223-226.

Haeger, Klaus A.: "Die Krankheit des Menschen im Werk F.Ks." *PPr,* XV (1961), 349-361.

Hahn, Ludwig: "F.Ks. 'Der Kübelreiter'," in *Interpretationen Moderner Prosa,* ed. by Fachgruppe Deutsch-Geschichte im Bayerischen Philologenverband. Frankfurt: Verlag Moritz Diesterweg, 1957, 49-54.

Hajek, Jirí: "Kafka und Wir." *PR,* 107-111; "Kafka und die sozialistische Welt." *Kürbiskern,* No. 1 (1967), 77-93.

Hajek, Siegfried: "F.K.: 'Der Nachbar'." *DU,* VII (1955), 5-12.

Hall, Calvin S. and Richard E. Lind: *Dreams, Life, and Literature. A Study of Franz Kafka.* University of North Carolina Press, 1970, 133 pp.

Hall, Vernon: "Kafka, Lessing and Vigny." CL, I, No. 1 (Winter 1949), 73-77.

Hamalian, Leo: "The Great Wall of Kafka." *Journal of Modern Literature*, I, No. 2 (1970), 254-261; (ed.): *Franz Kafka. A Collection of Criticism*. N.Y.: McGraw-Hill, 1974, 151 pp., with an "Introduction" by L.H., 1-17.

Hamburger, Käthe: "Erzählformen des modernes Romans." *DU*, IV (1959), 5-23, [On *The Trial*, 16-19].

Hamburger, Michael: "Kafka in England" in his *Zwischen den Sprachen: Essays und Gedichte*. Frankfurt: Fischer, 1966, 121-136; "Robert Musil, Robert Walser, Franz Kafka" in his *Vernunft und Rebellion*. Munich: Hanser, 1969, 139-168.

Han, Jean-Pierre: "La notion de fatigue." *Europe*, No. 511-512 (1971), 148-155.

Handler, Gary: "A Textual Omission in the English Translation of *Der Prozess*." *MLN*, LXXXIII (1968), 454-456; "A Note on the Structure of Kafka's *Der Prozess*." *MLN*, LXXXIV, No. 5 (1969), 798-799.

Harder, Marie-Luise: *Märchenmotive in der Dichtung Franz Kafkas*. Freiburg i. Br. University, 1962 (typ dis).

Hardt, Ludwig: "Erinnerung an Franz Kafka." *NR*, LVIII (1947), 239-242; "Recollections." *KP*, 32-36.

Hartung, Rudolf: "Anwärter der Gnade." *Eckart* (Witten/Berlin), (Apr.-Jun. 1952), 369-370; "Die Gestalt des Vaters in der modernen Literatur." *Eckart* (Witten/Berlin), (Oct.-Dec. 1953); "Ein neues Kafka-Bild: Amerkungen zu Canettis Essay *Der andere Prozess*." *TuK*, XXVIII (1970), 44-49; "*Briefe an Ottla*." *NDH*, XXII, No. 2 (1975), 385-389.

Harvey, William J.: *Franz Kafka and Friedrich Durrenmatt: A Comparison of Narrative Techniques and Thematic Approaches*. Texas University (Austin), 1973 (typ dis), *DAI*, 34: 772A-73A (1973).

Hassan, Ihab: *The Dismemberment of Orpheus. Toward a Postmodern Literature*. N.Y.: Oxford University Press, 1971, 110-138.

Hasselblatt, Dieter: "Kafka Russisch." *DM*, XVI No. 187 (1964), 84-89; *Zauber und Logik: Eine Kafka-Studie*.

Cologne: Verlag/Wissenschaft und Politik, 1964, 214 pp.; "F.K. Eine nicht-Biographie." *NDH,* 21 (1974), 698-716.

Hasselblatt, Ursula: *Das Wesen des Volksmärchen und das moderne Kunstmärchen.* Freiburg i Br. University, 1956 (typ dis), 191-198.

Hata, Setsuo: "Bürokratie und Individuum: Ein Versuch über Kafkas *Das Schloss. Doitsu Bungaku,* No. 27 (1961), 50-57.

Hatfield, Henry: "Franz Kafka," in his *Modern German Literature.* Indiana University Press, 1966, 84-94; "Life as Nightmare: Franz Kafka's 'A Country Doctor'," in his *Crisis and Continuity in Modern German Fiction.* Cornell University Press, 1969, 49-62.

Hatvani, Paul: "Einige Bemerkungen über das Werk des Dichters F.Ks. und über das Land." *LuK,* IV, No. 36-37 (1969), 421-428.

Hauser, Arnold: "Proust and Kafka," in his *Ursprung der modernen Kunst und Literatur.* Munich, 1964, 383-394, in tr. as *Mannerism: The Crisis of the Renaissance and the Origin of Modern Art.* N.Y.: Knopf, 1965, 2 vols.

Hebel, Franz: "Kafka: 'Zur Frage der Gesetze' und Kleist: 'Michael Kohlhaas'." *PPr,* 12 (1956), 632-638.

Hebel, Frieda: "Max Brod: *F.K. Eine Biographie,"* in Hugo Gold (ed.): *Max Brod: Ein Gedenkbuch.* Tel Aviv: Olamenu, 1969, 161-166.

Hecht, M.B.: "Uncanniness, Yearning and F.K." *AI,* IX, No. 1 (Apr. 1952), 45-55.

Heer, Friedrich: "Josef Weinheber aus Wien." *Frankfurter Hefte,* 8 (1953), 590-602.

Heger, Roland: *Der osterreischische Roman des 20. Jahrhunderts.* Vienna/Stuttgart, 1971, Part I, 49-85; Part II, 50-58.

Heidinger, Maurice M.: *Kafka Criticism in America, 1949-1963.* Indiana University, 1965 (typ dis).

Heinz, Heide: "Herman Melville's Erzählung 'Bartleby' in Vergleich zu F.Ks. Roman *Der Prozess."* Saarbrücker *Beiträge zur Ästhetik,* (1966), 59-66.

Heiseler, Bernt von: "Franz Kafka oder Sonnenfinsternis." *Zeitwender* (Munich), XXIII (Jan. 1, 1952), 436-440, reprinted in his *Ahnung und Aussage.* Gütersloh:

Bertelsmann, 1952, 232-240, and in his *Gesammelte Essays*. Stuttgart: Steinkopf, 1967, 2 vols., Vol. II, 71-77.

Helander, Lars: "Kafka i Österuropa." *Bonniers Litterära Magasin*, XXXIV (1965), 43-46.

Heldmann, Werner: *Die parabel und die parabolischen Erzählformen bei Franz Kafka*. Münster University. 1953 (typ dis).

Hellens, Franz: "Le phénomène Franz Kafka revu à travers le *Journal*." *Europe*, No. 511-512 (1971), 91-95.

Heller, Erich: "The World of Franz Kafka." *Cambridge Journal*, II, No. 1 (1948), 22 ff.; rep in *The Disinherited Mind*. Cambridge: Bowes & Bowes, 1952, 155-181; N.Y.: Farrar, Straus & Cudahy, 1957, 199-231; Penguin Books, 1961, 173-202; "Kafka's True Will. An Introductory Essay" to F.K.: *Letters to Felice*. N.Y.: Schocken, 1973, vii-xxiii; *TBL.; Franz Kafka*. N.Y.: Viking Press, 1975, 140 pp., London: Fontana, 1975 (paperback); [and Joachim Beug] (eds.): *Franz Kafka: Dichter über ihre Dichtungen*. Munich: Heimeran/S. Fischer, 1969; "The Imagery of Guilt" [On *The Trial*], *JRT*.

Heller, Peter: "The Autonomy of Despair: An Essay on Kafka." *Massachusetts Review*, I No. 2 (1960), 231-253; "The Futility of Striving," in his *Dialectics and Nihilism: Essays on Lessing, Nietzsche, Mann, and Kafka*. University of Massachusetts Press, 1966, 227-306 and 331-335; "Kafka and Nietzsche." *PCLS*, 71-95; "On Not Understanding Kafka." *GQ*, XLVII, No. 3 (1974), 373-393.

Hemmerle, Rudolf: *Franz Kafka. Eine Bibliographie*. Munich: Robert Lerche, 1958. 140 pp.

Henel, Heinrich: "Kafka's 'Der Bau', or How to Escape from a Maze," in P.F. Ganz (ed.): *The Discontinuous Tradition. Studies in German Literature in Honour of Ernst Ludwig Stahl*. Oxford: Clarendon Press, 1970, 224-246; "Das ende Kafkas 'Der Bau'." *GRM*, XXII (1972), 3-23.

Henel, Ingeborg: "Die Türhüterlegende und ihre Bedeutung für Kafkas *Prozess*." *DV*, XXXVII (1963), 50-70; tr. as "The Legend of the Doorkeeper." *JRT;* "Ein Hungerkünstler." *DV*, XXXVIII (1964), 230-247; "Die Deutbarkeit von Kafkas Werken." *ZDP*, LXXXVI (1967), 250-266; "Kafkas 'In der Strafkolonie': Form, Sinn und Stellung der Erzählung im Gesamtwerk," in Vincent J. Günther and Helmut Koopmann et al (eds.): *Untersuchungen zur Literatur als Geschichte: Festchrift für Benno von Wiese.* Berlin: E. Schmidt, 1973.

Hennecke, Hans: *Kritik. Gesammelte Essays zur modernen Literatur.* Gütersloh: 1958, 209-216.

Henrard, Annie: "Une source espagnole au *Chateau* de Kafka?" *RLV*, XXXI (1965), 444-453.

Hering, Gerhard F.: "Franz Kafkas *Tagebücher." Merkur,* II, No. 1 (1948), 96-109; "Kafka in drei Spiegeln." *Merkur,* XIII, No. 6 (1959), 582-589; No. 7, 685-690; No. 9, 883-889.

Herling-Grudzinski, Gustaw: "Kafka w Rosji" [Kafka in Russia]. *Kultura,* No. 218 (1965), 8-13; tr. into Italian in *Tempo Presente,* X (1965), 42-54.

Hermlin, Stephan: "F.K." *Die Fähre. Ein Almanach.* Munich: Willi-Weismann Verlag, 1946, 67-73; [and Hans Mayer]: *Ansichten über einige Bücher und Schrifsteller.* Berlin, 1947, [On *The Castle,* 158-163].

Hermsdorf, Klaus: "Briefe des Versicherungsangstellten F.K." *SuF,* IX, No. 4 (1957), 639-662; "Hinweis auf einen Aufsatz von F.K." *WB,* No. 4 (1958), 545-556; "Werfels und Kafkas Verhältnis zur tschechischen Literatur." *GP,* 3 (1964), 39-47; "Kunst und Künstler bei F.K." *WB,* X No. 3 (1964), 404-412, and in *PR,* 95-106; *F.Ks Roman-fragment "Der Verschollene"* [*Amerika*]. Humboldt University, Berlin, 1961 (typ dis); *Kafka: Weltbild und Roman.* Berlin: Rütten & Loening, 1961, (2nd ed., 1966), 300 pp.; "Nachwort" to F.K.: *Erzählungen. Der Prozess. Das Schloss.* Berlin: Rütten & Loening, 1965, 775-820; "Nachwort" to F.K.: *Amerika.* Berlin: Rütten & Loening, 1967, 303-317.

Hernàndez Aguirre, Mario: "El misterio de las puertas en la literatura de Franz Kafka." *Atenea* (Concepción, Chile), No. 375 (1957), 83-86.

Heselhaus, Clemens: "Kafkas Erzählformen." *DV,* XXVI, No. 3 (1952), 353-376.

Hesnard, Angelo Louis Marie: "Le message incompris de Kafka." *Psyché* (Paris) XII (1947), 1161-1173.

Hesse, Hermann. *Gesammelte Schriften,* Berlin: Suhrkamp,

1957, Vol. VII, 469-471; *Gesammelte Werke.* Frankfurt, 1970, Vol. XII, 477-491.

Heuer, Helmut: *Die Amerikavision bei William Blake und Franz Kafka.* Munich University, 1960 (typ dis, 139 pp.).

Hibberd, John: *Kafka. in Context.* London: Studio Vista, 1975, 152 pp.

Hillebrand, Bruno: "F.K.", in his *Theorie des Romans.* Munich, 1972, 2 vols., Vol. II, 133-144.

Hillmann, Heinz: *Franz Kafka: Dichtungstheorie und Dichtungsgestalt.* Bonn: Bouvier, 1964, 196 pp., (2nd ed., 1973, 259 pp.); "Franz Kafka," in Benno von Wiese (ed.): *Deutsche Dichter der Moderne: Ihre Leben und Werk.* Berlin: Schmidt, 1965, 258-279 (2nd ed., 1969, 262-283); "Das Sorgenkind Odradek." *ZDP,* LXXXVI, No. 2 (1967), 197-210; "Kafkas *Amerika.* Literatur als Problemlösungsspiel," in Manfred Brauneck (ed.): *Der deutsche Roman im 20. Jahrhundert.* Bamberg: C.C. Buchners Verlag, 1975; *"Amerika." KD.*

Hilsbecher, Walter: "Die Widersprüche des Daseins." *Frankfurter Hefte,* VII No. 10 (Oct. 1952), 797-799; "Kafkas *Das Schloss,*" in his *Wie modern ist eine Literatur?.* Munich: Nymphenburger, 1965, 113-138.

Hinze, Klaus-Peter: "Neue Aspekte zum Kafka-Bild: Bericht über ein noch unveröffentlichtes Manuskript." *MAL,* V, No. 3-4 (1972), 83-92.

Hirsch, Wolfgang: *Substanz und Thema in der Kunst.* Amsterdam/Stuttgart, 1961, 40-48.

Hlavacova, Jirina: "Franz Kafkas Beziehungen zu Jicchak Löwy." *Judaica Bohemiae,* I (1965), 75-78.

Hobson, Irmgard: "Oklahoma, USA, and the Nature Theater." *KD.*

Hodgart, Matthew: "K." *New York Review of Books,* 12 (Apr. 10, 1969), 3-4.

Hodin, J.P.: "Memories of Franz Kafka." *Horizon* (London), No. 97 (1948), 26-45; "Erinnerungen an Franz Kafka." *DM,* I No. 8-9 (Jun. 1949), 89-96; "The Fate of Franz Kafka." *The Literary Guide and Rationalist Review,* (London), LXIX, No. 11 (1954), 5-7; *The Dilemma of Being Modern.* London: Routledge, 1956, 3-22 N.Y.:

Noonday Press, 1959, 3-22; *Kafka und Goethe*. London/ Hamburg: Odysseus Verlag, 1968, 99 pp. [Includes "Die Dekadenz F.Ks."; "Kafka und Prag"; "Kafkas glückliche Jahre," 7-34].

Hoen, Christian: "Franz Kafka." *Nieuwe Vlaams Tijdschrift* (Antwerp), VII, No. 12, 1260-1291.

Höfele, Karl Heinrich: "Kafkas Selbsporträt und das Menschenbild Pascals." *ZRG*, V, No. 4 (1953), 372-375.

Hoff Stolk-Huisman, A.Z. van't: "Janouch gesprekken met Kafka." *De Nieuwe Stem*, XX (1965), 680-687.

Hoefert, Sigfrid: "Kafka in der DDR: Ein Bericht." *Seminar*, II, No. 2 (1966), 43-52.

Hoffer, Klaus: *Das Bild des Kindes im Werk Franz Kafkas*. Graz University, 1971 (typ dis).

Hoffman, Frederick J.: *Freudianism and the Literary Mind*. Louisiana State University Press, 1945, 181-192, (2nd ed., 1957, 177-207); "Escape from Father," *KP*, 214-246; "Kafka's *The Trial:* The Assailant as Landscape." *Bucknell Review* (Bucknell University), IX (May 1960), 89-105.

Hoffman, Leonard R.: *Melville and Kafka*. Stanford University, 1951, (typ dis).

Hoffmann, Werner: *Franz Kafkas Aphorismen*. Bern, 1974, 120 pp.; "Kafka und die jüdische Mystik." *SZ*, XCVII No. 190 (1972), 230-248. "Ks. Legende 'Vor dem Gesetz'." *Boletin de Estudios Germanicos*, VIII (1970), 107-119.

Hofrichter, Laura: "From Poe to Kafka." *University of Toronto Quarterly*, XXIX (Jul. 1960), 405-417.

Holland, Norman N.: "Realism and Unrealism: Kafka's 'Metamorphosis'." *MFS*, IV (Summer 1958), 143-150.

Honegger, Jürg B.: *Das Phänomen der Angst bei Kafka*. Berlin: Erich Schmidt, 1974, 320 pp. (Phil. Stud. und Quellen, 81).

Honig Edwin: *Dark Conceit*. N.Y.: Oxford University Press, 1966 (2nd. ed.), 63-68.

Höntzsch, Alfred: "Gericht und Gnade in der Dichtung Franz Kafkas." *Hoch*, XXXI, No. 8 (May 1934), 160-167.

Hoog, Armand: "Kafka et la grande peur." *La Nef* (Paris), No. 13 (1945), 107-112.

Hora, Josef: *"Le Chateau." Europe,* No. 511-512(1971), 10-12.

Horst, Karl August: "Von Kafka zu Kasack." *DZ,* XXV, No. 4 (1954), 260-264.

Hosaka, Muneshige: "Die erlebte Rede in 'Die Verwandlung' von Franz Kafka." *Doitsu Bungaku,* XLI (1968), 39-47.

Houska, Leos: "Franz Kafka und Prag, 1963" *PP,* VI, No. 4 (1963), 491-494; "F.K. bibliographisch." *PP,* No. 4(1964), 413-418.

Howey, Nicholas P.: *Who's Afraid of Franz Kafka? An Introduction to Theatre Activity in Czechoslovakia, 1969.* Wayne State University, 1971 (typ dis) DAI 31:3695A-96A.

Hubben, William: *Four Prophets of Our Destiny: Kierkegaard, Dostoevsky, Nietzsche, Kafka.* N.Y.: Macmillan, 1952, 129-144; 2nd. ed., 1954; rep. under the title *Dostoevsky, Kierkegaard, Nietzsche, and Kafka.* N.Y.: Collier Books, 1970, 135-155.

Hutchinson, Peter: "Red Herrings or Clues?" *KD.*

Huyghe, René: "Das Zeitalter des Absurden." *Die Quelle* (Konstanz/Leipzig), I, No. 1 (1947) 6-20.

Hyde, Virginia M.: "From the Last Judgment to Kafka's World," in *The Gothic Imagination.* N.Y. & London, 1974, 128-149.

I

Ide, Heinz: "Existenzerhellung im Werke Kafkas." *JWB*, (1957), 66-104; "F.K.: 'Der Gruftwächter' und 'Die Truppenaushebung': Zur 'religiösen' Problematik im Kafka Werk." *JWB*, V (1961), 7-27; "F.Ks. *Der Prozess.* Interpretation des ersten Kapitels." *JWB*, VI (1962), 19-57.

Ingram, Forrest L.: *Representative Short Story Cycles of the Twentieth Century: Studies in a Literary Genre.* The Hague: Mouton, 1971, 234 pp.

Ionesco, Eugene: "Dans les armes de la ville." *CCMR*, L, No. 20 (1957), 3-5 [On "The City Coat of Arms"].

Ironside, Robin: "Kafka." *Polemic* (London), 8 (1946), 39-45.

Isermann, Gerhard: *"Unser Leben, unser Prozess: theologischen Fragen bei F.K."* Wuppertal: Jugenddienst-Verlag, 1969, 29 pp.

Ita, J.M.: "Note on Willa and Edwin Muir's translation of Kafka's novel *Das Schloss.*" *Ibadan,* 29 (1971), 102-105; "Laye's *Radiance of the King* and Kafka's *Castle.*" *Odù,* 4 (1970), 18-45.

Iyengar, K.R.S.: "Franz Kafka," in *The Adventure of Criticism.* London: Asia Publishing House, 1962, 568-582.

J

Jacob, Heinrich Eduard: "Kafka oder die Wahrhaftigkeit." *Der Feuerreiter* (Berlin), (Aug.-Sept. 1924), 61-66; "Truth for Truth's Sake," *KP,* 53-59.

Jacobi, Hansres: "Kafkas Briefe an seine Verlobte Felice." *Univ,* XXIII, No. 3 (1968), 297-302.

Jacobi, Walter: "Kafkas Roman *Amerika* im Unterricht: Eine Untersuchung seiner Motive und Symbole und deren Bedeutung für Kafkas Gesamtwerk." *DU,* XIV, No. 1 (1962), 63-78.

Jaeger, H.: "Heidegger's Existential Philosophy and Modern German Literature." *PMLA,* LXVII, No. 5 (1952), 655-683 [On *The Castle, The Trial,* "The Burrow," 670-673].

Jaffe, Adrian H.: "Franz Kafka et le héros solitaire dans le roman americain contemporain." *Roman* (Saint-Paul-de-Vence), 2 (Mar. 1951), 142-149; *The Process of Kafka's "Trial."* Michigan State University Press, 1967, 150 pp.; [and Virgil Scott]: "Analysis of 'In the Penal Colony,'" in their *Studies in the Short Story.* N.Y.: Dryden Press, 1949, 468-471.

Jäger, Manfred: "Keine Kapitulation vor Kafka: Ein Literatur-Bericht." *Europäische Begegnung,* VI (1966), 447-452.

Jahn, Wolfgang: "Kafka und die Anfänge des Kinos." *JDSG,* VI (1962), 447-452; "Kafkas Handschrift zum *Verschollenen"* [*Amerika*]. *JDSG,* IX (1965), 541-552; *Kafkas Roman "Der Verschollene"* [*Amerika*]. Stuttgart: Metzler, 1965, 157 pp.

Jakob, Dieter: "Das Kafka-Bild in England: Zur Aufnahme des Werkes in der journalistischen Kritik 1928-1966." *OGS,* V (1970), 90-143; *Das Kafka-Bild in England: Eine Studie zur Aufnahme des Werkes in der journalistischen Kritik (1928-1966). Darstellung. Dokumente, Bibliographie.* Oxford and Erlangen: Selbstverl., 1971, 2 vols., 710 pp.

Jakubec, Joël: *Kafka contre l'absurde.* Lausanne: Cahiers de la Renaissance Vaudoise, 1962, 109 pp.

Jancke, Oskar: *Kunst und Reichtum deutscher Prosa. Von Lessing bis Thomas Mann.* Munich: Piper, 1954, 425-443.

Janouch, Gustav: "Erinnerungen an Franz Kafka." *NR*, LXII, No. 1 (1951), 49-64; *Gespräche mit Kafka. Erinnerungen und Aufzeichnungen.* Frankfurt: S. Fischer, 1951, 138 pp. enlarged ed., 1968; *Conversations with Kafka. Notes and Reminiscences.* Tr. by Goronwy Rees. N.Y.: F.A. Praeger, London: Verschoyle, 1953, 109 pp.; enlarged ed. London: Deutsch, 1971, 219 pp.; N.Y.: New Directions, 1971, 219 pp.; *Franz Kafka und sein Welt. Eine Bildbiographie.* Vienna: Deutsch, 1965, 188 pp.; "Kafka in Stegliz." *Die Diagonale*, (Berlin), I, No. 2 (1966), 26-34.

Järv, Harry: *Konsten som livssurrogat. Kafkas analys av konstnärskapets problematik.* [On "A Report to an Academy"]. Upsala University, 1953 (typ dis) 123 pp.; *Die Kafka-Literatur.* Malmö & Lund: Bo Cavefors Verlag, 1961, 380 pp.; *Varaktigare än Koppar: Fran Homeros till Kafka, författer Porträtt.* Malmö & Lund: Cavefors, 1962, 205-274; *Introduktion til Kafka.* Vasa: Horisont, 1962; *Lasarmekanismer. Essaer och utblickar.* Malmo, 1971 [On Kafka, 252-329].

Jens, Inge: *Studien zur Entwicklung der expressionistischen Novelle.* Tübingen University, 1954 (typ dis, 318 pp.) [On "Description of a Struggle," pp. 80-108].

Jens, Walter: "Franz Kafka. Eine vorläufige Analyse seiner Welt und seines Werkes." *Deutsche Universitäts-Zeitung* (Göttingen), VI No. 1 (1951), 13-17; "Der Mensch und die Dinge. Die Revolution der deutschen Prosa." *Akz*, IV, No. 4 (1957), 319-334; "Ein Jude namens Kafka" in T. Koch: *Porträts deutsch-jüdischer Geistesgeschichte.* Cologne, 1961, 179-203; *Un ebreo di nome Kafka e altri saggi di letterature contemporanee.* Urbino: Argalia, 1964.

Jesenska, Milena: "Franz Kafka." *Europe*, No. 511-512 (1971), 5-6; "La malédiction des meilleures qualités." *Europe*, No. 511-512 (1971), 6-9; "Milenas Nachruf auf Kafka: Mit einem Kommentar von Ruben Kingsberg." *Forum*, IX (1962), 28-29.

Jolas, Eugene: "Franz Kafka's Stories and Ascending Realism," in his *Vertical Yearbook.* N.Y.: Gothem Book Mart, 1941, 169-172.

Jonas, Klaus, W.: "Franz Kafka: An American Bibliography." *Bulletin of Bibliography* (Boston), XX, No. 9 (Sept.-Dec. 1952), 212-216; No. 10 (Jan.-Apr. 1953), 231-233; "Die Hochschulschriften über Franz Kafka und sein Werk." *Philobiblon,* XII (Sept. 1968), 194-203.

Jorge, Ruy A.: *Interpretaçao de Kafka.* Sao Paulo: L. Oren, 1968, 269 pp.

Juliet, Charles: "La littérature et le theme de la mort chez Kafka et Leiris." *Critique*, No. 126 (1957), 933-945.

Jungmann, Milan: "Kafka and Contemporary Czech Prose." *Mosaic,* III, No. 4 (1970), 178-188.

K

Kafka, Frantisek: "F.Ks. Handschrift." *Zeitschrift für die Geschichte der Jüden*, VI (1969), 75-81.

Kafka, Franz: *Das Kafka-Buch. Eine innere Biographie in Selbszeugnissen*. Edited by Heinz Politzer. Frankfurt: Fischer Bücherei, 1965, 271 pp.; *Dichter über Dichtungen: F.K.* Ed. by Erich Heller and Joachim Beug. Munich: Heimeran, 1969, 186 pp.; *I am a Memory Come Alive*. Ed. by Nahum N. Glatzer. N.Y.: Schocken, 1974, 264 pp. [Autobiographical Writings].

Kaiser, Gerhard: "Franz Kafkas *Prozess*. Versuch einer Interpretation." *Euphorion*, LII, No. 1 (1958), 23-49.

Kaiser, Helmuth: *Franz Kafkas Inferno. Ein psychologische Deutung seiner Strafphantasie*. Vienna: Internationaler Psychoanalytischer Verlag, 1931, 65 pp. Originally published in *Imago* (Vienna), XVII, No. 1 (Feb. 1931), 41-104; *PFK*, 69-142.

Kaiser, Joachim: "Glück bei Kafka." *Frankfurter Hefte*, IX, No. 4 (1954), 300-303 [On *Amerika*].

Karp, Friedrich: "Ein Flug um die Lampe herum—ein bekanntes Werk von Kafka?" *LuK*, I (1966), 105-107.

Karpfen, Otto Maria: "Franz Kafka oder Der Durchbruch." *Die Erfüllung* (Vienna-Leipzig) I (1934/1935), 22-29.

Karst, Roman: "Franz Kafka. Studium." *Twórczosc* (Cracow), 6 (1958), 78-110; *Drogi samotnosci. Rzecz o Franzu Kafce*. Warsaw: Czytelnik, 1960; *Wstep. Kafka, Nowele i miniatury*. Warsaw, 1961; "Unbewegliche Uhrzeiger." *WZ*, IX, No. 7 (1963), 1-12; "Ein Versuch zur Rettung des Menschen." *PR*, 141-148; "Franz Kafka: Word-Space-Time." *Mosaic*, III, No. 4 (Summer 1970), 1-13.

Kartiganer, Donald M.: "Job and Joseph K.: Myth in Kafka's *The Trial*." *MFS*, VIII (1962), 31-43.

Kassel, Norbert: *Das Groteske bei Franz Kafka*. Munich: W. Fink, 1969, 176 pp.

Kassner, Rudolf: "Stil und Gesicht. Swift, Gogol, Kafka."

Merkur, VIII, No. 8 (1954), 737-752 and No. 9 (1954), 834-845; rep. in his *Der goldene Drachen. Gleichnis und Essay.* Zurich/Stuttgart: E. Rentsch, 1957; "Fin ou limite." *CCMR,* L (1965), 46-65.

Kauf, Robert: "Once Again—Kafka's 'Report to an Academy'." *MLQ,* XV, No. 4 (Dec. 1954), 359-366; "*Verantwortung:* The Theme of Kafka's *Landarzt* Cycle." *MLQ,* XXXIII, No. 4 (1972), 420-432.

Kautmann, Frantisek: "Franz Kafka und die tschechische Literatur." *PR,* 141-148; "Kafka et la Boheme." *Europe,* No. 511-512 (1971), 56-72.

Kavanagh, Thomas M.: "Kafka's *The Trial:* The Semiotics of the Absurd." *Novel,* V, No. 3 (1972) 242-253; *JRT.*

Kayser, Rudolf: "Dem Gedächtnis F.Ks." *Deutsche Blätter* (Santiago, Chile), IV, No. 34 (1946), 24-27.

Kayser, Werner and Horst Gronemeyer: *Max Brod.* Hamburg: Hamburger Bibliographien, 1972, Vol. XII [On Kafka, 108-125].

Kayser, Wolfgang: "Die Erzähler des Grauens," in his *Das Groteske. Seine Gestaltung in Malerei und Dichtung.* Oldenburg/Hamburg: Gerhard Stalling Verlag, 1957, 149-161. *The Grotesque in Art and Literature.* Tr. by Ulrich Weisstein. Indiana University Press, 1963, N.Y.: McGraw-Hill Paperback Edition, 1966, 145-150.

Kazin, Alfred: *The Inmost Leaf.* N.Y.: Harcourt, Brace, 1955, (new ed., 1959, 142-148).

Keller, Fritz: "Das Phänomen der Angst im Werke F.Ks.," in his *Studien zum Phänomen der Angst in der modernen deutschen Literatur.* Winterthur: P.G. Keller, 1956, 87 pp. [On Kafka, 43-78].

Kellerman, Seymour: *The Kafkaesque. An Iconography.* SUNY (Buffalo) typ dis DA 34 (1973/74) 5179 A.

Kelly, John: "Franz Kafka *Trial* and the Theology of Crisis." *Southern Review* (Baton Rouge, La.) V (Spring 1940), 748-766; "*The Trial* and the Theology of Crisis," *KP,* 151-171.

Kemp, Friedhelm: "Entwicklung eines Negativs. Zum Beginn der deutschen Ausgabe von Franz Kafkas Werken." *Die*

Neue Zeitung (Munich/Berlin/Frankfurt), (Nov. 11, 1950), 24-29.

Kemp, Robert: "Qui était Franz Kafka?" *Les Nouvelles Littéraires* (Paris), V, (Nov. 22, 1945).

Kemper, Hans-Georg: "Gestörte Kommunikation. Franz Kafka: 'Das Urteil'," in Silvio Vietta and H.G. Kemper (eds.): *Expressionismus.* Munich: Fink, 1975, 286-305.

Kerkhoff, Emmy: "Franz Kafka." *Levende Talen* (Groningen), No. 172 (Dec. 1953), 488-509; "Noch einmal: Franz Kafkas 'Von den Gleichnissen.' Vorgreifliche Bemerkungen zu einer Deutung," in Ferdinand van Ingen and others (eds.): *Dichter und Leser.* Groningen: Wolters Noordhoff, 1972, 191-194.

Kern, Edith: "Reflections on the Castle and Mr. Knott's House: Kafka and Beckett." *PCLS*, 97-111.

Kilian, Ernst R.: *Die verfremdete Wirklichkeit in den Erzählungen Hugo von Hofmansthals und F. Ks.* University of Vienna, 1971 (typ dis).

Kirshner, Sumner: "Kafka's Gnostic Imagery." *GN*, IV (1973), 42-46.

Kisch, Guido: "Kafka-Forschung auf Irrwegen." *ZRG*, XXIII (1971), 339-350.

Klarman, Adolf D.: "Franz Kafkas 'Der Heizer': Versuch einer stilkritischen Studie." *Bibliotheque de la Faculté de Liege, Langue et Littérature,* Fascicule CLXI (1961), 287-289; "Franz Kafkas 'Der Heizer': Nach einer stilistischen Studie." *WZ*, VIII, No. 8 (1962), 35-39.

Klatt, Reinhard: *Bild und Struktur in der Dichtung F.Ks.* Freiburg University, 1963 (typ dis).

Klausing, Helmut: "Das Schicksal der Familie Franz Kafkas." *NDL*, IV (May 1956), 154-155.

Klee, Wolfhart G.: *Die characteristischen Motive der expressionistisches Erzählungsliteratur.* Berlin, 1934, 151 pp. [On "Der Heizer," 21-22 and *Der Prozess,* 84-90]. (University of Leipzig dis).

Kleinschmidt, Gert: "'Ein Landarzt'," in Albrecht Weber and Others: *Interpretationen zu F.K.* Munich: Oldenbourg, 1972 (3rd. ed.), 106-121.

Klempt, Heinrich: "Die Deutung des Lebens in dichterischer Gestaltung." *WW*, XIV, No. 6 (1964), 414-423 [On "Auf der Galerie," 421-423].

Klinge, Reinhold: "Mensch und Gesellschaft im Spiegel neuerer Romane." *DU*, XXIII, No. 2 (1971), 86-102 [On *Amerika*, 94-96].

Kloocke, Kurt: "Zwei späte Erzählungen Kafkas." *JWB*, XII (1968), 79-91.

Klossowski, Pierre: "Introduction au Journal Intime de F.K." *CdS*, XXII, No. 270 (1945), 148-160; "Kafka nihiliste?" *Critique*, VII, No. 30 (1948), 963-975.

Knieger, Bernard: "Kafka's 'The Hunter Gracchus'." *Explicator*, XVII (Mar. 1959), Item 39.

Kobs, Jürgen: *Kafka: Untersuchungen zu Bewusstein und Sprache seiner Gestalten*. Edited by Ursula Brech. Bad Homburg: Athenäum, 1970, 559 pp.

Koch, Hans: "Fünf Jahre nach Bitterfeld." *NDL*, XII (1964), 5-21.

Kock, Erich: "F.K. in der Optik Max Brods." *WoW*, VII (1954), 543-544.

Kofler, Leo: "F.K. und die Besonderheit seines Nihilismus," in his *Zur Theorie der modernen Literatur*. Neuwied/Berlin: 1962, 238-267.

Köhnke, Klaus: "Das Gericht und die Helfer: Untersuchungen zu Kafkas Roman *Der Prozess*." *AG*, V (1970), 177-201; "Kafkas *guoter sündere*: Zu der Erzählung 'Die Verwandlung'." *AG*, VI (1971), 107-120.

Kokis, Sérgio: *Franz Kafka e a expressao da realidade*. Rio de Janeiro: Tempo Brasileiro, 1967, 140 pp.

Kolman, Maria A.: *The Literary Fortune of F.K.: A Critical Survey of the German, English, and Slavic Secondary Literature*. University of Colorado, 1973 (typ dis). *DAI* 34: 1918A (Colo).

Komlovski, Tibor: "Kafka's *Schloss* und das Fortuna-Schloss des Comenius. *Acta Literaria*, X (1968), 83-93.

Konder, Leandro: *Kafka*. Rio de Janeiro: José Alvaro, 1966, 210 pp.

Konig, Gerd: *F.Ks. Erzählungen und kleine Prosa*. University of Tübingen, 1954 (typ dis, 234 pp.)

Kono, Osamu: "Zu Kafkas Darstellungsform." *Forschungberichte der deutschen Literatur* (Osaka/Kobe), III (1961), 39-51.

Korst, Marianne R.: *Die Beziehung zwischen Held und Gegenwelt in F.Ks. Romanen.* University of Marburg, 1953 (typ dis, 138 pp.).

Kosta, Oscar: "Wege Prager deutscher Dichter zum tschechischen Volk." *Aufbau* (Berlin), XIV (1958), 559-581.

Kowal, Michael: *F.K.: Problems in Interpretation.* Yale University, 1962, (typ dis), *DAI*28 (1967), 682A; "Kafka and the Emigrés: A Chapter in the History of Kafka Criticism." *GR,* XLI (1966), 291-301.

Kracauer, S.: "Zu 'Beim Bau der chinesischen Mauer'," in his *Das Ornament des Masse.* Frankfurt: Suhrkamp, 1963, 256-268.

Kraft, Herbert: *Kafka: Wirklichkeit und Perspektive.* Bebenhausen: Rotsch, 1972, 82 pp.

Kraft, Werner: "Über F.Ks. 'Elf Söhne'." *Die Schildgenossen* (Augsburg), XII, No. 2-3 (1932), 120-132; "Über den Tod. Zu F.Ks. 'Ein Traum'." *Morg,* XI, No. 2 (1935), 81-85; "F.K. und das Religiöse." *Die F, II, No. 1 (1947), 13-19;* "F.Ks. Erzählung 'Das Ehepaar'." *Wand,* IV, No. 2 (1949), 155-160; *Franz Kafka: Durchdringung und Geheimnis.* Frankfurt: Suhrkamp; 1968, 214 pp.

Kramer, Dale: "The Aesthetics of Theme: Kafka's 'In the Penal Colony'." *SSF,* V, No. 4 (1969), 362-367.

Krammer, Jenö: "Kafka in Ungarn." *PR,* 79-80.

Kreitner, L.B.: "Kafka as a Young Man." *Connecticut Review,* III, No. 2 (1970), 28-32.

Krejci, Karel: "F.K. et Jakub Arbes." *Europe,* No. 511-512 (1971), 156-168.

Krell, Max: "Der Heizer." *NR,* XXVIII (Jan.-Jul. 1917), 270-277.

Kreuzer, Helmut: "Die paradoxen Bildskizzen in Hebbels Tagebüchern: Materialien zum Thema Kafka und Hebbel." *Augenblick,* IV No. 4 (1960), 55-57.

Krieger, Murray: *The Tragic Vision: Variations on a Theme in Literary Interpretation.* N.Y.: Holt, Rinehart & Winston, 1960, 114-144.

Krock, Marianne: "Franz Kafkas 'Die Verwandlung'." *Euphorion*, LXIV No. 3-4 (1970), 326-352; *Oberflächen- und Tiefenschicht im Werke Kafkas 'Der Jaeger Grachus' als Schlüsellfigur*. Marburg: Elwert 1974, 169 pp.

Krolop, Kurt: "Herder-Blätter." *PP*, VI, No. 2 (1963), 211-212; "Ein Manifest der 'Prague Schule'." *PP*, VII, No. 4 (1964), 329-335; "Hinweis auf eine verschollene Rundfrage: "Warum haben Sie Prag verlassen?'" *GP*, IV (1966), 47-64; "Zu den Erinnerungen Anna Lichtensterns an Franz Kafka." *GP*, V (1968), 21-60; "Zur Geschichte und Vorgeschichte der Prager deutschen Literatur des 'expressionistischen Jahrzehnts'," in E. Goldstücker (ed.): *Weltfreunde*, 47-96.

Krotz, Frederick W.: "Franz Kafka 'Der Hungerkünstler': Eine Interpretation." *MAL*, V, No. 3-4 (1972), 93-119.

Krüger, Hans-Peter: "F.Ks. Dramenfragment 'Der Gruftwächter'." *Proceedings of the Department of Foreign Languages and Literatures* (University of Tokyo), IX, No. 5 (1962), 1-27.

Kruntorad, Paul: "Bruno Schulz: Ein Vergleich mit F.K." *WZ*, XI, No. 3 (1965), 9-19.

Krusche, Dietrich: "Die kommunikative Funktion der Deformation klassischer Motive 'Der Jäger Gracchus': Zur Problematik der Kafka-Interpretation." *DU*, XXV, No. 1 (1973), 128-140; *Kafka und Kafka-Deutung*. Munich: W. Fink, 1974, 172 pp. "Kommunikationsstruktur und Wirkpotential." *DU*, XXVI, No. 4, (1974), 110-122.

Kudszus, Winfried: "Erzählhaltung und Zeitverschiebung in Kafkas *Prozess* und *Schloss*." *DV*, XXXVIII, No. 2 (1964), 192-207; PFK 331-350; "Between Past and Future: Kafka's Later Novels." *Mosaic*, III, No. 4 (Summer 1970), 107-118; "Erzählperspektive und Erzählgeschehen in Kafkas *Prozess*." *DV*, XLIV, No. 2 (1970), 306-317.

Kuepper, Karl J.: "Gesture and Posture as Elemental Symbolism in Kafka's *The Trial*." *Mosaic*, III, No. 4 (Summer 1970), 143-152, and *JRT*.

Kügler, Hans: "Zur Ortsbestimmung der Menschen in den Parabeln Franz Kafkas," in his *Weg und Weglosigkeit: 9 Essays*. Heldenheim: Heldenheimer Verlagsansalt, 1969, 105-125.

Kuhn, Ira: *Kafka and the Theater of the Absurd: Transformation of an Image.* Kansas University, 1970, DAI 31 (1970): 2924A (Kan.); "The Metamorphosis of *The Trial." Sym,* XXVI, No. 3 (1972), 226-241.

Kühne, Jörg: *"Wie das Rascheln in gefallen Blättern." Versuch zu F.K.* Tübingen/Bebenhausen: Verlag Lothar Rotsch, 1975, 87 pp.

Kuhr, Alexander: "Neurotische Aspekte bei Heidegger und Kafka." *Zeitschrift für Psychosomatische Medizin* (Göttingen), I No. 3 (1955), 217-227.

Kumar, Satish: "Franz Kafkas 'In der Strafkolonie'." *DUA,* XIII (1963), 147-156.

Kuna, Franz: "Art as Direct Vision: Kafka and Sacher-Masoch." *Journal of European Studies,* II (1972), 237-246 and *KD; Franz Kafka: Literature as Corrective Punishment.* Indiana University Press, 1974, 196 pp.; "Rage for Verification: Kafka and Einstein." *TBL.*

Kurella, Alfred: "Der Frühling, die Schwalben und F.K." in *Kritik in der Zeit.* Berlin, 1970, 532-544.

Kurz, Paul Konrad: "Standorte der Kafkadeutung." *SZ,* CLXXVII (1966), 196-218; "Verhängte Existenz" F.Ks. Erzählung 'Ein Landartz'." *SZ,* CLXXVII (1966), 432-450, both of these essays in his *Über moderne Literatur.* Frankfurt: Knecht, 1967, 38-71 and 171-202, tr. by Sister Mary Frances McCarthy as "Perspectives in Kafka Interpretation" and "Doomed Existence: F.K.'s Story 'A Country Doctor'," in *On Modern German Literature.* University of Alabama Press, 1967, 30-55 and 149-172.

Kurzweil, Baruch Benedikt: "Die Fragwürdigkeit der Jüdischen Existenz und das Problem der Sprachgestaltung." *Bulletin des Leo Baeck Instituts,* VIII, No. 29 (1965), 28-40; "Franz Kafka: Jüdische Existenz ohne Glauben." *NR,* LXVIII No. 3 (1966), 418-436.

Kusák, Alexej: "Bemerkungen zu Marxistischen Interpretationen Franz Kafkas." *PR,* 169-180.

L

Lachmann, Eduard: "Das Türhütergleichnis in Kafkas *Prozess.*" *Innsbrucker Beiträge zur Kulturwissenschaft,* (1959), 265-270, and in K.K. Klein and E. Thurner (eds.): *Germanistische Abhandlungen.* Innsbruck University, 1960, 265-270.

Ladendorf, Heinz: "Kafka und die Kunstgeschichte." *Wallraf-Richartz Jahrbuch,* (Cologne), XXIII (1961), 293-326 and XXV (1963), 227-262.

Lainoff, Seymour: "The Country Doctors of Kafka and Turgenev." *Sym,* XVI No. 2 (1962), 130-135.

Lakin, Michael: "Hofmannsthals *Reitergeschichte* und Kafkas 'Ein Landarzt'." *MAL,* III, No. 1 (1970), 39-50.

Lamprecht, Helmut: "Mühe und Kunst des Anfangs. Ein Versuch über Kafka und Kleist." *NDH,* VI, No. 66 (1960), 935-940.

Lancelotti, Mario A.: *El universo de Franz Kafka.* Buenos Aires: Argos, 1950, 189 pp.; *De Poe a Kafka. Para una teoría del cuento.* Buenos Aires: Eudeba, 1965, 61 pp.; *Como leer a Kafka.* Buenos Aires: Emecé, 1969, 155 pp.

Landsberg, Paul L.: "Kafka et *La Métamorphose.*" *L'Esprit* (Paris), CXXII, (Sept. 1938), 671-684, rep. in his *Problèmes du personnalisme.* Paris: Editions du Seuil, 1952, 83-98; "The Metamorphosis." *KP,* 122-133.

Langer, Jaroslav: "'Ein Flug um die Lampe herum' ist keine Fälschung." *LuK,* XVI-XVII (1967), 409-419.

Langguth, Carl W.: *Narrative Perspective and Consciousness in Franz Kafka's "Trial".* Stanford University, 1969, *DAI* 29: 4006A (Stanford).

Laporte, Roger: "Kafka: Le dehors et le dedans." *Critique* XXIII No. 240 (1967), 407-419.

Lavrin, Janko: "Franz Kafka." *Review 43* (London), I, No. 1 (1943), 8-12.

Lawson, Richard H.: "Kafka's "Ein Landarzt'." *Monatshefte,* XLIX, No. 5 (Oct. 1957), 265-271; *"Ungeheures Ungezief-*

er in Kafka's 'Die Verwandlung'." *GQ,* XXXIII, No. 3 (1960), 216-219; "Kafka's Use of the Conjunction *Bis* in the sense of *As Soon As." GQ,* XXXV, (Mar. 1962), 165-170; "Kafka's Parable 'Der Kreisel': Structure and Theme." *TCL,* XVIII, (1972), 199-205.

Lecomte, Marcel: "Note sur Kafka et le rêve," in André Breton (ed.): *Rêve. Documents.* Paris, 1938, 61-62; "'Le plus proche village'." *CdS,* XXII No. 270 (Mar.-Apr. 1945), 147; "Kafka." *Disque Vert* (Paris), No. 4 (Nov.-Dec. 1953).

Ledgard, Rodolfo: "La realidad de Franz Kafka." *Tres* (Lima), (Mar.-Jun. 1941), 84-91.

Léger, François: "De Job a Kafka." *CdS,* XXII No. 270 (Mar.-Apr. 1945), 161-165.

Lehmann, Peter L.: "Kafka" in his *Meditationen um Stefan George.* Düsseldorf & Munich: Helmut Küpper, 1965, 233-254.

Leibfried, Erwin: *Kritische Wissenschaft vom Text.* Stuttgart, 1970 [On "Gibs auf!", 188-191; "Schakale und Araber", 337-342, etc.].

Leiris, Michel: "Faut-il bruler Kafka?" *Action* (Paris), No. 90 (May 24, 1946).

Leisegang, Dieter: *Lücken im Publikum: Relatives und Absolutes bei Kafka.* Frankfurt: Heiderhoff, 1972, 56 pp.

Leiter, Louis H.: "A Problem in Analysis: Franz Kafka's 'A Country Doctor'." *Journal of Aesthetics & Art Criticism* (Baltimore), XVI No. 3 (Mar. 1958), 337-347.

Lenz, Hermann: "Franz Kafka und die 'Machte'." *Weltstimmen* (Stuttgart), XVIII, No. 12 (1949), 1-8.

Leopold, Keith: "Franz Kafka's Stories in the First Person." *JAU,* No. 11 (Sept. 1959), 56-62; "Breaks in Perspective in Franz Kafka's *Der Prozess." GQ,* XXXVI, No. 1 (1963), 31-38.

Lerner, Max: *Ideas for the Ice Age.* N.Y.: Viking Press, 1941, 143-151; "The Human Voyage." *KP,* 38-46.

Lesser, Simon O.: "The Sources of Guilt and the Sense of Guilt: Kafka's *The Trial." MFS,* VIII No. 1 (1962), 44-60; "Reflections on Pinter's *The Birthday Party." Contemporary Literature,* XIII (1972), 34-43.

Levi, Djak: "On Brod and Kafka," in E.T. Beck: *Kafka and the*

Yiddish Theater. Wisconsin University Press, 1971, 220-223.

Levi, Mijal: *Kafka and Anarchism*. N.Y.: Revisionist Press, 1972, 11 pp.

Levi, P. Margot: "K., an Exploration of the Names of Kafka's Central Characters." *Names*, XIV, No. 1 (1966), 1-10.

Levinsky, Ruth: "In Search of Kafka—Summer 1970." *PCLS*, 157-164.

Liehm, Antonin: "The Mosaic of the Czech Culture in the Late 1960's: The Inheritors of the Kafka-Hasek Dialectic." *Mosaic*, I, No. 3 (1967-1968), 12-27; "Franz Kafka dix ans après." *TM*, No. 323 (1973), 2253-2296. "Kafka and his Communists Critics." *Part*, XLII, No. 3 (1975), 406-415.

Linde, Ebbe: "Drömstilen hos Strindberg och Kafka." *Bonniers Litterära Magasin* (Stockholm), IX (Nov. 1946), 760-765.

Lindsay, J.M.: "Kohlhaas and K.: Two Men in Search of Justice." *GLL*, XIII, (Apr. 1960), 190-194.

Lion, Ferdinand: *Die Geburt der Aphrodite. Ein Gang zu den Quellen des Schönen*. Heidelberg: W. Rothe, 1955, 130-135.

Livermore, Ann L.: "Kafka and Stendhal's *De l'Amour*." *RLC*, XLIII (1969), 173-218.

Lockemann, Fritz: *Gestalt und Wandlungen der deutschen Novelle*. Munich, 1957, 357-363.

Loeb, Ernst: "Bedeutungswandel der Metamorphose bei Franz Kafka und E.T.A. Hoffmann: Ein Vergleich." *GQ*, XXXV (Jan. 1962), 47-59.

Loeblowitz-Lennard, Henry: "Some Leitmotifs in Franz Kafka's Works Psychoanalytically Explored." *University of Kansas City Review*, XIII, No. 2 (1964), 115-118.

Loeffel, Hartmut: "Das Raumerlebnis bei Kafka und Eichendorff. Untersuchungen an Eichendorffs *Taugenichts* und Kafkas *Amerika*." *Aurora*, XXXV (1975), 78-98.

Loewenson, Erwin: *Der Weg zum Menschen*. Hildesheim: A. Lax, 1970, 199 pp.

Lombardo Radice, L.: *see* Radice, L. Lombardo.

Loose, Gerhard: *Franz Kafka und "Amerika."* Frankfurt: Klostermann, 1968, 89 pp.

Lortz, Helmut: "F.K.: 'Ein Bericht für eine Akademie'." *Neue Literarische Welt* (Berlin), III, No. 4 (1952), 5.

Louzil, Jaromir: "Ein unbekannter Zeitungsabdruck der Erzählung 'Josephine' von Franz Kafka." *ZDP,* LXXXVI (1967), 317-319.

Ludvik, Dusan: "Kafka bei den Jugoslawen." *PR,* 229-236.

Lührsen, Hans Detlef: "Franz Kafka. Einführung und Bibliographie." *Europa-Archiv* (Frankfurt), V, No. 22 (1950), 3527-3534.

Lukács, Georg: "Franz Kafka oder Thomas Mann?" in his *Wider den missverstandenen Realismus.* Hamburg: Claasen, 1958, 49-96; *La signification présente du réalisme critique.* Paris: Gallimard, 1960, 86-168, tr. by J. and N. Mander as "Franz Kafka or Thomas Mann?" in *The Meaning of Contemporary Realism.* London: Merlin Press, 1962, retitled *Realism in Our Time.* N.Y.: Harper & Row, 1964.

Luke, F.D.: "Kafka's 'Die Verwandlung'." *MLR,* XLVI, No. 2 (1951), 232-245; *"The Metamorphosis." FKT,* 25-44.

Lüth, Paul E.H.: "Franz Kafka, Dichter, 1924." *Der Bogen* (Wiesbaden), II, No. 1 (1947), 22-24; "Kafka und Kasack." *Der Bogen* (Wiesbaden), III, No. 2 (1948), 69-70.

Lyons, Nathan: "Kafka and Poe—and Hope." *Minnesota Review,* V (1965), 158-168.

M

Mac Andrew, M. Elizabeth: "A Splacknuck and a Dung-Beetle: Realism and Probability in Swift and Kafka." *CE*, XXXI, No. 4 (1969), 376-391.

Macklem, M.: "Kafka and the Myth of Tristan." *Dalhousie Review* (Halifax, N.S.), XXX, No. 4 (1950), 335-345.

Madden, William A.: "A Myth of Meditation: Kafka's 'Metamorphosis'." *Th*, XXVI, No. 101 (Summer 1951), 246-266.

Madeheim, Helmuth: "Die Rolle des Fürsprechers bei Kafka." *DU*, XV, No. 3 (1963), 44-47.

Magny, Claude-Edmonde: "Kafka ou L'Écriture objective de l'absurde." *CdS*, (Nov. 1942), 12-36; rep. in *Les Sandales d'Empédocle*. Neuchatel: La Baconniére, 1945, 173-266; "The Objective Depiction of Absurdity." *KP*, 75-96; "L'Influence de Kafka en France." *Litterair Paspoort* (Amsterdam), (Aug.-Sept. 1949), 99-101; *Essais sur les limites de la littérature*. Paris: Payot, 1968, 272 pp.

Mahler, Karl-Werner: *Eigentliche und uneigentliche Darstellung in der modernen Epik. Der parabolische Stil Franz Kafkas*. Marburg University, 1958, (typ dis).

Mahoney, Jon L.: "Symbolism and Calvinism in the Novels of Kafka." *Renascence* (N.Y.), XV (1963), 200-207.

Maier, Anna: *Franz Kafka und Robert Musil als Vertreter der ethischen Richtung des modernen Romans*. University of Vienna, 1949, (typ dis, 185 pp.).

Maione, Italo: *Franz Kafka*. Naples: Libreria Scientifica Editrice, 1952, 81 pp. (rev. ed., 1955).

Majerová, Marie: "Eröffnungsansprache." *PR*, 7-9.

Mallac, Guy de: "Kafka in Russia." *Russian Review*, XXXI (1972), 64-73.

Mallea, Eduardo: "Introducción al mundo de Franz Kafka." *Sur* (Buenos Aires), No. 39 (Dec. 1937), 7-37; rep. in *El sayal y la púrpura*. Buenos Aires: 1941.

Malmsheimer, Richard R.: "Kafka's 'Nature Theater of

Oklahoma': The End of Karl Rossman's Journey to Maturity." *MFS*, XIII (1967), 493-501.

Mann, Klaus: "Preface" to F.K.: *Amerika*. N.Y.: New Directions, 1946, iii-x; *H*, 133-139; "Franz Kafka" in his *Prüfungen: Schriften zur Literatur.* Munich: Nymphenburger, 1968, 286-296.

Mann, Thomas: "Homage to F.K." *The Literary World* (N.Y.), No. 3 (Jul. 1934), 1; "Homage", foreword to F.K.: *The Castle.* N.Y.: Knopf, 1941, v-xvi, rep. in T.M.: *Gesammelte Werke.* Frankfurt, 1960, 12 vols., Vol. X, 771-779.

Marache, Maurice: "La Métaphore dans l'oeuvre de Kafka." *EG*, XIX (1964), 23-41; "Les Lettres à Felice." *EG*, XXIV (1969), 58-61; "L'Image fonctionnelle dans *Le Procès* de Kafka: Structuralisme et évolution des formes." *Annales de la Faculté des Lettres et Sciences Humaines de Nice.* Paris: Les Belles Lettres, 1969, 157-169.

Marcenac, Mathieu: "Préparatifs pour les noces d'Ariane et de Franz Kafka; En italique: *'La presence de la loi'.''* Europe, No. 511-512 (1971), 89-90.

Mares, Michal: "Wie ich F.K. kennenlernte," in Klaus Wagenbach: *F.K. Eine Biographie seiner Jugend.* Bern: Francke Verlag, 1958, 270-276.

Margeson, John: "Franz Kafka, a Critical Problem." *University of Toronto Quarterly,* XVIII (Oct. 1948), 30-40.

Margetts, John: "Satzsyntaktisches Spiel mit der Sprache: Zu Franz Kafkas 'Auf der Galerie'." *Colloquia Germanica,* IV, No. 1 (1970), 76-82.

Margolis, Joseph: "Kafka vs. Eudaimonia and Duty." *Philosophy and Phenomenological Research* (Buffalo, N.Y.), XIX No. 1 (1958), 27-42. [On *The Metamorphosis*].

Maria, Giorgio de: "Ipotesi di lavoro su Kafka, dopo una rilettura di Walter Benjamin." *Paragone* (Florence), XXIV, No. 282 (1973), 95-103.

Marion, Denis: *"La Métamorphose* par Franz Kafka." *NRF,* No. 297 (Jun. 1938), 1034-1037.

Marson, Erich L.: "Franz Kafka's 'Das Urteil'." *JAU,* No. 16 (1961), 167-178; [and Keith Leopold]: "Kafka, Freud, and 'Ein Landarzt'" *GQ,* XXXVII, No. 2 (Mar. 1964), 146-159; "Justice and the Obsessed Character in *Michael*

Kohlhaas, Der Prozess, and *L'Etranger." Seminar,* II, No. 2 (1966), 21-33; "Die *Prozess-*Ausgaben: Versuch eines textkritischen Vergleichs." *DV,* XLII (1968), 760-772; *An Analytical Interpretation of F.K.'s "Der Prozess"* University of Queensland, 1966 (typ dis); *Kafka's "Trial,"* University of Queensland Press, 1975; *Kafka's Trial. The Case Against Josef K.* Atlantic Highlands, N.J.: Humanities Press, Inc., 1975, 353 pp.

Martin, Peter A.: "The Cockroach as an Identification, with reference to Kafka's *Metamorphosis." AI,* XVI, No. 1 (1959), 65-71.

Martin, W.B.J.: "Significant Modern Writers: Franz Kafka." *Expository Times* (Edinburgh), LXXI (Jun. 1960), 309-331.

Martínez Estrada, Ezequiel: "Intento de señalar los bordes del 'mundo' de Kafka." *La Nación* (Buenos Aires), (May 14, 1944), 2nd Section, 1; "Acepción literal del mito de Kafka." *Babel* (Santiago, Chile), XIII, No. 53 (1st Semester 1950), 24-28; "Apocalipsis de Kafka." *Israel y América Latina* (Buenos Aires), XII, No. 98 (Apr. 1960), 7-9; all aforementioned rep. in *En torno a Kafka y otros ensayos.* Barcelona; Seix Barral, 1967, 274 pp., 21-41; "Intuition." *KP,* 348-353.

Martini, Fritz: "Franz Kafka: *Das Schloss.* Text und Interpretation," in his *Das Wagnis der Sprache.* Stuttgart: Klett, 1954, 287-335; "Franz Kafka" in Hans Schwerte & Wilhelm Spengler (eds.): *Gestalter unserer Zeit.* Oldenburg/Hamburg, 1954, 191-201; "Ein Manuskript Franz Kafkas: 'Der Dorfschullehrer'." *JDS,* II (1958), 266-300.

Masini, Ferruccio: "La diallettica esistenziale in Kafka." *Aut-Aut* (Milan), XLV (1959), 116-137.

Mast, Günther: "Ein Beispiel moderner Erzählkunst in Missdeutung und Erhellung." *Neue Sammlung,* II, No. 3 (1962), 237-247 [On 'Auf der Galerie'].

Matt, Peter von: "Canetti über Kafka." *Schweizer Monatshefte für Politik, Wirtschaft, Kultur,* XLVIII (1968-1969), 1134-1136.

Matteucci, Benvenuto: "Franz Kafka o l'allegoria del Vecchio Testamento." *Vita e Pensiero* (Milan), XXXV, No. 3 (1952), 157-164.

Mauer, Otto: "Kommentar zu zwei Parabeln von Franz Kafka ['Eine kaiserliche Botschaft' and 'Der Schlag ans Hoftor']." *WoW,* I (1946), 29-34.

Mauriac, Claude: "Franz Kafka" in his *L'Alittérature contemporaine.* Paris: 1958, 13-32; *The New Literature.* N.Y.: Braziller, 1959, 15-34.

Mayer, Hans: "Kafka und kein Ende? in his *Ansichten: Zur Literatur der Zeit.* Reinbek: Rowohlt, 1962, 54-70; "Literatur und Kommunismus." *DM,* XVI, No. 185 (Feb. 1964), 49-56; "The Struggle for Kafka and Joyce." *Encounter* (London), XXII, No. 5 (1965).

McDaniel, T.R.: *Two Faces of Bureaucracy. A Study of the Bureaucratic Phenomenon in the Thought of Max Weber and Franz Kafka.* Johns Hopkins University, 1971 (typ dis).

Meidinger-Geise, Inge: "Franz Kafka und die junge Literatur." *WoW,* VII, No. 6 (1952), 189-194.

Meissner, Frank A.: "A Social Ecology of the German Jews in Prague." *Dalhousie Review* (Halifax, N.S.), XXXIX No. 4 (1960), 511-523.

Mellen, Joan: "Joseph K. and the Law." *Texas Studies in Literature and Language,* XII (1970-1971), 295-302.

Mellown, Elgin W.: "The Development of a Criticism: Edwin Muir and Franz Kafka," *CL,* XVI, No. 4 (1964), 310-321.

Memmi, Germaine: "Motivations inconscientes et formes dans 'La verdict' de Franz Kafka." *Revue de l'Allemagne,* 5 (1973), 785-800.

Mendelsohn, Leonard R.: "Kafka's 'In the Penal Colony' and the Paradox of Enforced Freedom." *SSF,* VIII, No. 2 (1971), 309-316.

Menezes, Oliveira de: *Kafka—o outro: componentes psicosexuais.* Porto Alegre: Ediçoes Flama, 1970, 70 pp.

Merleau-Ponty, Maurice: "Faut-il bruler Kafka?" *Action* (Paris), No. 97 (Jul. 12, 1946).

Mesnil, Michel: "Orson Welles et le jugement." *Esprit* (Paris), No. 423 (1973) 973-985.

Metzger, Michael and Erika: "Franz Kafkas 'Ein altes Blatt' im Deutschunterricht." *KFLQ,* XIII (1966), 30-36.

Micha, René: "Le Fantastique kafkaien sur le plan de l'art." *L'Arche* (Paris), No. 16 (Jun. 1946), 43-50; "Une nouvelle littérature allégorique." *La Nouvelle NRF*, No. 16 (1954), 697-706.

Michael, Wolfgang: "The Human Simian." *The Library Chronicle* (Philadelphia), XIX, No. 1 (1952-1953), 35-44.

Michaels, L.: [F.K.] "Life, Works and Locus." *N.Y. Times Book Review*, (Nov. 21, 1971), 1, 12, 14, 16 & 18.

Michaelson, L.W.: "Kafka's 'Hunger Artist' and Baudelaire's 'Old Clown'." *SSF*, V No. 3 (1968), 293.

Michel, Kurt: *Adalbert Stifter und die transzendente Welt.* Graz: Stiasny Verlag, 1957, 160 pp. [On 'In the Penal Colony', pp. 135-146].

Michel-Michot, P.: "Franz Kafka and William Sansom Reconsidered." *RLV*, XXXVII (1971), 712-718.

Michl, Josef B.: "Franz Kafka und die moderne skandinavischen Literatur." *Schweizer Monatshefte*, XLVIII, No. 1 (1968), 57-71; "Über die Beziehung der skandinavischen Moderne zu Franz Kafka," *PR*, 257-260.

Middelhauve, Friedrich: *Ich und Welt im Frühwerk Franz Kafkas.* University of Freiburg i. Br., 1957, (typ dis).

Middleton, J.C.: "The Picture of Nobody." *RLV*, XXIV (1958), 404-428.

Miles, David H.: "Kafka's Hapless Pilgrims and Grass' Scurrilous Dwarfs. Notes on Representative Figures in the Anti-Bildungsroman." *Monatshefte*, LXV (1973), 341-350.

Milfull, John: "From Kafka to Brecht: Peter Weiss's Development towards Marxism." *GLL*, XX, No. 1 (1966), 61-71.

Miller, Dorothy: "Cultural Tremors in East Germany: the Kafka Discussions." *East Europe* (N.Y.), XIII, No. 5 (May 1964), 30.

Miller, J.H. Jr.: "Franz Kafka and the Metaphysics of Alienation," in Nathan A. Scott, Jr. (ed.): *The Tragic Vision and the Christian Faith.* N.Y.: Association Press, 1957, 281-305.

Miller, Norbert: "Erlebte und verschleierte Rede." *Akz*, V, No.

3 (1958), 213-226; "Die moderne Parabel." *Akz,* VI, No. 3 (1959), 200-213.

Mingelgrun, Albert: "Kafka à la rencontre de Flaubert." *Europe,* No. 511-512 (1971), 168-178.

Misselbeck, Maria: "Franz Kafka: 'Ein Landarzt." *DU,* X, No. 6 (1958), 36-46.

Mitchell, Breon: "Kafka's 'Elf Sohne.' A New Look at the Puzzle." *GQ,* XLVII (1974), 191-203.

Mittenzwei, Werner: "Brecht und Kafka." *SuF,* XV, No. 4 618-625, and *PR,* 119-129; "Brecht et Kafka." *La Nouvelle Critique. Revue du Marxisme Militant* (Paris), No. 163 (1965), 114-123.

Mittner, Ladislao: "Kafka senza kafkismi," in his *La letteratura tedesca del Novecento e altri saggi.* Turin: Einaudi, 1960, 249-294; *Storia della letteratura tedesca del realismo alla sperimentazione.* Turin: Einaudi, 1971, 2 vols., Vol. II, 1159-1188.

Miyai, Toyo: "Motiv zu Franz Kafkas Erzählung 'Das Urteil'." *Jahresberichte des germanisch-romanischen Instituts von Kwanseigakuin Universität,* II (1968), 41-55.

Modern, Rodolfo: "Introducción a Kafka." *La Torre* (Puerto Rico), XI, No. 44 (1963), 11-26.

Moeller, Charles: "Franz Kafka ou La terre promise sans espoir," in his *Littérature du XXe. siècle et Christianisme.* Paris, 1957, 193-210.

Molitor, Jan: *Asmodai in Praag. Franz Kafka, zijn tidj en Werk.* 's Graveland: De Driehoek, Paria Reeks, 1950, 141 pp.

Monserrat, Santiago: *Franz Kafka y el oscuro presente.* Córdoba (Argentina), 1956.

Morand, Jean: "Le *Journal* de Kafka, ou l'irréductible interiorité." *Europe,* No. 511-512 (1971), 95-111.

Morao, Artur: "Sentido e Nao-sentido em Franz Kafka." *Brotéria,* LXXXIII (1966), 87-96.

Morrison, Jean Antoine: *Kafka als Hungerkünstler.* Tulane University, 1963 (typ dis).

Moseley, Edwin M.: "The American Dream Becomes Nightmare: Franz Kafka and Others," in Miloslav Rechcigl (ed.): *Czechoslovakia Past and Present*. The Hague: Mouton, 1968, 1012-1021.

Moss, Leonard: "A Key to the Door Image in 'The Metamorphosis'." *MFS*, XVII (1971), 37-42.

Motekat, Helmut: "Franz Kafkas 'Ein Landarzt'," in *Interpretationen moderner Prosa*, ed. by Fachgruppe Deutsch-Geschichte im Bayerischen Philologenverband. Frankfurt: Verlag Moritz Diesterweg, 1957, 7-27 [new ed., 1968].

Motyljova, T.: "Der Streit um den Roman," *KuL*, XII (1964), 350-377.

Mouligneau, Michel: "Kafka, ou La vie privée." *Europe*, No. 511-512 (1971), 129-132.

Mounier, Guy-Fernand: *Étude Psychopathologique sur l'écrivain Kafka*. University of Bordeaux, 1951 (dissertation), Bordeaux: Imprimerie Samie, 1951.

Moyer, Patricia: "Time and the Artist in Kafka and Hawthorne." *MFS*, IV, No. 4 (1958), 295-306.

Mueller, William R.: "The Theme of Judgment: Franz Kafka's *The Trial*," in his *The Prophetic Voice in Modern Fiction*. N.Y.: Association Press, 1959, 83-109; *Celebration of Life*. N.Y., 1972, [On *The Castle*, 232-250].

Mühlberger, Josef: *Hugo von Hofmannsthal-F. Kafka: Zwei Vorträge*. Esslingen: Bechtle Verlag, 1953, 31-70; "Zum 75. Geburstag Franz Kafkas." *Sudetenland*, I (1958-1959), 38-48: "Einleitung" to F.K.: *Die kaiserliche Botschaft*. Graz/Vienna: Stiasny Bücherei, 1960, 5-28.

Mühler, Günther: "Narciss und der phantastische Realismus," in his *Dichtung der Krise*. Vienna, 1951, 407-539; "Über das Zeitgerüst des Erzählens." *DV*, XXV, No. 1 (1950), 1-31 [On *The Castle*, 29-31].

Muir, Edwin: "Franz Kafka." *The Bookman* (N.Y.), Nov. 1930), 235-241; "Franz Kafka." *Life and Letters* (London), (Jun. 1934), 341-351; "Introductory Note" to F.K.: *The Castle*. N.Y.: Knopf, 1930, v-xi; "Introductory Note" to F.K.: *The Great Wall of China and Other Pieces*. London: Secker, 1933, vii-xvi; *Transition*. N.Y.: Viking Press, 1954, 120-124; "Franz Kafka." *FKM*, 55-66, and *GK*, 33-44; *Essays on Literature and Society*. Harvard University Press, 1956, 120-124.

Müller, Joachim: "Erwägungen an dem Kafka-Text. 'Ein Landarzt'." *Orbis Litterarum* (Copenhague), XXIII (1968), 35-54; "F.Ks. Briefe." *Univ,* XXX (1975), 595-598.

Münnich, Horst Richard: "Der Dichter Franz Kafka." *Der Zwiebelfisch* (Munich), XXV, No. 1 (1946), 16-21.

Murrill, V. and W.S. Marks: "Kafka's 'The Judgment' and *The Interpretation of Dreams." GR,* XLVIII (1973), 212-228.

Muschg, Walter: "Über Kafka." *VHS-Blätter für Wissenschaft und Kunst* (Zurich) III (1929), 80-85; "Der Unbekannte Kafka," in his *Von Trakl zu Brecht.* Munich: Piper, 1961, 149-173; "Franz Kafka: Der Künstler," in his *Gestalten und Figuren.* Bern/Munich: Francke, 1968, 103-126; Über Franz Kafka," in his *Pamphlet und Bekenntnis.* Olten: Walter, 1968, 101-107 "Der Ruhm Franz Kafkas," in his *Die Zerstörung der deutschen Literatur.* Bern: List Bücher, 1956, 1958, 200-213 (4th ed., 1960, 160-171.

Musil Robert: "Literarische Chronik." *NR,* XXV, No. 8 (1914), 1169-1170, rep. in his *Tagebücher, Aphorismen, Essays und Reden,* ed. by A. Frisé. Hamburg, 1955, 687-688; "Note sur Kafka." *CCMR,* L (1965), 43-45.

Musurillo, Herbert: "Healing Symbols in Kafka." *The Month* (N.Y.), XIX (Jun. 1958), 334-340.

N

Nadeau, Maurice: "Kafka et 'L'Assaut contre les frontières'." *Les Lettres Nouvelles* (Paris), XXIV (Feb. 1955), 260-267.

Nag, Martin: "Kunstneren Franz Kafka i dag." *Samtiden* (Stockholm), LXXVIII (1969), 237-252.

Nagel, Bert: *"Jud Süss* und *Strafkolonie.* Das Exekutionsmotiv bei Lion Feuchtwanger und F.K." *Beiträge zur Geschichte der deutschen Sprache und Literatur* (Tubingen), XCIV (1972), 597-629; *Franz Kafka. Aspekte zur Interpretation und Wertung.* Berlin: Erich Schmidt Verlag, 1974, 398 pp.

Nägele, Rainer: "Auf der Suche nach dem verlorenen Paradies. Versuch einer Interpretation zu Kafkas 'Der Jäger Gracchus'." *GQ,* XLVII, No. 1 (1974), 60-72.

Naumann, Dietrich: "Kafkas Auslegungen," in Reinhold Grimm and Conrad Wiedemann (eds.): *Literatur und Geistesgeschichte: Festgabe für Heinz Otto Burger.* Berlin: Schmidt, 1968, 280-307.

Navarro, Oscar: *Kafka, la crisi della fede.* Turin: Taylor, 1949, 109 pp.

Neesen, Peter: *Vom Louvrezirkel zum "Prozess": Franz Kafka und die Psychologie Franz Brentanos.* Göppingen: Kümmerle, 1972, 235 pp.

Neider, Charles: "The Cabalists." *KP,* 398-445; *The Frozen Sea.* N.Y.: Oxford University Press, 1948, 195 pp.; N.Y. Russell & Russell, 1962; retitled *Kafka: His Mind and Art.* London: Routledge & Kegan Paul, 1949.

Németh, André: *Kafka ou Le Mystère juif.* Paris: Jean Vigneau, 1947, 201 pp.

Nerlich, Michael: "La finestra: Note a Mallarmé, Kafka e Gide." *Sigma,* XIV (1967), 61-74.

Neumann, E.: "Aus dem ersten Teil des Kafka-Kommentars: 'Das Gericht'. 'Das Domkapitel.'," in *Geist und Werk. Aus der Werkstatt unserer Autoren. Zum 75. Geburtstag von Dr. Daniel Brody.* Zurich: Rhein-Verlag, 1958, 175-196.

Neumann, Gerhard: "Umkehrung und Ablenkung: Franz

Kafkas 'Gleitendes Paradox'." *DV,* XLII (1968), 702-744 and *PFK;* "'Ein Bericht fur die Akademie'." *DV,* XLIX (1975), 166-183.

Neumarkt, Paul: "Kafka's 'A Hunger Artist': The Ego in Isolation." *AI,* XXVII (Summer 1970), 109-121.

Neumeister, Sebastian: *Der Dichter als Dandy: Kafka, Baudelaire, Thomas Bernhard.* Munich: Fink, 1973, 134 pp., 9-39.

Neumeyer, Peter F.: *The Modern German Novel in England, with Special Emphasis on the Work of F.K. and Thomas Mann.* University of California, Berkeley, 1963 (typ dis); "F.K. and Jonathan Swift." *Dalhousie Review* (Halifax, N.S.) XLV (1965), 60-65; "Franz Kafka, Painter Manqué." *University Review* (Kansas City), XXXI (1965), 217-218; "Frank Kafka and William Sansom." *WSCL,* VII (1966), 76-84; "Franz Kafka and England." *GQ,* XL (1967), 630-642; *Twentieth Century Interpretations of "The Castle."* Englewood Cliffs, N.J.: Prentice Hall, 1969, 122 pp.; "Franz Kafka, Sugar Baron." *MFS,* XVII (1971) 5-19; "Janouch *Conversations* with Kafka: Some Questions." *MFS,* XVII (1971-1972), 555-556.

Neuse, Werner: "Franz Kafka." *BA,* IX (Summer 1935), 266-268.

Nicholson, Hubert: "Some American Nightmares," in his *A Voyage to Wonderland and Other Essays.* London; 1947, 128-148.

Nicholson, Norman: *Man and Literature.* London: Student Christian Movement Press, 1943, 162-185.

Nicolai, Ralf R.: "Erziehung zum Kollektiv." *Humanitas* (Nuevo León, Mexico), (1971), 203-215; "Kafkas Stellung zu Kleist und der Romantik." *SN,* XLV (1973), 80-103; "Diskussionsbeitrage zu Kafkas 'Die Sorge des Hausvaters'." *RLV,* XLI (1975), 156-161.

Nivelle, Armand: "Kafka und die marxistische Literaturkritik," in J. Hösle and W. Eitel (eds.): *Beiträge zur vergleichenden Literaturgeschichte.* Tübingen: Niemeyer, 1972, 331-354.

Noble, C.A.M.: "Kafkas Männer ohne Eigenschaften." *LuK,* LXVI-LXVII (1972), 387-398.

Noon, William T.: "God and Man in Twentieth Century Fiction." *Th*, XXXVII (1962), 35-56.

Northey, Anthony D.: "Kafkas Advokaten." *MLN*, LXXXIX (1974), 469; *"Amerika"*, *KD*.

Nowak, Ernst: *Figurenpaar und Triad in den Werken Franz Kafkas*. University of Vienna, 1974 (typ dis).

O

Ogawa, Satoru: "Das Problem des Monologs in den Erzäh-lungen Kafkas." *Die Deutsche Literatur,* VIII (1962), 48-65.

Ohrgaard, Per: "Franz Kafka," in Sven M. Kistensen (ed.): *Fremmede digtere i det 20 arhundrede.* Copenhagen: G.E.C. Gad, 1968, Vol. II, 311-325.

Olafson, Frederick A.: "Kafka and the Primacy of the Ethical." *Hudson Review* (N.Y.), XIII (Spring 1960), 60-73.

Oliass, Heinz-Günther: "Franz Kafka." *WuW,* IV, No. 2 (1949), 52-56.

Olivieri, Uta: "Analisi statistica dei racconti di Kafka." *Studi Urbinati di Storia, Filosofia e Letteratura* XLII (1969), 369-437.

Ong, Walter J.: "Kafka's Castle in the West." *Th.,* XXII, No. 86 (Sept. 1947), 439-460; "Finitude and Frustration." *Modern Schoolman* (St. Louis), XXV (1948), 173-182.

Osborne, Charles; *Kafka.* Edinburgh/London: Oliver & Boyd, 1967, 120 pp., and N.Y.: Barnes & Noble, 1967, 120 pp.

P

Paci, Enzo: "Contemporary Art as the Expression of the Social and Political Situation." *Confluence,* I (Sept. 1952), 12-18; "Kafka e la Sfida del Teatro di Oklahoma." *SG,* V, No. 13 (1967), 240-252.

Paoli, Rodolfo: "Introduzione" to F.K.: *La metamorfosi.* Florence: Vallecchi, 1934; "Sulle 'Lettere a Milena'." *Annali della Facolta di Lettere dell'Universita di Cagliari,* XXI, Part 2 (1953); "Nota a Kafka" in F.K.: *Descrizione di una battaglia.* Milan: Mondadori, 1960, 9-24; "L'amico de Kafka." [On Max Brod]. *Approdo Letterario* (Rome), XLV (1969), 83-88.

Paraf, Pierre: "L'univers de Kafka." *Europe,* No. 511-512 (1971), 50-55.

Parigi, Ingrid: "Dino Buzzati und sein Verhältnis zu Franz Kafka." *Prisma* (Munich), No. 17 (1948), 26-29.

Parry, Idris F.: "Kafka and Gogol." *GLL,* VI, No. 2 (Jan. 1953), 141-145; "Letters to Milena." *The Listener* (London), L, No. 1294 (Dec. 17, 1953), 1057; *"The Castle," The London Magazine,* I. No. 4 (May 1954), 78-81; "Wedding Preparations." *The London Magazine,* (Dec. 1954), 80-84; "Kafka, Gogol, and Nathanael West." *GK,* 85-90; "Kafka's Modern Mythology." *Bulletin of the John Rylands Library,* LIII, No. 1 (1970), 210-226; "Co-defendants" *Times Literary Supplement* (London), No. 3808 (Feb. 25, 1975), 231.

Pascal, Roy: *The German Novel.* University of Toronto Press, 1956, (new ed., 1965), 215-257, and Manchester University Press, 1956; "Dickens and Kafka." *The Listener* (London), LV (Apr. 26, 1956), 504-506; "Parables from No Man's Land." *Times Literary Supplement* (London), No. 3770 (Jun. 7, 1974), 611-612; *KD.*

Pasche, Wolfgang: *Der religiöse Mittler im Werke Franz Kafkas.* Capetown University, 1964 (typ dis); "Die Frage nach dem Weltbild Kafkas anhand einer kritischen Auseinandersetzung mit der wichtigsten Kafka-Literatur." *AG,* 2 (1967), 75-80.

Pasley, Malcolm: "Frank Kafka MSS; Description and Select Inedita." *MLR,* LVII (Jan. 1962), 53-59; "Franz Kafka: 'Ein Besuch im Bergwerk'." *GLL,* XVIII (1964), 40-46; "Two Kafka Enigmas: 'Elf Söhne' and 'Die Sorge des Hausvaters'." *MLR,* LIX (1964), 73-81; [and Klaus Wagenbach]: "Versuch einer Datierung sämtlicher Texte Franz Kafkas" *DV,* XXXVIII (1964), 149-167, rep. in *KS,* 55-83; "Rilke und Kafka: Zur Frage ihrer Beziehungen." *LuK,* XXIV (1965), 218-225; "Drei literarische Mystifikationen Kafkas." ['Elf Sohne,' 'Die Sorge des Hausvaters' and 'Ein Besuch in Bergwerk']. *KS,* 21-37; "Zur äusseren Gestalt des Schloss-Romans." *KS,* 181-188; "Asceticism and Cannibalism. Notes on an Unpublished Kafka Text." *OGS,* I, (1966), 102-113; "Die Sorge des Hausvaters." *Akz,* XIII, No. 4 (1966), 303-309; "Introduction" and "Notes" to his edition of "Der Heizer," "In der Strafkolonie" and "Der Bau." Cambridge University Press, 1966 and *KD;* "Two Literary Sources of Kafka's *Der Prozess." Forum of Modern Language Studies* (University of St. Andrews, Scotland), III (1967), 142-147; "Zur Entstehunggeschichte von Franz Kafkas Schloss-Bild," in Eduard Goldstücker (ed.): *Weltfreunde.* Neuwied: Luchterhand, 1967, 241-251; "Kafka's Semi-private Games." *OGS,* VI (1971), 112-131 and *KD;* "Rilke und Kafka." *LuK,* III, No. 24 (1968), 218-225; ed. & tr. F.K.: *Shorter Works.* London: Secker & Warburg, 1974, 196 pp.

Paucker, Henri: "Der Einbruch des Absurden: Zwei Interpretationen der Struktur von Kafkas Denken." *Neophilologus,* LV (1971), 175-190.

Paul, David: "A View of Kafka." *Polemic,* No. 4 (Jul.-Aug. 1946), 30-33.

Paulsen, Wolfgang: "Franz Kafka." *Monatshefte,* XXIX, No. 8 (Dec. 1937), 373-388.

Pazi, Margarita: "F.K. und Ernst Weiss." *MAL,* VI, No. 3-4, (1973), 52-92; *Max Brod. Werk und Persönlichkeit.* Bonn: Bouvier, 1970, 178 pp., 6-17.

Pearce, Donald: *"The Castle:* Kafka's Divine Comedy." *FKT,* 165-172

Périlleux, G.: "Kafka et le groupe suédois '40 tal." *RLV,* XXXVI (1970), 637-645.

Perniola, Mario: "Metaletteratura e alienazione dell'arte in Cervantes e Kafka." *Rivista di Estetica* (University of Padua), XVI (1971), 83-92.

Pestalozzi, Karl: "Nachprüfung einer Vorliebe: Franz Kafkas Beziehung zum Werk Robert Walsers." *Akz,* XIII, No. 4 (1966), 322-344.

Peters, F.G.: "Kafka and Kleist: A Literary Relationship." *OGS,* I (1966), 114-162.

Peters, Heinrike: *Die Wahrheit im Werk F.Ks.* Tubingen Fotodruck Präzis, 1967, 112 pp.

Petr, Pavel: "Franz Kafka und der Weg zur Synthese." *PR,* 239-244.

Petry, Walter: "Franz Kafka oder Bemerkungen zu Prinzipien der Prosa." *Die Neue Bücherschau* (Berlin), VI, No. 1 (1926-1927), 14-20.

Pfeiffer, Johannes: "Franz Kafka: 'Eine kleine Frau'. Eine parabolisches Selbstgespräch," in his *Wege zur Erzählkunst. Über den Umgang mit dichterischer Prosa.* Hamburg: Wittig, 1953, 108-116, [4th ed., 1958]; "Über Franz Kafkas Novelle 'Die Verwandlung'." *Die Sammlung* (Göttingen), XIV (1959), 297-302, tr. as "The Metamorphosis" in *GK,* 53-59; "Ahnung und Offenbarung: Zur Deutung der Kunst bei Karl Jaspers," in his *Die dichterische Wirklichkeit.* Hamburg: R. Meinen, 1962, 153-166; "La question des Chateaux." *Obliques* (Paris), No. 3 (2nd trimester 1973), 17-21.

Philippi, Klaus-Peter: *Reflexion und Wirklichkeit: Untersuchungen zu Kafkas Roman "Das Schloss".* Tübingen: Niemeyer, 1966; 248 pp.; "Parabolisches Erzählen: Anmerkungen zu Form und möglicher Geschichte." *DV,* XLIII (1969), 297-332 [On "Von den Gleichnissen", 316-326].

Pick, Otto: "Zwanzig Jahre deutsches Schrifttum in Prag." *Witiko,* (Kassel-Wilhelmshöhe), II, (1929), 116-120; "Prager Dichter" in *Das jüdisch Prag.* Prague: Verlag der Selbstwehr, 1917.

Pilard, Philippe: "Kafka et le cinéma contemporain." *Europe,* No. 511-512 (1971), 192-197.

Pingaud, Bernard: "La doute de Kafka." *TR,* No. 89 (1955), 91-94.

Pivasset, Jean: *L'univers politique de Kafka.* Paris: Editions Cujas, 1965, 137 pp.

Platzer, Hildegard: *A Study of the Relationship between Technique and Theme in the Shorter Works of Kafka.* University of Southern California, 1962 (typ dis, 303 pp.); "Kafka's View of Institutions and Traditions." *GQ,* XXXV, No. 4 (Nov. 1962), 492-503; "Kafka's 'Double-Figure' as a Literary Device." *Monatshefte,* LV (1963), 7-12; "Sex, Marriage, and Guilt: The Dilemma of Mating in Kafka." *Mosaic,* III, No. 4 (Summer 1970), 119-130.

Plavius, Heinz: "Realismus in Entwicklung." *WB,* No. 2 (1964), 262-285.

Pocar, Ervinio: *Introduzione a Kafka.* Milan: Il Saggiatore, 1974.

Podestà, Giuditta: "Kafka e Pirandello." *Humanitas* (Brescia), XI (1956), 230-244; *Franz Kafka e i suoi fantasmi nell'itinerario senza meta.* Turin: Società Editoriale Internazionale, 1956, 175 pp., and Genoa: Libreria Universitaria Pacetti, 1957, 175 pp.

Poggioli, Renato: "Mitologia di Franz Kafka." *Solaria* (Florence), (1934-1935), 1-10; *Pietre di paragone.* Florence: Parenti, 1939, 161-173; "Kafka and Dostoyevsky." *KP,* 97-107; "Mythology of Franz Kafka," in his *The Spirit of the Letter.* Harvard University Press, 1965, 254-263.

Politzer, Heinz: "Nachwort," to Franz Kafka: *Vor dem Gesetz.* Berlin: Schocken Verlag, 1934, 75-80; "Franz Kafkas Autograph." *Die Schrift* (Brünn), I (1935), 94-97; "Franz Kafka. Versuch einer Deutung der Anekdote 'Gibs auf!'." *Jüdische Welt-Rundschau* (Jerusalem), XIII (Jun. 9, 1939), 5; "'Give It up!'." *KP,* 117-121; "Franz Kafka und diese Zeit." *Der Turm* (Vienna), II, No. 1 (1946-1947), 66-69; "Problematik und Probleme der Kafka-Forschung." *Monatshefte,* XLII, No. 6 (1950), 273-280; "Franz Kafka's Letter to His Father." *GR,* XXVIII, No. 3 (1953), and *FKT,* 221-237; "Franz Kafka: Metaphysical Anarchist." *Renascence* (N.Y.), VI (1954), 106-111; "Prague and the Origins of R.M. Rilke, F.K., and Franz Werfel." *MLQ,* XVI, No. 1 (1955), 49-62; "Der Prozess gegen das Gericht: Zum Verständnis von F.Ks. Roman *Der Prozess.*" *WoW,* XIV (1959), 279-292; "F.K. and Albert Camus: Parables of Our Time." *Chicago Review,* XIV, No. 1 (1960), 47-65;

"The Puzzle of Kafka's Prosecuting Attorney." *PMLA*, LXXV, No. 4 (1960), 432-438; "Eine Parabel F.Ks." *JDSG*, IV (1960), 463-483; "F.K's Language." *MFS*, VIII, No. 1 (1962), 16-22; *Franz Kafka: Parable and Paradox.* Cornell University Press, 1962, 376 pp. (rev. and expanded, 1966, 398 pp., tr. as *Franz Kafka, der Künstler.* Frankfurt: Fischer, 1968, 530 pp.; "Kafka im 'Bau'." *Forum* (Vienna), IX (1962), 405-408 and 455-458; "Kafka in der alten Heimat." *Forum* (Vienna), XII, (1965), 188-191; "Das Schweigen der Sirenen." *DV*, XLI (1967), 444-467; (ed.): *Das Kafka-Buch. Eine innere Biographie in Selbst zeugnissen.* Frankfurt: Fischer, 1965; (ed.): *Franz Kafka. Wege der Forschung.* Darmstadt: Wissenschaftliche Buchgesellschaft, 1973, 560 pp.; "Franz Kafka's Completed Novel: His Letters to Felice Bauer." *The Centennial Review* (Michigan State University), XIII (1969), 268-290; "Die Verwandlung des Armen Spielmanns." *Jahrbuch der Grillparzer-Gesellschaft*, III, No. 4 (1965), 55-64; *Das Schweigen der Sirenen.* Stuttgart, 1968, 13-41 and 42-69; "Das entfremdete Selbst—ein Schlüssel zu Kafkas *Schloss*," and "F.Ks. vollendeten Roman. Zur Typologie seiner Briefe an Felice Bauer," in his *Hatte Ödipus einen Ödipus-Komplex?* Munich, 1974, 9-28 and 56-77.

Pondrom, Cyrena N.: "Purdy's *Malcolm* and Kafka's *Amerika*: Analogues with a Difference." *PCLS*, 113-133; "Kafka and Phenomenology: Josef K's Search for Information." *WSCL*, VIII (1967), 78-95; "Coherence in Kafka's 'The Judgment': Georg's Perceptions of the World." *SSF*, IX (1972), 59-79.

Pongs, Hermann: "Kleist und Kafka." *WuW*, VII, No. 11 (1952), 379-380, rep. *Im Umbruch der Zeit. Das Romanschaffen der Gegenwart.* Göttingen: Göttinger Verlagsansalt, 1956 (2nd. ed.), 66-95; *Franz Kafka: Dichter des Labyrinths.* Heidelberg: W. Rothe, 1960, 136 pp.; "'Die Verwandlung' zwischen Ost und West," and "Kafkaesker Stil," in his *Dichtung im gespaltenen Deutschland.* Stuttgart: Union-Verlag, 1966, 262-285 and 286-298; "Franz Kafka: *Das Bild in der Dichtung.* Marburg: Elwert, 1969, Vol. III, 435-463.

Popelová, Jirina: "Die Kategorie der Vereisamung in Kafkas Werk." *PR*, 113-117.

Pott, Hans-Günter: *Die aphoristischen Texte Franz Kafkas. Stil und Gedankenwelt.* Freiburg i. Br. University, 1958 (typ dis).

Praag, Siegfried van: "Franz Kafka." *De Nieuwe Gids* (Brussels and The Hague), XLV, No. 1 (1930), 688-698.

Pratt, Audrey E. (McKim): *Franz Kafka und sein Vater: des Verhältnis der beiden und dessen Einwirkung auf Kafkas Werk.* McGill University, 1949 (typ dis).

Preisner, Rio: "Franz Kafka and the Czechs." *Mosaic.* III, No. 4 (Summer 1970), 131-141.

Prévost, Claude: "A la recherche de Kafka (esquisse d'un bilan très provisoire). *Europe,* No. 511-512 (1971), 13-49.

Prigge-Kruhoeffer, Maria: "Eine andere Welt. Franz Kafka." *Die Literatur* (Stuttgart), XXXI, No. 3 (Oct. 1928), 19-21.

Pryce-Jones, David: "Introduction" and "Appreciation" in F.K.: *The Trial.* Geneva: Edito-Service, distributed in London by Heron Books, 1968, xiii-xvi and 255-278.

Pujmanova, Marie: "Franz Kafka est mort." *Europe,* No. 511-512 (1971), 3.

Pulver, Max: "Spaziergang mit Franz Kafka," in his *Erinnerungen an eine europäische Zeit.* Zurich: Orell Füssli, 1953, 50-57.

Purdy, Strother B.: "A Talmudic Analogy to Kafka's Parable 'Vor dem Gesetz'. *PLL,* IV (1968), 420-427; "Religion and Death in Kafka's *Der Prozess." PLL,* V (1969), 170-182.

Pybus, Rodney: "A Kafka Legacy" *European Judaism* (London), VIII, No. 2 (Summer 1974), 30-32.

Q

Quentin, Max-Pol: "Adapter *Le Chateau.*" *CCMR*, V, No. 20 (Oct. 1959), 13-16.

Quinn, Sister M. Bernetta, O.S.F.: "Butterfly on a Skull: Tragedy as Metamorphosis." *Greyfriar*, VI (1963), 22-28.

Quintero Alvárez, Alberto: "La fatalidad en Kafka." [On *The Metamorphosis*]. *Taller* (Mexico), I, No. 2 (Apr. 1939), 37-39.

R

Raabe, Paul: "F.K. und der Expressionismus." *ZDP,* LXXXVI, No. 2 (1967),161-175 and *PFK,* 386-405; "F.K. und Franz Blei, samt einer wiederntdeckten Buchbesprechung Kafkas." *KS,* 7-20

Rabi, Wladimir: "Le juif de Prague." *Esprit* (Paris), (Jan. 1953), 154-159; "Kafka et la néo-Kabbale." *La Terre Retrouvé*e (Paris), XXIV, No. 10 (Feb. 15, 1955), and *TR,* No. 123 (Mar. 1958), 116-128.

Raboin, Claudine (ed.): *Les critiques de notre temps et Kafka.* Paris: Garnier, 1973, 191 pp.

Radice, L. Lombardo: "F.K." in his *Gli accusati.* Bari: De Donato, 1972, 11-131.

Rahv, Philip: "The Hero as Lonely Man." *The Kenyon Review* (Gambier, Ohio), I, No. 1 (Winter 1939), 60-74; "Death of Ivan Ilyich and Joseph K." *Southern Review* (Baton Rouge, La.), (Summer 1939), 174-185; "Exegetical Notes" in Franz Kafka: *The Great Wall of China.* N.Y.: Schocken, 1946, 309-315; *Image and Idea.* N.Y.: New Directions, 1949, 105-119, (rev. ed., 1957, 121-139); "Introduction" in Franz Kafka: *Selected Short Stories.* N.Y.: Modern Library, 1952, vii-xxii, rep. in his *Literature and the Sixth Sense.* Boston: Houghton, Mifflin, 1969, 38-54 and 183-196.

Raine, Kathleen: "A Comment on Kafka." *Fo,* 44-45.

Rajan, B.: "Kafka—A Comparison with Rex Warner." *Fo,* 7-14.

Rákos, Petr: "Über die Vieldeutigkeit in Kafkas Werk." *PR,* 81-86.

Ramm, Klaus: *Reduktion als Erzählprinzip bei Kafka.* Frankfurt: Athenäum, 1971, 172 pp., (1972 ed., 240 pp.).

Rang, Bernhard: "Franz Kafka. Versuch eines Hinweises." *Die Schildgenossen* (Augsburg), XII, No. 2-3 (1932), 107-119; "Der weltanschauliche Roman." *WuW,* (1951), 131-134.

Rasmussen, Sten: "Uudgrundelighedens offer: Nogle betragtninger over Franz Kafkas roman *Der Prozess." Exil* (Nordisk tidsskrift for eksistentials-tisk debat), III (1968-1969), 89-94.

Rattner, Josef: *Kafka und das Vater-Problem: Ein Beitrag zum tiefenpsychologischen Problem der Kindererziehung: Interpretation von Kafkas "Brief an den Vater."* Munich: Reinhardt, 1964, 58 pp.

Raynoschek, Gustav: *Realismus und Symbolismus im Werke Franz Kafkas.* University of Vienna, 1956 (typ dis, 278 pp.).

Reed, Eugene E.: "Moral Polarity in Franz Kafka's *Der Prozess* and *Das Schloss." Monatshefte,* XLVI No. 6 (Nov. 1954), 317-324; "Franz Kafka: Possession and Being." *Monatshefte,* L No. 7 (Dec. 1958), 359-366; "Franz Kafka: The Futile Messenger." *RLV,* XXVIII, No. 5 (1962), 415-419.

Reed, T.J.: "Kafka und Schopenhauer: Philosophisches Denken und dichterisches Bild." *Euphorion,* LIX, No. 1-2 (1965), 160-172.

Rees, Goronwy: "A Visa for Kafka." *Encounter* (London), XXIII, No. 3 (1964), 27-34.

Reh, Albert M.: "Psychologische und psychoanalytische Interpretationsmethoden in der Literaturwissenschaft," in Wolfgang Paulsen (ed.): *Psychologie in der Literaturwissenschaft.* Heidelberg: Stiehm, 1971, 34-55 [On "Der Steuermann," 46-51].

Rehfeld, Werner: *Das Motiv des Gerichtes im Werke Franz Kafkas. Zur Deutung des "Urteils," der "Strafkolonie," des "Prozess."* J.W. Goethe University (Frankfurt), 1960 (typ dis, 212 pp.).

Reichmann, Peter: "Franz Kafka and New Trends in Europe." *Canadian Bookman* (Toronto), (June 1939), 17-19.

Reinmann, Paul: "Die gesellschaftliche Problematik in Kafkas Romanen." *WB,* III, No. 4 (1957), 598-618, rep. in his *Von Herder bis Kisch: Studien zur Geschichte der deutsch-österreichisch-tschechischen Lieraturbeziehungen.* Berlin: Dietz, 1961, 150-173; "Kafka und die Gegenwart," "Über den fragmentarischen Charakter von Kafkas Werk," and "Schlusswort." *PR,* 13-21, 221-227 and 289-292.

Reiss, Hans S.: "Franz Kafka." *GLL,* I, No. 3 (Apr. 1948), 186-194; "Franz Kafka's Conception of Humour." *MLR,* XLIV, No. 4 (Oct. 1949), 534-542; "Zwei Erzählungen Franz Kafkas. Eine Betrachtung." ["Der Schlag ans Hoftor" and "Die Prüfung"]. *Triv,* VIII, No. 3 (1950), 218-242; *Franz Kafka. Eine Betrachtung seines Werkes.* Heidelberg: Lambert Schneider, 1952, 195 pp., [2nd. ed., 1956, 223 pp.]; "Eine Neuordnung der Werke Kafka?" *Akz,* II, No. 6 (1955), 553-555; "A Comment on 'die beiden Zettel Kafkas'." *Monatshefte,* XLVIII, No. 3 (1956), 152-153; "Recent Kafka Criticism—A Survey." *GLL,* IX, No. 4 (1956), 294-305, and in *GK,* 163-177; "Kafka on the Writer's Task." *MLR,* LXVI, No. 1 (1971), 113-124.

Rendi, Aloisio: "Influssi letterari nel *Castello* di Kafka." *AION-SG,* IV (1961), 75-93.

Renner, Ida: "F.K.: 'Die Prüfung': Ein Deutungsversuch mit Hilfe anderer Aussagen des Dichters." *DU,* X, No. 6 (1958), 47-57.

Rexroth, Kenneth: "F.K. and *The Trial*" in Marshall Lee (ed.): *The Trial of Six Designers.* Lock Haven, Penn.; Hammermill Paper Co., 1968, 15-22.

Rhein, Phillip A.: *The Urge to Live: Kafka's "Der Prozess" and Camus' "L'Etranger".* University of North Carolina Press, 1964, 123 pp.; "Two Examples of Twentieth-Century Art: Giorgio di Chirico and Franz Kafka," in Siegfried Mews (ed.): *Studies in German Literature of the 19th and 20th Centuries. Festschrift for Frederic E. Coenen.* University of North Carolina Press, 1972 (2nd. ed.), 201-209.

Richard, Lionel: "Kafka et la déchirure." *Europe,* No. 511-512 (1971), 141-148.

Richli, Urs: "Jaspers, Musil und Kafka." *Reformatio* (Zurich), XI (1962), 208-215 and 339-351.

Richter, Fritz K.: "'Verwandlungen' bei Kafka und Stehr: Eine Studie zum Surrealismus," in Alfred Hayduk (ed.): *Schlesische Studien.* Munich: Kelp, 1970; also in *Monatshefte,* LXIII, No. 2 (1971), 141-146.

Richter, Helmut: "Im Masstab der Kritik. Zu einigen Prosastücken Franz Kafkas." *SuF,* XI No. 5-6 (1959), 837-871; "Zu einigen neuren Publikationen über Franz Kafka."

WB, No. 4 (1959), 568-578; *Franz Kafka. Werk und Entwurf.* Berlin: Rütten & Loening, 1962, 348 pp.; "Entwurf und Fragment: Zur Interpretation von Kafkas *Prozess.*" *ZDP,* LXXXIV (1965), 47-73; "Zur Nachfolge Kafkas in der westdeutschen Literatur." *PR,* 181-197.

Richter, Peter: [D. Krusche's *Kafka und Kafka-Deutung*]. *Poetica,* VI (1974), 519-521.

Rickert, Richard F.: *"Aesthetic Interpreting and Describing: Their Functions in Regard to the 'Transinterpretive' Art of Kafka and Zen."* University of North Carolina, 1973, DAI 33:4480A (N.C. Chapel Hill).

Rieder, Heinz: "Vierzig Jahre nach Kafka: Zur Geschichte seines Nachruhms." *SR,* LXIII, No. 5 (1964), 343-346, and in *WZ,* X, No. 6 (1964), 22-26; "Kafka und Musil" in his *Österreichische Moderne: Studien zum Weltbild und Menschenbild in ihrer Epik und Lyrik.* Bonn: Bouvier, 1968, 44-47.

Ries, Wiebrecht: "Kafka und Nietzsche." *Nietzsche Studien* (Berlin/N.Y.), II (1973), 258-275.

Ripellino, A.M.: *Praga Magica.* Turin: Einaudi, 1973.

Robbe-Grillet, A.: *Pour un nouveau roman.* Paris, 1963, tr. by B. Wright as *Toward a New Novel.* N.Y., 1965; "Über F.K." *PFK,* 328-330.

Robert, Marthe: *Introduction à la lecture de Kafka.* Paris: Editions du Sagittaire, 1946, 46 pp.; *"Amérique." L'Arche* (Paris), No. 25 (1947), 152-156; "L'Humour de Franz Kafka." *Revue de la Pensée Juive* (Paris), No. 6 (1951), 61-72; "La lecture de Kafka." *TM,* VIII (Oct.-Nov. 1952), 646-660; "Une figure de Whitechapel. Notes inédites de Dora Dymant sur Kafka." *Evidences* (Paris), No. 28 (1952), 38-42; "Introduction" to *Journal de Kafka.* Paris: B. Grasset, 1954, v-xxi; "Kafka et l'art." *MdF,* CCCXXXVII (Oct. 1959), 206-219; *Kafka.* Paris: Gallimard, 1960, 299 pp., new ed. 1968, 223 pp.; "L'imitation souveraine." *TM,* XVI (Mar. 1961), 1124-1149; "Kafka en France." *MdF,* (Jun. 1961), 241-255; "F.K. et la paradoxe de la littérature." *MdF,* CCCLIV (1965), 457-470; (ed.): "Lettres a Minze E." *NRF,* XIII (Oct. 1965), 635-662; "F.K. et la loi de son oeuvre" in F.K.: *Oeuvres completes.* Paris: Cercle du Livre

Précieux, 1963-1965, 8 vols., Vol. I, 11-123; *L'ancien et le nouveau: De Don Quichotte à Kafka.* Paris: Grasset, 1963, 311 pp.; *Sur le papier. Essais.* Paris, 1967, 45-79, 173-179 and 181-219; "Introduction" a F.K.: *Correspondance 1902-1924.* Paris: Gallimard, 1965, 7-17.

Rochefort, Robert: *Kafka ou l'Irréductible espoir.* Paris: R. Julliard, 1947, 254 pp.; "La culpabilité chez Kafka." *Psyché* (Paris), III (Apr.-May 1948), 483-495; "Une oeuvre liée mot pour mot à une vie." *CCMR,* XX (1957), 41-45.

Rogers, Joseph A.: "Kafka's 'An Old Manuscript'."*SSF,* II, No. 4 (1965), 367-368.

Rohl, Freda K.: *A Study of Kafka's Irony.* University of Manchester, 1955 (typ dis); "Kafka's Background as the Source of his Irony." *MLR,* LIII, No. 3 (1958), 380-392.

Rohner, Wolfgang: *Franz Kafkas Werkgestaltung.* University of Freiburg, 1950 (typ dis, 357 pp.) *"Das Schloss"—Der Prozess." Univ,* No. 4 (1952), 412-413; "Briefe an Milena" *Psyche* (Heidelberg, Stuttgart), No. 4 (1953), 70-74; "Hochzeitsvorbereitungen auf dem Lande." *Psyche* (Heidelberg, Stuttgart), No. 12 (1954), 211-216; *Franz Kafka.* Mühlacker: Stieglitz Verlag, 1967, 140 pp.

Rolleston, James: *Kafka's Narrative Theater.* Pennsylvania State University Press, 1974, 165 pp.; "The Judgment," *PJ.;* (ed.): *Kafkas "The Trial."* Englewood Cliffs, N.J.: Prentice-Hall, 1976 (20th Century Interpretations Series); *"The Trial," KD.*

Rommerskirch, Erich: "Prozess gegen Gott." *Geist und Leben* (Würzburg), XXII, No. 2 (1949), 81-90.

Roque de Costa, Constancio: "Franz Kafka visto por um oriental." *Atlantico* (Lisbon), 3rd Series, No. 2 (1949), 89-92.

Rösch, Ewald: "Getrübte Erkenntnis: Bemerkungen zu Franz Kafkas Erzählung. 'Ein Landarzt," in Rainer Schonhaar (ed.): *Dialog.* Berlin: E. Schmidt, 1973, 205-243.

Rosenfeld, Anatol: *Doze estudos.* Sao Paulo, Brazil: Conselho Estadual de Cultura, Comissao de Literatura, 1960.

Rosenthal, Erwin T. [and Others]: *Introduçao a obra de Franz Kafka.* Universidad de Sao Paulo, 1966.

Rost, Nico: "Persoonlijke outmoetingen met F.K. en mijn Tsjechische vrienden." *De Vlaamse Gids* (Brussels), XLVIII (1964), 75-97.

Rosteutscher, Joachim: "Kafkas Parabel 'Vor dem Gesetz' als Antimärchen." *Festschrift für Friedrich Beissner.* Bebenhausen: Rotsch Verlag, 1974, 359-363.

Roudaut, Jean: "En hommage à la littérature." *Preuves* (Paris), No. 171 (1965), 30-37.

Rougemont, Denis de: *Les personnes du drame.* N.Y.: Pantheon, 1945, 105-126, in tr. *Dramatic Personages.* N.Y., 1964, 75-95.

Roy, Gregor: *Kafka's "The Trial," "The Castle" and Other Works. A Critical Commentary.* N.Y.: Distributed by Monarch Press, 1966, 96 pp.

Rubbini, Carlo: "Franz Kafka e 'Il medico di campagna'," *Ferrara Viva,* III, No. 7-8 (1962), 85-100.

Rubinstein, William C.: "'A Hunger Artist'." *Monatshefte,* XLIV, No. 1 (Jan. 1952), 13-19; "Franz Kafka's 'A Report to an Academy'." *MLQ,* XIII, No. 4 (1952), 372-376, and in *FKT,* 55-60; "Kafka's 'Jackals and Arabs'." *Monatshefte,* LIX, No. 1 (1967), 13-18.

Ruf, Urs: *Franz Kafka: Das Dilemma der Söhne.* Berlin: E. Schmidt, 1974, 103 pp.

Ruhleder, Karl H.: "Franz Kafka's "Das Urteil': An Interpretation." *Monatshefte,* LV (Jan. 1963), 13-22; "Biblische Parallelen in Franz Kafkas *Der Prozess.*" *Literatur in Wissenschaft und Unterricht* (Kiel), II, No. 2 (1969), 98-107; "Die theologische Dreizeitenlehre in Franz Kafkas 'Die Verwandlung'." *Literatur in Wissenschaft und Unterricht (Kiel)* IV (1971), 106-114.

Ruland, Richard F.: "A View from Back Home: Kafka's *Amerika.*" *American Quarterly,* XIII (1961), 33-42.

Russell, Francis: "An Examination of Kafka." *Catacomb* (London), (Winter 1951-1952), 194-205, rep. in his *Three Studies in Twentieth Century Obscurity.* Aldington, Ashford, Kent: The Head and the Flower Press, 1954, 45-65, and Chester Springs, Pa.: Dufour, 1961, 45-65; N.Y.: Haskell House, 1966; N.Y.: Gordon Press, 1973, 124 pp.

Rutt, Theodor: "Betrachtung zu 'Der Nachbar' von Franz

Kafka," in Wilhelm L. Hoffe (ed.): *Sprachpädagogik Literaturpädagogik.* Frankfurt: Diesterweg, 1969, 261-271.

Ryan, Judith: "Die zwei Fassungen der 'Beschreibung eines Kampfes': Zur Entwicklung von Kafkas Erzähltechnik." *JDSG,* XIV (1970), 546-572.

Ryan, Lawrence: "'Zum letzten Mal Psychologie!': Zur psychologischen Deutbarkeit der Werke Franz Kafkas," in Wolfgang Paulsen (ed.): *Psychologie in der Literaturwissenschaft.* Heidelberg: L. Stiehm, 1971, 157-173.

Rying, Matts: "Kafka." *Folklig Kultur* (Stockholm), No. 3 (1946), 101-104.

S

Sacharoff, Mark: "Pathological, Comic, and Tragic Elements in Kafka's 'In the Penal Colony'." *Genre,* IV (1971), 392-411.

Sahl, Hans: *"Das Schloss."* Das Tagebuch (Berlin/Munich), VIII (1927), 150-152.

Saillet, Maurice: "Franz Kafka ou La traversée de la nuit." *CdS,* No. 209 (Oct. 1938), 722-725.

Sainmont, J.H.: "De l'onanisme théologal." *Les Lettres Nouvelles* (Paris), (Oct. 1954), 559-569.

St. Leon, R.: "Religious Motives in Kafka's *Der Prozess:* Some Textual Notes." *JAU,* XIII No. 19 (1963), 21-38.

Salinger, Herman: "More Light on Kafka's 'Landarzt'." *Monatshefte,* LIII, No. 3 (1961), 97-104.

Sapper, T.: "Akribie und 'analytische' Präzision." *LuK,* VII (1972), 424-27.

Sandbank, Shim'on: "Structures of Paradox in Kafka." *MLQ,* XXVIII (1967), 462-472; "Surprise Techniques in Kafka's Aphorisms." *Orbis Litterarum* (Copenhagen), XXV (1970), 261-274; "Action as Self Mirror. On Kafka's Plots." *MFS,* XVII, No. 1 (1971), 21-29; "The Unity of Kafka's "Beschreibung eines Kampfes." *Archiv für das Studium der neuren Sprachen und Literaturen,* CCX, Jahrg. 125, No. 1 (1973), 1-21.

Sarraute, Nathalie: "De Dostoievski à Kafka." *TM,* III, No. 25 (Oct. 1947), 664-685, rep. in her *L'Ere du soupçon.* Paris: Gallimard, 7-52, in tr. *The Age of Suspicion.* N.Y.: Braziller, 1963.

Sartre, Jean-Paul: *"Aminadab* ou Le Fantastique considéré comme un langage," in his *Situations I.* Paris: Gallimard, 1947, 122-142, tr. by Annette Michelson as *"Aminadab* or the Fantastic Considered as a Language" in his *Literary Essays.* N.Y.: Philosophical Library, 1957, 56-72; "Symposium on the Question of Decadence." *Streets,* (May-Jun. 1965), 46-55, rep. in Lee Baxandall (ed.): *Radical Perspectives in the Arts.* Hardmondsworth: Penguin Books, 1972, 224-239.

Saurat, Denis: "Homage to Kafka." *The Literary World* (N.Y.) No. 3 (Jul. 1934), 3; *Modernes*. Paris, 1935, 230-236; "A Note on *The Castle.*" *KP,* 181-183.

Sautermeister, Gerd: "Sozialpsychologische Textanalyse. Franz Kafkas Erzählung 'Das Urteil'," in Dieter Kimpel and Beate Pinkermeil (eds.): *Methodische Praxis der Literaturwissenschaft.* Kronberg/Ts.: Scriptor-Verlag, 1975, 179-221. "Die sozialkritische und sozialpsychologische Dimension in Franz Kafkas 'Die Verwandlung'." *DU,* XXVI (1974), 99-109.

Savage, D.S.: "Franz Kafka: Faith and Vocation." *Fo,* 1326, and *Sewanee Review,* LIV (1946), 222-240, and *KP,* 319-336.

Schaufelberger, Fritz: Kafkas Prosafragmente." *Triv,* VII (1949), 1-15; "Kafka und Kierkegaard." *Reformatio* (Schauffhausen/Zurich), (Jul. 1959), 387-400 and (Aug. 1959), 451-456; "Franz Kafka." *DU,* XV (1963), 32-43.

Scherer, Michael: "Das Versagen und die Gnade in Kafkas Werk. Zu Kafkas Erzählung 'Ein Landarzt'." *SZ,* LXXXI, No. 2 (1955-1956), 106-117.

Schild, Kurt W.: *Formen des Verschlüsselns in F.Ks. Erzählkunst.* University of Cologne, 1970 (typ dis, 234 pp.).

Schillemeit, Jost: "Welt im Werk F.Ks." *DV,* XXXVIII (1964), 170-191; "Zur neueren Kafka-Forschung." *Göttingische Gelehrte Anzeigen,* CCXVII, No. 1-2 (1965), 156-179; "Zum Wirklichkeitsproblem der Kafka-Interpretation." *DV,* XL (1966), 577-596.

Schlant, Ernestine: "Kafka's *Amerika:* The Trial of Karl Rossmann." *Criticism,* XII (1970), 213-225.

Schlingmann, Carsten: "Die Verwandlung" and "Kleine Prosastücke" ["Der plötzliche Spaziergang," "Das nächste Dorf," "Kleine Fabel" and "Laufst du immerfort vorwarts"], in Albrecht Weber [and Others]: *Interpretationen zu Franz Kafka.* Munich: Oldenbourg, 1968, 81-105 and 122-137, (3rd. ed., 1972).

Schmidt, Verne V.: *Strindberg's Impact on Kafka.* University of Texas, 1967, (typ dis), DA27(1967)2545A Tex.

Schmiele, Walter: *Dichter und Dichtung in Briefen, Tagebüchern und Essays.* Darmstadt, 1955, 305-312.

Schneeberger, Irmgard: *Das Kunstmärchen in der ersten Hälfte des 20. Jahrhunderts.* University of Munich, 1960 On "Das Urteil," "In der Strafkolonie" and "Die Verwandlung," 17-46] (typ dis).

Schneider, Jean-Claude: "Kafka ou le refus du bonheur." *NRF,* XIV (Aug. 1966), 311-317; "Lectures de Kafka." *NRF,* XVI (Sept. 1968), 303-307. "Robert Walser." *NRF,* No. 229 (Jan. 1972), 59-62.

Schneller, Christian: "Bekenntnis zu Franz Kafka." *Deutsche Beiträge* (Munich), IV, No. 3 (1950), 193-198.

Schoeps, Hans-Joachim: "Die geistige Gestalt Kafkas." *Die Christliche Welt* (Gotha), XLIII, No. 16-17 (1929), 761-771; "Das verlorene Gesetz. Zur religiösen Existenz Franz Kafkas." *Morg,* X, No. 2 (1934), 71-75; "Franz Kafka oder Der Glaube in der Tragischen Position," in his *Gestalten an der Zeitenwende.* Berlin, 1936, 54-76; "The Tragedy of Faithlessness." *KP,* 287-297; "Theologische Motive in der Dichtung Franz Kafkas." *NR,* LXII (Jan-Mar. 1951), 21-37; "Franz Kafka und der Mensch unserer Tage." *Univ,* XVI (Jan.-Feb. 1961), 163-171; "Franz Kafka and the Modern Man." *Univ* [English edition], V (1962), 235-243.

Schouten, J.H.: "Franz Kafka." *Duitse Kroniek* (The Hague), IV, No. 4 (1952), 91-97; "Kafka's brief aan zijn vader." *De Gids* (Amsterdam), CXVII, No. 2 (1954), 359-372.

Schubardt, Wolfgang: "Die neuesten Arbeiten von Ernst Bloch und die Franz Kafka Diskussion." *Wissenschaftliche Zeitschrift der Universität Jena,* XIII (1964), 325-327.

Schubiger, Jürg: *Franz Kafka: "Die Verwandlung": Eine Interpretation.* Zurich: Atlantis Verlag, 1969, 106 pp.

Schüddekopf, Jürgen: "Rätzel der Faszination. Zu F.Ks. Erzählung 'Die Verwandlung'." *Athena* (Berlin), II, No. 7 (1948), 40-43.

Schultz-Behrend, G.: "Kafka's 'Ein Bericht für eine Akademie: An Interpretation." *Monatshefte,* LV, No. 1 (1963), 1-6.

Schulze, Hans: "Anwärter der Gnade." *Tagebuch V 1955. Veröffentlichung der Evangelischen Akademie Tutzing.* No. 6. Munich, 1956, 25-34 [On "Eine kaiserliche Botschaft," "Ein Landarzt," and "Die Verwandlung"].

Schumacher, Ernst: "Kafka vor der neuen Welt." *PR,* 245-256.

Schumann, Thomas B.: "Ein anderer, unkomplizierter K." *SR,* LXXIV (1975), 285-287 [On *Briefe an Ottla*].

Schwartzman, Félix: "Fantasía y realidad en Kafka." *Babel* (Santiago, Chile) XIII (1950), 61-68.

Schweckendiek, Adolf: "Fünf moderne Satiren im Deutschunterricht." *DU,* XVIII, No. 3 (1966), 39-50.

Scott, Nathan A., Jr.: "Franz Kafka: The Sense of Cosmic Exile," in his *Rehearsals of Discomposure.* N.Y.: King's Crown Press, 1952, 11-65; "Kafka's Anguish," in his *Forms of Extremity in the Modern Novel.* Richmond, Va.: John Knox Press, 1965, 13-34.

Sebald, W.G.: "Thanatos: Zur Motivstruktur in Kafkas *Schloss.*" *LuK,* VII, No. 66-67 (1972), 399-411; "The Undiscovered Country: The Death Motif in Kafka's *Castle.*" *Journal of European Studies,* II, No. 1 (Mar. 1972), 22-34; and *KD;* "The Law of Ignominy: Authority, Messianism and Exile in *The Castle.*" *TBL.*

Sedlacek, Peter: *August Strindberg und Franz Kafka. Versuch einer vergleichenden Betrachtung von Persönlichkeit und Werk.* University of Vienna, 1966 (typ dis).

Seidel, Bruno: "Franz Kafkas Vision des Totalitarismus. Politische Gedaken zu Kafkas Roman *Das Schloss* und George Orwells Utopie *1984. Die Besinnung* (Nuremberg), VI, No. 1 (1951), 11-14.

Seidler, Ingo: *"Zauberberg* und *Strafkolonie:* Zum Selbstmord zweier reaktionärer Absolutisten." *GRM,* XIX, No. 1 (1969), 94-103; "'Das Urteil': 'Freud natürlich'? Zum Problem der Multivalenz bei Kafka." in Wolfgang Paulsen (ed.): *Psychologie in der Literaturwissenschaft.* Heidelberg: Stiehm, 1971, 174-190.

Seidler, Manfred: *Strukturanalysen der Romane "Der Prozess" und "Das Schloss" von Franz Kafka.* Bonn University, 1953 (typ dis, 166 pp.) Summary in the *Jahrbuch der Dissertationen der Phil. Fak. der Rheinischen Friedrich-Wilhelms-Universität zu Bonn.* Bonn, 1956, 41-42; "Franz Kafka: Leben, Dichtung und Bedeutung." *Die Kirche in der Welt* (Münster) VII, Lfg. 1 (1954), 119-122; "F.K.: Ein Vortrag." *PPr,* XVI (1962), 299-312; "F.K., der Prager Dichter." *Emuna* (Cologne), III (1968), 159-166.

Seidlin, Oskar: "F.K.—Lackland. An Austro-German Jew from Bohemia." *BA,* XXII, No. 3 (1948), 244-246; "The Shroud of Silence." *PMLA,* LXVIII, No. 2 (1953), 45 ff., and *GR,* XXVIII, No. 4 (1953), 154-261.

Serrano Plaja: Arturo: "Kafka y la segunda consulta al Doctor Negro." *Sur,* XVII, No. 73 (1949), 79-87.

Servotte, Hermann: "Franz Kafka: 'Der Landarzt'." *DUA,* VIII, No. 2 (1958), 33-38.

Seyppel, Joachim H.: "The Animal Theme and Totemism in Franz Kafka." *Literature and Psychology* (N.Y.), IV, No. 4 (1954), 49-63, and in *AI,* XIII (Spring 1956), 69-93, and *Univ,* IV, No. 2 (1961), 163-172.

Sgorlon, Carlo: "Pagine di critica Kafkiana." *Annali della Scuola Normale Superiore di Pisa.* Serie II, No. 2 Lettere, Storia e Filosofia, No. 24 (1955), 50-66; *Kafka narratore.* Venice: Neri Pozza, 1961.

Sheppard, Richard W.: "Kafka's 'Ein Hungerkünstler': A Reconsideration." *GQ,* XLVI (1973), 219-233; *On Kafka's Castle: A Study.* N.Y.: Harper & Row, 1973, 234 pp.; London, Croom Helm, 1974, 227 pp.; *"The Trial/The Castle:* Toward an Analytical Comparison." *KD.*

Shmueli, Efraim: "Entrapments, Absurdities and Absolutes. A Reinterpretation (50 Years after his Death)." *DU,* XLIX (1975), 546-569.

Siebenschein, Hugo: "Franz Kafka und sein Werk." *Wissenschaftliche Annalen* (Berlin), 6 (1957), 793-811, and Beiheft 1957, 2-20.

Siefken, Hinrich: "Man's Inhumanity to Man—Crime and Punishment: Kafka's Novel *Der Prozess* and Novels by Tolstoy, Dostoyevsky, and Solzhenitsyn." *Trivium* (St. David's College), VII (1972), 28-40.

Siegel, Klaus: "Kafka in de dagelijkse omgang." *De Gids* (Amsterdam), CXXXI, No. 8 (1968), 131-140.

Singer, Carl S.: "Kafka and *The Trial:* The Examined Life." in John Unterrecker (ed.): *Approaches to the Twentieth Century Novel.* N.Y.: Crowell, 1965, 182-187: *Discovery of America by Accident: A Study of the Form and Value of the Novel in Kafka's Art.* Columbia University, 1971 (typ dis) *DAI* 32:456A (Columbia) 1971.

Slochower, Harry: "Franz Kafka, Pre-Fascist Exile," in *FKM,* 7-30; "Secular Crucifixion: Franz Kafka" in his *No Voice Is Wholly Lost.* N.Y.: Creative Age Press, 1945, 103-125; "The Limitations of Franz Kafka." *American Scholar* (Williamsburg, Va.), XV (Summer 1946), 291-297; "The Vogue of Franz Kafka." *FKM* [enlarged ed., 1946], 110-118; "The Use of Myth in Kafka and Mann" in R. Hopper (ed.): *Spiritual Problems in Contemporary Literature.* N.Y., Harper, 1952, 117-126.

Slotnick, Linda: *The Minotaur Within: Varieties of Narrative Distortion and Reader Implication in the Works of Franz Kafka, John Hawkes, Vladimir Nabokov and Alain Robbe-Grillet.* Stanford University, 1971 *DAI* 31:607A-72A (Stanford).

Smith, Agnes W.: *"The Castle." New Yorker,* VI (Sept. 20, 1930), 95-96.

Smith, David E.: *The Use of Gesture as a Stylistic Device in Heinrich von Kleist's 'Michael Kohlhaas' and Franz Kafka's "Der Prozess"* Stanford University, 1972 *DAI* 32 (1972) 4634A.

Soergel, Albert and Curt Hohoff: "Franz Kafka," in their *Dichtung und Dichter der Zeit.* Düsseldorf: August Bagel. 1964, 2 vols., Vol. II, 495-511.

Sofovich, Luisa: "Reordenación de Kafka." *Cuadernos del Congreso por la Libertad de la Cultura* (Paris), No. 97 (1965), 76-80.

Sokel, Walter H.: "Kafka's 'Metamorphosis': Rebellion and Punishment." *Monatshefte,* XLVIII, No. 4 (Apr.-May 1956), 203-214; *Franz Kafka. Tragik und Ironie. Zur Struktur seiner Kunst.* Munich/Vienna: Albert Langen-Georg Müller, 1964, 586 pp.; *Franz Kafka.* N.Y.: Columbia University Press, 1966, 48 pp.; "Das Verhältnis der Erzählperspektive zu Erzählgeschehen in 'Vor dem Gesetz', 'Schakale und Araber,' und *Der Prozess:* Ein Beitrag zur Unterscheidung von Parabel und Geschichte bei Kafka." *ZDP,* LXXXVI, No. 2 (1967), 267-300; "Kafka und Sartres Existenzphilosophie." *Arcadia,* V, No. 3 (1970), 262-277; "Franz Kafka as a Jew." *Yearbook of the Leo Baeck Institute,* VIII (1973), 233-238; "Zwischen Drohung und Errettung. Zur Funktion Amerikas in

Kafkas Roman 'Der Verschollene'," in Sigrid Bauschinger, Horst Denkler and Wilfried Malsch (eds.): *Amerika in der deutsche Literatur. Neue Welt—Nord Amerika—USA.* Stuttgart: Reclam, 1975, 246 ff.; "The Judgment," *PJ;* "The Opaqueness of *The Trial,*" *JRT;* "The Three Endings of Joseph K." *KD.*

Solier, René de: "Les Voies de l'inversion." *Cahiers de la Pléiade* (Paris), 2 (Apr. 1947), 27-32.

Sommavilla, Guido: "Kafka era un santo." *Letture* (Milan), XII (1957), 485-489; "La disperazione religiosa di Franz Kafka." *Letture* (Milan), XVI (1961), 323-338; "La vertiginosa incognita divino demoniaca di Franz Kafka," in his *Incognite religiose.* Milan, 1963, 173-181; "Kafka, un nuovo Abramo." *Letture* (Milan), XX (1965), 675-692.

Sonnenfeld, Marion: "Parallels in [Goethes] *Novelle* und *Verwandlung.*" *CIBÀ Symposium* (Basel), XIV (1960), 221-225; "Die Fragmente *Amerika* und *Der Prozess* als Bildungsromane." *GQ,* XXXV (Jan. 1962), 34-46; "Eine Deutung der *Strafkolonie,*" in M. Sonnenfeld and Others (eds.): *Wert und Wort. Festschrift für Else M. Fleissner.* Aurora, N.Y.: Wells College, 1965, 61-68.

Sorensen, Willy: *Kafkas Digtning.* Copenhagen: Gyldendal, 1968, 216 pp.

Sötemann, August L.: *Over het lezen van Kafka.* Amsterdam: De Boekvink Series, 1957, 29 pp.

Spahr, Blake Lee: "Kafka's 'Auf der Galerie': A Stylistic Analysis." *GQ,* XXXIII, No. 3 (1960), 211-215; "Franz Kafka: The Bridge and the Abyss." *MFS,* VIII No. 1 (1962), 3-15.

Spaini, Alberto: "Prefazione" to F.K.: *Il Processo.* Milan: Mondadori 1933, 4-18; *"The Trial." KP,* 143-150; Prefazione to F.K. *Amerika.* Milan: Mondadori, 1947, 7-15.

Spann, Meno: "Die beiden Zettel Kafkas." *Monatshefte,* XLVII, No. 7 (Nov. 1955), 321-328; "Franz Kafka's Leopard." ["A Hunger Artist']. *GR,* XXXIV, No. 2 (Apr. 1959), 85-104; "Don't Hurt the Jackdaw." ['A Hunger Artist)]. *GR,* XXXVII (1962), 68-78; "The Minor Kafka Problem." *GR,* XXXII (1957), 163-177; "F.K." in J. Gealey & W. Schumann (eds.): *Einführung in die deutsche Literatur.* N.Y., 1964, 401-426.

Sparks, Kimberly: "Drei schwarze Kaninchen: Zu einer Deutung der drei Zimmerherren in Kafkas 'Die Verwandlung'." *ZDP*, LXXXIV (Sonderheft 1965), 73-82; "Kafka's *Metamorphosis:* On Banishing the Lodgers." *Journal of European Studies,* III (1973), 230-240, "Radicalization of Space in Kafka's Stories." *TBL.*

Späth, Ute: "Parallelismus: Semantisch-syntaktische Untersuchungen an motivverwandter Dichtung: E.T.A. Hoffmann-Franz Kafka." *WW,* XXIII, No. 1 (1973), 12-44.

Spector, Robert D.: "Kafka's 'The Stoker' as Short Story." *MFS,* II (May 1956), 80-81; "Kafka and Camus: Some Examples of Rhythm in the Novel." *KFLQ,* V (1958), 205-211; "Kafka's Epiphanies." *KFLQ,* X (1963), 47-54.

Spender, Stephen: *The Destructive Element.* N.Y.: Random House, 1936, 236-250; *"The Trial."* *New Republic* (N.Y.) (Oct. 27, 1937), 347; *"Amerika".* *Living Age* (N.Y.), Vol. 355 (Dec. 1938), 382; "Franz Kafka." *Daily Worker* (London), (Jul. 28, 1937), 7; *"The Trial* and *Metamorphosis" Life and Letters Today* (London), (Autumn 1937), 185-186.

Spilka, Mark: *Dickens and Kafka: A Mutual Interpretation.* Indiana University Press, 1963, 315 pp.; and London: Dennis Dobson, 1963, 315 pp.; Gloucester: P. Smith, 1969; *"Amerika:* Its Genesis." *FKT,* 95-116; "Kafka's Sources for the 'Metamorphosis'." *CL,* XI, No. 4 (1959), 289-307; "David Copperfield as Psychological Fiction." *Critical Quarterly* (Hull/London), I (1959), 292-301; "Kafka and Dickens: The Country Sweetheart." *AI,* XVI (1959), 367-378; "Dickens and Kafka: The Technique of the Grotesque." *Minnesota Review,* I (1961), 441-458.

Spiro, Solomon J.: "Verdict—Guilty! A Study of *The Trial."* *TCL,* XVII, No. 3 (1971), 169-179.

Spittler, Ella: "Franz Kafkas 'Gesetz' unter dem Aspekt des Atems." *RLV,* XXXI (1965), 439-443.

Springer, Mary D.: *"The Metamorphosis"* in her *Forms of the Modern Novella.* University of Chicago Press, 1976.

Spycher, Peter: "Franz Kafka." *Reformatio* (Zurich) (Jun. 1958), 275-289.

Stahl, August: "Konfusion ohne Absicht? Zur Interpretation von Kafkas Erzählung 'Die Sorge des Hausvaters'," in

Rudolf Malter and Alois Brandstetter (eds.): *Saarbrücken Beiträge zur Ästhetic*. Saarbrücken: Verlag der Saarbrücker Zeitung, 1966, 67-78.

Stallman, Robert W.: "Kafka's Cage." *Accent* (Urbana, Illinois), No. 8 (1948), 117-125; "The Hunger Artist," in R.W. West and R.W. Stallman (eds.): *Art of Modern Fiction*. N.Y.: Rinehart, 1949, 366-372; also in R.W. Stallman and R.E. Watters: *The Creative Reader*. N.Y.: Ronald, 1954, 318-323; "A Hunger Artist." *FKT,* 61-70.

Stamer, Uwe: "Sprachstruktur und Wirklichkeit in Kafkas Erzählung 'Auf der Galerie'," in Rose B. Schäfer-Maulbetsch [and Others]: *Festschrift für Kurt Herbert Halbach zum 70. Geburstag*. Cologne/Vienna: Böhlau, 1972, 427-452.

Standaert, Eric: "Psychografie van F.K." *Nieuw Vlaams Tijdschrift* (Antwerp), X (1956), 166-183; "'Gibs auf!': Ein Kommentar zu dem methodologischen Ausgangspunkt in Heinz Politzers Kafka-Buch." *Studia Germanica Gandensia* (Ghent), VI (1964), 249-272; *Franz Kafka:* Van *Mens tot Werk,* Ghent University 1954 (typ dis).

Starobinski, Jean: "Figure de Franz Kafka" preface to Franz Kafka: *La Colonie Pénitentiaire*. Paris: Egloff, 1945, 9-67; "Le Rêve architecte (à propos des intérieurs de Franz Kafka)." *Lettres* (Geneva/Paris), (Feb. 1947), 24-33, rep. in *CCMR,* L (1965), 21-29; "Kafka et Dostoievski." *CdS,* No. 304 (1950), 466-475, rep. in *Obliques* (Paris), No. 3 (2nd trimester 1973), 40-44; "Kafka's Judaism." *European Judaism.* (London), VIII, No. 2 (Summer 1974), 27-30.

Staroste, Wolfgang: *Raum und Realität in dichterischer Gestaltung: Studien zu Goethe und Kafka*. Heidelberg: Stiehm, 1971, 123-155.

Stefani, Giuseppe: "Franz Kafka, Impiegato delle Generali." *Bollettino delle Assicurazioni Generali* (Prague), (Dec. 1952); "Kafka e Italia." *Nuova Antologia* (Rome), 470 (1957), 67-68.

Steinberg, Erwin R.: "A Kafka Primer." *CE,* XXIV (1962), 230-232; "The Judgment in Kafka's 'The Judgment'." *MFS,* VIII, No. 1 (1962), 23-30; "Kafka and the God of Israel." *Judaism,* XII (1963), 142-149; "K. of *The Castle:* Ostensible Land-Surveyor." *CE,* XXVII (1965), 185-189, and *H,* 126-132.

Steinberg, M.W.: "Franz Kafka: The Achievement of Certitude." *Queen's Quarterly* (Kingston, Ontario), LXVIII (1961), 90-103.

Steiner, George: *Language and Silence.* London: Faber & Faber, 1967, 141-149; "Central European." *New Yorker,* XLVIII (Jul. 15, 1972), 75-78.

Steinhauer, Harry: "Hungering Artist or Artist in Hungering: Kafka's 'A Hunger Artist'." *Criticism,* IV (1962), 28-43.

Steinhoff, P.A.: "Franz Kafka, Dichter." *Aufbau* (Berlin), III, No. 6 (1947), 481-487.

Steinmetz, Horst: *Aber bij Kafka.* Leiden Universitaire Pers, 1971, 22 pp.

Stelzmann, Rainulf A.: "Kafka's *The Trial* and Hesse's *Steppenwolf:* Two Views of Reality and Transcendence." *Xavier University Studies,* V (1966), 165-172.

Stéphane, Nelly: "K par K." *Europe,* No. 511-512 (1971), 197-201; "Chronologie de Kafka." *Europe,* No. 511-512 (1971), 197-201.

Stern, Guy: "Explication de Texte: 'Der Heizer'." *MLJ,* XLI (1957), 37-38.

Stern, J.P.: "Franz Kafka: The Labyrinth of Guilt." *Critical Quarterly,* VII (1965), 35-47; "Franz Kafka's 'Das Urteil': An Interpretation." *GQ,* XLV (1972), 114-129; "The Law of *The Trial." TBL,* "The Judgment," *PJ.*

Stierle, Karlheinz: "Mythos als 'bricolage' und zwei Endstufen des Prometheus-Mythos," in M. Fuhrmann (ed.): *Poetik und Hermeneutik 4.* Terror und Spiel. Probleme der Mythenrezeption. Munich, 1971, 455-472 [On "Prometheus", 463-467].

Stokes, John L.: *F.K.: A Study in Imagery.* Drew University, 1969, *DAI* 30 (1969) 2045A (Drew).

Stolze, A.O.: "Un-Wirklichkeit in der modernen Dichtung." *WuW,* VII, No. 8 (1952), 265-266.

Stolzl, Christoph: *Kafkas böses Böhmen. Zur Sozialgeschichte einer Prager Juden.* Munich: Edition text und kritik, 1975.

Storch-Marien, O.: "Alchimistengässchen Nr. 22. Unbekanntes über F.K." *Im Herzen Europas,* (Prague) No. 10 (Oct. 1963), 7 and 17.

Storz, Gerhard: "Über den 'monologue intérieur' oder die

'Erlebte Rede'." *DU,* VII, No. 1 (1955), 41-53 [On *Der Prozess*]; *"Der Prozess,"* in his *Sprache und Dichtung.* Munich, 1957, 201-204.

Strauss, Walter A.: "Albert Camus's *Caligula:* Ancient Sources and Modern Parallels." *CL,* III, No. 2 (1951), 160-173; "F.K.: Between the Paradise and the Labyrinth." *Centennial Review,* V (1961), 206-222.

Street, James B.: "Kafka through Freud. Totems and Taboos in 'In der Strafkolonie'." *MAL,* VI, No. 3-4 (1973), 93-106.

Strelka, Joseph: *Kafka, Musil, Broch und die Entwicklung des modernen Romans.* Vienna/Hanover/Basel: Forum Verlag, 1959, 110 pp.

Strich, Fritz: "Franz Kafka und das Judentum." *Festschrift des Schweizerischen Israelitischen Gemeinbundes.* Basel, 1954, 273-289, and in his *Kunst und Leben. Vorträge und Abhandlungen zur deutschen Literatur.* Bern/Munich: Francke, 1960, 139-151.

Strohschneider-Kohrs, Ingrid: "Erzähllogik und Verstehensprozess in Kafkas Gleichnis 'Von den Gleichnissen," in Fritz Martini (ed.): *Probleme des Erzählens in der Weltliteratur.* Stuttgart: Klett, 1971, 303-329.

Strolz, Walter: "Platon, Newman, Kafka und die Musik." *Der Grosse Entschluss* (Vienna), (Nov. 1956), 80-91.

Struc, Roman S.: *Food, Air, and Ground: A Study of Basic Symbols in Kafka's Short Stories.* University of Washington, 1962 (typ dis); "Critical Reception of F.K. in the Soviet Union." *Annals of the Ukranian Academy of Arts and Science in the U.S.,* II (1964-1968), 129-142; "Franz Kafka in the Soviet Union: A Report." *Monatshefte,* LVII (1965), 193-197; "The Doctor's Predicament: A Note on Turgenev and Kafka." *Slavic and East European Journal,* IX (1965), 174-180; "Zwei Erzählungen von E.T.A. Hoffmann und Kafka: Ein Vergleich." *RLV,* XXXIV (1968), 227-238; "Madness as Existence." *Research Studies* (Washington State University), XXXVIII, No. 2 (1970), 75-94; "Categories of the Grotesque: Gogol and Kafka." *PCLS,* 135-154.

Stuart, Dabney: "Kafka's 'A Report to an Academy': An Exercise in Method." *SSF,* VI, No. 4 (1969), 413-420.

Stumpf, Walter: "Das religiöse Problem in der Dichtung Franz

Kafkas." *Orient und Okzident* (Leipzig), No. 5 (1931), 48-63; "Franz Kafka." *Die Furch* (Berlin), XVIII, No. 3 (1932), 249-262; "Franz Kafkas Werdegang." *Die Schildgenossen* (Augsburg), XIV, No. 4 (1935), 351-366; "Franz Kafka: Persönlichkeit und geistige Gestalt." *Die Fähre* (Munich), II, No. 7 (1947), 387-397; "Franz Kafka. Der Mensch und sein verlorenes Einst." *Literarische Revue* (Munich), III, No. 5 (1948), 281-284 [On "Investigations of a Dog" and "In the Penal Colony"].

Sturmann, Manfred: "Erinnerungen an Franz Kafka." *Allgemeine Zeitung* (Munich), No. 329 (1924); "Franz Kafkas Sendung." *Jüdische Rundschau* (Marburg/Berlin), XXXIII, No. 20 (1928), 143-144; "Franz Kafka. Ein Versuch aus Anlass seines zehnten Todestages." *Bayerische Israelitische Gemeindezeitung* (Munich), X, No. 14 (1934), 289-290.

Suchkov, Boris: "Kafka: His Fate and Work." *Studies in Soviet Literature,* (Spring 1966), 10-46, (Summer 1966), 58-93. See also *Soviet Literature,* No. 5 (1965), 141-148: "Kafka's Work in the Estimation of Soviet Critics."

Süskind, W.E.: "Der Dichter Franz Kafka." *Der Neue Merkur* (Stuttgart/Berlin), VII, Band 12, No. 2 (1924), 1010-1014.

Susman, Margarete: "Das Hiob-Problem bei Franz Kafka." *Morg.* V, No. 1 (1929), 31-49, reprinted in her *Gestalten und Kreise.* Stuttgart: Diana Verlag, 1954, 348-366, and *PFK,* 48-68.

Sviták, Ivan: "Kafka: Ein Philosoph." *PR,* 87-94, and *PFK,* 378-385.

Swander, Homer: "The Castle: K's Village." *FKT;* 173-192; "Zu Kafkas *Schloss,*" in Jost Schillemeit (ed.): *Deutsche Romane von Grimmelshausen bis Musil.* Frankfurt: Fischer, 1966, 269-289.

Swiatlowski, Zbigniew: "Das Erkenntnisproblem und die Gerechtigkeitsfrage bei F.K." *Germanica Wratislaviensa,* XV (1971), 85-98; "Kafkas 'Oktavhefte' und ihre Bedeutung im Werk des Dichters." *Germanica Wratislaviensia,* XX (1974), 97-116.

Sykes, Gerald: *"The Castle." The Nation* (N.Y.), (Oct. 15, 1930), 411.

Symons, Julian: "A Comment." *Fo,* 43.

Szamek, Pierre, Mark Van Doren and Lyman Bryson: *"The Trial." Invitation to Learning* (N.Y.), II (Spring 1952), 48-55.

Szanto, George H.: *Narrative Consciousness: Structure and Perception in the Fiction of Kafka, Beckett and Robbe-Grillet.* University of Texas Press, 1972, 189 pp. [On "Metamorphosis," "The Judgment," and the novels, 15-68 and 173-180].

T

Taaning, Tage: "Franz Kafka og Milena Jesenska." *Det Danske Magasin* (Copenhague), IV (1954), 286-289.

Taberner, Victor: "Anotaciones en torno a Kafka." *Letras de Deusto* (Spain), I, No. 2 (1971), 187-196.

Tauber, Herbert: *Franz Kafka. Eine Deutung seiner Werke.* Zurich: Oprecht Verlag, 1941, 237 pp.; *Franz Kafka, an Interpretation of His Works.* Yale University Press, 1948, 252 pp.; London: Secker & Warburg, 1948; Port Washington, N.Y.: Kennikat Press, 1968.

Taylor, Alexander: "The Waking: The Theme of Kafka's 'Metamorphosis'." *SSF,* II, No. 4 (1965), 337-342.

Tedlock, E.W., Jr.: "Kafka's Imitation of *David Copperfield.*" *CL,* VII, No. 1 (Winter 1955), 52-62.

Terras, Victor: "Zur Aufhebung bei Kafkas und Dostojewski." *PLL,* V (1969), 156-169.

Terray, Elemir: "Einige Bemerkungen zu *Herder-Blättern* und der Prager Avantgarde." *PR,* 147-154.

Thalmann, Jörg: *Wege zu Kafka. Eine Interpretation des Amerikaromans.* Frauenfeld/Stuttgart: Huber, 1966, 298 pp.

Thieberger, Friedrich: "Erinnerungen an Franz Kafka." *Eckart* (Witten/Ruhr/Berlin), XXIII (Oct.-Dec. 1953), 49-53.

Thieberger, Richard: "Kafka trente-cinq ans après." *Critique,* XV (May 1959), 387-399; "Kafka, Camus, et la sémantique historique." *CLS,* IV, No. 3 (1967), 319-326; "Ein Käfig ging einen Vogel suchen." *Luk,* (1974), 403-407; *Le genre de la nouvelle dans la littérature allemande.* Paris, 1968.

Thierry, Werner: "Hvad er meningen med Kafka?" *Dialog* (Copenhagen), No. 1 (1950), 91-96.

Thomas, Hugh: "Notes towards a Better Understanding of Kafka and the Logic of Failure." *Cambridge Review,* LXXII (1951), 530.

Thomas, J.D.: "The Dark at the End of the Tunnel: Kafka's "In the Penal Colony." *SSF,* IV (1966) 12-18.

Thomas, R.H.: "Franz Kafka and the Religions Aspect of Expressionism." *GLL,* II (Oct. 1937), 42-49.

Thorlby, Anthony: *Kafka: A Study.* London: Heinemann, 1972, 101 pp., and Totowa, N.J.: Rowman & Littlefield, 1972, 101 pp.; *A Student's Guide to Kafka.* London: Heinemann Educational Books, 1972, 101 pp.; "Anti-Mimesis: Kafka and Wittgenstein." *TBL.*

Thurston, Jarvis: "'The Married Couple'." *FKT,* 83-91.

Tiburzio, Enrico: "Note sull'opera di Franz Kafka." *Belfagor,* XXV (1970), 135-162.

Tiefenbrun, Ruth: *Moment of Torment: An Interpretation of Franz Kafka's Short Stories.* Carbondale, Ill.: South Illinois University Press, 1973, 160 pp.

Tilton, John W.: "Kafka's *Amerika* as a Novel of Salvation." *Criticism,* III (Fall 1961), 321-332.

Timmer, Charles B.: "Kafka in de spiegel van de Russische critiek." *Litterair Paspoort* (Amsterdam), (Aug.-Sept. 1949), 115-116.

Timmermans, R.: *Franz Kafka. De mens-zijn werkzijn betekenis.* Leuven University, 1954 (typ dis, 199 pp.).

Tindall, William York: *The Literary Symbol.* N.Y.: Columbia University Press, 1955, 63-64, 139-142, 174-176.

Tinturier, André: *Form und Inhalt bei Broch, Freud und Kafka.* University of Zurich, 1970 (typ dis).

Todorov, Tzvetan: *Einführung in die fantastische Literatur.* Munich, 1972 [On "The Metamorphosis"].

Tomanek, Thomas J.: "The Estranged Man: Kafka's Influence on Arreola." *RLV,* XXXVII (1971), 305-308.

Tomberg, Friedrich: "Kafkas Tiere und die bürgerliche Gesellschaft." *Das Argument,* VI, No. 1 (1964), 1-13.

Tomlinson, K.C.: *"The Castle." Nation & Athenaeum* (London), (May 10, 1930), 182.

Torberg, Friedrich: "Kafka the Jew." *Commentary* (N.Y.), IV (Aug. 1947), 189-190.

Tragtemberg, Mauricio: "Franz Kafka—O romancista do 'absurdo'." *Alfa,* I (1964) 81-95.

Trahan, Elizabeth: "'A Common Confusion': A Basic Approach to Franz Kafka's World." *GQ,* XXXVI No. 3 (1963), 269-278.

Tramer, Friedrich: "August Strindberg und Franz Kafka." *DV,* XXXIV, No. 2 (1960), 249-256.

Tramer, Hans: "Prague, City of Three People." *Leo Baeck Institute Yearbook* (London), IX (1964), 305-339.

Trost, Pavel: "Franz Kafka und das Prager Deutsch." *GP* III (1964), 29-37; "Zur Interpretationsmethode von Kafkas Werken." *PR,* 237-238.

Tucholsky, Kurt: "'In der Strafkolonie'," in his *Gesammelte Werke.* Reinbek: Rowohlt, 1960, Vol. I, 664-666, reprinted from *Die Weltbühne* (Berlin), (Mar. 6, 1920), also in *KS,* 154-156; "*Der Prozess,*" in his *Gesammelte Werke.* Reinbek: Rowohlt, 1961, Vol. II, 372-376, reprinted from *Die Weltbühne* (Berlin), (Sept. 3, 1926).

Turkov, Mark: "Frants Kafkas Prag." *Der Veg* (Mexico City), (Jan. 24, 1967).

Turner, Allison: "Kafka's Two Worlds of Music." *Monatshefte,* LV No. 4 (Oct. 1963), 265-276.

Tuverlin, Jacques: "Les derniers travaux sur Kafka." *Allemagne d'Aujourdhui* (Paris), II (Feb. 1953), 181-186.

Tyler, Parker: "Kafka and the Surrealists." *Accent* (Urbana, Ill.), VI (Autumn 1945), 23-27; "Kafka's and Chaplin's *Amerika.*" *Sewanee Review*, LVIII (Spring 1950), 299-311; rep. as "The Dream-Amerika of Kafka and Chaplin," in his *The Three Faces of the Film.* N.Y. & London, 1960, 94-101.

U

Uematsu, Kenro: "Ein Problem vom Bewusstsein in Kafkas 'Beschreibung eines Kampfes'." *Forchungsberichte zu Germanistik,* VI (Osaka/Kobe), VI (1964) 20-37.

Ulshöfer, Robert: "Die Wirklichkeitsauffassung in der modernen Prosadichtung." *DU,* VII, No. 1 (1955), 13-40 [On 'Die Verwandlung,' 27-36].

Urzidil, Gertrude: "Notes on Kafka." *PCLS,* 11-16.

Urzidil, Johannes: "Franz Kafka, Novelist and Mystic." *Menorah Journal* (N.Y.), XXX, No. 1 (1943), 272-283; "Personal Notes on Franz Kafka." *Life and Letters Today* (London) XLII (Sept. 1944), 134-140; "Recollections." *KP,* 20-24; "The Oak and the Rock." *KP,* 276-286; "Franz Kafka and Prague." *GR,* XXVI, No. 2 (1951), 163-165 and *H,* 21-26; "Meetings with Franz Kafka." *Menorah Journal* (N.Y.), XL (Apr.-Jun. 1952), 112-116; "Das Reich des Unerreichbaren: Kafka-Deutungen." *GR,* XXXVI (Oct. 1961), 163-179; "Edison and Kafka." *DM,* XIII (1961), 31-35; "L'Amérique revée par Kafka." *Preuves* (Paris), No. 137 (1962), 31-35; "Brand: Erinnerung an einen Prager Weggefähreten Kafkas und Werfels." *WoW,* XIX, No. 6-7 (1964), 457-462; "Kafkas Bestattung und Totenfeier." *Merkur,* XVIII (1964), 595-599; *Da geht Kafka.* Zurich: Artemis Verlag, 1965 and Munich: Deutscher Taschenbuch Verlag, 1966, 125 pp., tr. by Harold A. Basilius as *There Goes Kafka.* Wayne State University Press, 1968, 231 pp.; "Der Lebendige Anteil des jüdischen Prag an der neuren deutschen Literatur." *Bulletin des Leo Baeck Instituts* (Tel Aviv), X (1967), 276-297; "Epilog zu Kafkas Felice-Briefen," in Wolfgang Paulsen: *Das Nachleben der Romantik in der modernen deutschen Literatur.* Heidelberg: Stiehm, 1969, 212-219; "Cervantes und Kafka," in Hugo Gold (ed.): *Max Brod: Ein Gedenkbuch.* Tel Aviv: Olamenu, 1969, 107-126; "Cervantes und Kafka." *Hoch,* LXIII (1971), 333-347.

Usmiani, Renate: "Twentieth Century Man, the Guilt-Ridden Animal." *Mosaic,* III, No. 4 (Summer 1970), 163-168.

Utitz, Emil: "Erinnerungen an Franz Kafka," in Klaus Wagenbach: *F.K.: Eine Biographie seiner Jugend.* Bern: Francke, 1958, 267-269.

Uyttersprot, Herman: "Beschouwingen over Franz Kafka: (1) Kafka, Praeceptor lectoris." *De Vlaamse Gids* (Brussels), No. 8 (1953), 449-458; (2) "Kafka, stijl als wisselstroom," No. 9 (1953), 534-548; (3) "Legende en werkelijkheid over Rimbaud en Kafka," No. 9 (1954), 541-554 and No. 10 (1954), 595-605; "Zur Struktur von Kafkas *Der Prozess.* Versuch einer Neu-Ordnung." *RLV,* V, No. 42 (1953), 333-376 and Brussels: Marcel Didier, 1953, 44 pp.; "Zur Struktur von Kafkas Romanen." *RLV,* XX (Oct. 1954), 367-382, also Nynwegen: Tijschrift voor Levende Talen, 1954, 18 pp.; "F.K., de 'Aber-mann'." *RLV,* XX, No. 6 (1954), 452-457; *"The Trial:* Its Structure." *FKT,* 127-144; *Kleine Kafkaiana.* Brussels: Didier, 1955, 22 pp. [Contains "F.K., de 'Aber-mann'," and "F.K. of de processie te Echternach"]; *Eine neue Ordnung der Werke Kafkas? Zur Struktur von "Der Prozess" und "Amerika".* Antwerp: C. de Vries-Brouwers, 1957, 85 pp.; *Praags Cachet.* Antwerp: Uitgeverij Ontwikkeling, 1963, 277 pp. [Essays on Rilke and Kafka]; "F.Ks. 'Der Verschollene'." *Merlyn,* III (1965), 409-424; "De kogel door de kerk? Nuchtere beschouwingen over een Kafka-Colloquium." *De Vlaamse Gids* (Brussels), L (1966), 209-213; "Franz Kafka und immer noch kein Ende: Zur Textgestaltungsfrage." *Studia Germanica Gandensia,* VIII (1966), 173-246.

V

Václavík, Antonín: "Franz Kafka und seine Kunst der psychologischen Analyse." *PR,* 267-275.

Vahanian, Gabriel: *Wait without Idols.* N.Y.: Brazillier, 1964.

Vallette, Rebecca M.: *"Der Prozess* and *Le Procès:* A Study in Dramatic Adaptation." *Modern Drama,* X (1967), 87-94.

Van Alphen, Albert W.: *A Study of the Effects of Inferiority Feelings on the Life and Works of Kafka.* Louisiana State University, 1970 DAI 30 (1970) 3028A (La. State, Baton Rouge).

Vasata, Rudolf: "Dickens and Kafka." *The Central European Observer* (London), XXII, No. 3 (Feb. 9, 1945), 49-50; *"Amerika* and Charles Dickens." *KP,* 134-139.

Vennberg, Karl: "Franz Kafka." *Horisont* (Stockholm), V (1944), 39-55, reprinted in Karl Vennberg and Werner Aspenström: *Kritiskt 40-tal.* Stockholm, 1948, 359-376.

Vialatte, Alexander: "Note" [On Kafka: "Le Terrier"]. *NRF,* (Apr. 1933), 607-615; "Introduction." to Kafka's *Le Procès.* Paris: Gallimard, 1957 (7th ed.), 31-41; "'Empereur a dépeché un de ses messagers." *CCMR,* L (1965), 6-11; *L'Histoire secrète du "Procès".* Liege: Editions Dynamo, 1968.

Vianec, Mihael: "The Struggle for Kafka and Joyce." *Encounter* (London), XXIII (1964), 92.

Victoroff, David: "Quelques aspects de la personne dans l'oeuvre de Kafka." *Etudes Philosophiques* (Paris), No. 3 (1957), 471-473.

Vietta, Egon: "Franz Kafka und unsere Zeit." *NSR,* XXIV, No. 8 (1931), 565-577; "The Fundamental Revolution." *KP,* 337-347.

Vietta, S. and H.G. Kemper: *Expressionismus.* Munich: W. Fink, 1975 [On "Das Urteil", 286-305.

Vigée, Claude: "Les artistes de la faim." *TR,* (Apr. 1957), 43-64, and *CL,* No. 2 (1957), 43-64; *Les artistes de la faim.* Paris, 1960, 211-248.

Vivas, Eliseo:: "Kafka's Distorted Mask." *Kenyon,* X (Winter 1948), 51-70, and *GK,* 133-146; *Creation and Discovery. Essays in Criticism and Aesthetics.* N.Y.: Noonday Press, 1955, 29-46.

Vogelmann, D.J.: "Datos para una clave de Kafka." *La Nación* (Buenos Aires), (Apr. 6 and Apr. 20, 1941), Section II, p. 3; "Raigambre y desarraigo de Franz Kafka." *Heredad* (Buenos Aires), (Jan.-Feb. 1946), 13-22, and *Babel* (Santiago, Chile), Año XI, Vol. 13 (1950), 13-22.

Vogelsang, Hans: "Franz Kafka: Satiriker der Angst und Ausweglosigkeit." *Österreich in Geschichte und Literatur* (Vienna), IX (1965), 134-147.

Vogelweith, Guy: "Kafka et Kierkegaard." *Obliques* (Paris), No. 3 (2nd. trimestre, 1973), 45-50.

Volkening, Ernesto: *"La Metamorfosis* de Kafka." *Revista de las Indias* (Bogotá), (Mar.-May 1948), 465-475.

Volkmann-Schluck, Karl Heinz: "Bewusstein und Dasein in Kafkas *Prozess." NR,* LX, No. 1 (1951), 38-48.

Vortriede, Werner: *"Letters to Milena:* The Writer as Advocate to Himself." *FKT,* 239-248.

Votaw, Albert: "The Literature of Extreme Situations." *Horizon* (London), No. 117 (1949), 145-160.

Vuarnet, Jean-Noël: "Le Labyrinthe de l'absence." *Europe,* No. 511-512 (1971), 73-80.

W

Wagenbach, Klaus: *Franz Kafka. Eine Biographie seiner Jugend, 1883-1912.* Bern: Francke Verlag, 1958, 345 pp., (French translation): *Franz Kafka, les années de jeunesse 1883-1912.* Paris: Mercure de France, 1967, 277 pp.; (Spanish translation): *La juventud de Franz Kafka.* Caracas: Monte Avila, 1970, 368 pp.; "Ein Autor und sein Nachruhm." *NR,* LXXIV (1963), 509-512; *Franz Kafka in Selbstzeugnissen und Bilddokumenten.* Reinbek bei Hamburg: Rowohlt Taschenbuch Verlag, 1964, 1965, 1966, 150 pp., (Spanish translation): *Franz Kafka en testimonios personales y documentos gráficos.* Madrid: Alianza Editorial, 1970, 191 pp.; "Ein unbekannter Brief Franz Kafkas." *NR,* LXXVI (1965), 426-433; [with Jürgen Born, Ludwig Dietz, Malcolm Pasley and Paul Raabe]: *Kafka-Symposion.* Berlin: Verlag Klaus Wagenbach, 1965, 189 pp.; "Julie Wohryzek, die zweite Verlobte Kafkas." *KS,* 39-54; "Wo liegt Kafkas Schloss?" *KS,* 161-180; *Franz Kafka 1883-1924. Manuskripte Erstdrucke/Dokumente/Photographien.* Berlin: Akademie der Künste, 1966, 110 pp.; "Où peut-on situer le chateau de Kafka? *Lettres Nouvelles* (Paris), Jul.-Sept. 1967), 38-55; (ed.): *Kafka par lui-même.* Paris: Editions du Seuil, 1968, 192 pp.

Wagner, Klaus: "Hiob im Büro." *Der Spiegel* (Hamburg), VII, No. 32 (1953), 27-31.

Wagner Marianne: "Franz Kafka." *Der Bücherwurm* (Berlin/Dachau), XVI, No. 10 (1931), 276-280.

Wahl, Jean: "Kierkegaard and Kafka." *KP,* 262-275.

Waidson, H.M.: "The Starvation-Artist and the Leopard." *GR,* XXXV, No. 4 (1960), 262-269; "Kafka: Biography and Interpretation." *GLL,* XIV, No. 1-2 (Oct. 1960-Jan. 1961), 26-33; *"Das Schloss,"* in A. Closs: *XXth Century German Literature.* N.Y.: Barnes & Noble, 1969, pp. 122-128.

Waismann, F.: "A Philosopher Looks at Kafka." *Essays in Criticism* (Oxford), III, No. 2 (Apr. 1953), 177-190.

Waldeck, Peter B.: "Kafka's 'Die Verwandlung' and 'Ein Hungerkünstler' as Influenced by Leopold von Sacher-Masoch." *Monatshefte,* LXIV (1972), 147-152.

Waldmeir, Joseph J.: "Anti-Semitism as an Issue in *The Trial* of Kafka's Joseph K." *BA,* XXXV (1961), 10-15.

Walker, Augusta: "Allegory, a Light Conceit." *Part,* XXII, No. 4 (Fall 1955), 480-490 [On "The Burrow"].

Waldmann, Werner: "Auf dem Weg zum Klassiker: Franz Kafka." *WuW,* 28 (1973), 257-267.

Walser, Martin: *Beschreibung einer Form. Versuch über Franz Kafka.* Munich: Hanser, 1961, (3rd. ed., 1968), 156 pp.; (Spanish translation: *Descripción de una forma. Ensayo sobre Franz Kafka.* Buenos Aires: Sur, 1970, 128 pp.; "Arbeit am Beispiel: Über Franz Kafka," in his *Erfahrungen und Leserfahrungen.* Frankfurt: Suhrkamp, 1965, 143-147.

Walter, Siegfried: *Die Rolle der fuhrenden und schwellenden Elemente in Erzählungen des 19. und 20. Jahrhunderts.* Bonn University, 1952 (typ dis).

Walzel, Oskar: "Logik und Wunderbaren." *KS,* 140-146; *PFK,* 33-38.

Ware, Malcolm: "Catholic Ritual and the Meaning of Kafka's 'Das Ehepaar'." *Sym,* XIX, No. 1 (1965), 85-88.

Warren, Austin: "Kosmos Kafka." *Southern Review* (Baton Rouge, La.), VII (Autumn 1941), 350-365; "Kosmos Kafka." *KP,* 60-74; "The Penal Colony." *KP,* 140-142; *Rage for Order.* University of Chicago Press, 1948, 104-118.

Warshow, Robert: "Kafka's Failure." *Part,* XVI, No. 4 (Apr. 1949), 428-431.

Wasserstrom, William: "In Gertrude's Chest." *Yale Review,* XLVIII (1959), 245-265.

Waterman, Arthur E.: "Kafka's 'The Hunger Artist'." *CE,* XXIII, No. 3 (1961) 9.

Weber, Albrecht and Carsten Schlingmann and Gert Kleinschmidt: *Interpretationen zu Franz Kafka: "Das Urteil," "Die Verwandlung," "Ein Landarzt," "Kleine Prosastücke."* Munich: Oldenbourg, 1968, (2nd ed., 1970), 140 pp.

Webster, Peter Dow: "Arrested Individuation or The Problem of Joseph K. and Hamlet." *AI,* V (1948), 225-245; "A Critical Fantasy or Fugue." [Shakespeare's "Venus and Adonis" and Kafka's "A Country Doctor"]. *AI,* VI (1949), 297-309; "'Dies Irae' in the Unconscious, or The Significance of Franz Kafka." *CE,* XII (1950), 9-15 and *H,* 118-125; "A Critical Examination of Franz Kafka's *The Castle."* *AI,* VIII (1951), 36-60; "Franz Kafka's 'In the Penal Colony'." *AI,* XIII (1956), 399-407; "Franz Kafka's 'Metamorphosis' as Death and Resurrection Fantasy." *AI,* XVI (1959), 349-365.

Weidlé, Wladimir: *Les Abeilles d'Aristée. Essai sur le destin actuel des lettres et des arts.* Paris and Bruges, 1936, 260-267, (2nd. ed., Paris, 1954, 309-313); "The Negative Capability." *KP,* 354-362.

Weidner, Walthier: "Goethe weniger lebensnotwendig als Kafka?" *Die Besinnung* (Nuremberg), IV, No. 4-5 (1949), 147-151.

Weigand, Hermann J.: "Franz Kafka's 'The Burrow': An Analytical Essay." *PMLA,* LXXXVII No. 2 (1972), 152-166.

Weinberg, Helen A.: *The New Novel in America: The Kafkan Mode in Contemporary Fiction.* Cornell University Press, 1970, 248 pp.

Weinberg, Kurt: "F.Ks. 'Erste Veröffentlichung'." *ZDP,* LXXXI (1962), 496-500; *Kafkas Dichtungen: Die Travestien des Mythos.* Bern/Munich: Francke, 1963, 509 pp. [On "Die Verwandlung," 235-317; on "Das Urteil," 318-350].

Weinstein, Leo: "Kafka's Ape: Heel or Hero?" *MFS,* VIII (Spring 1962), 75-79.

Weiss, Ernst: "Bemerkungen zu den Tagebüchern und Briefen Franz Kafkas." *Mass und Wert* (Zurich), I, No. 2 (Nov.-Dec. 1937), 319-325; "The Diaries and Letters." *KP,* 207-213.

Weiss, T.: "The Economy of Chaos." *KP,* 363-375.

Weiss, Walter: "Dichtung und Grammatik: Zur Frage der grammatischen Interpretation." *Jahrbuch des Instituts für Deutsche Sprache.* Düsseldorf: Schwann, 1965-1966, 235-256.

Weitzmann, Siegfried: *Studie über Kafka.* Tel Aviv: Olamenu, 1970, 130 pp.

Weltmann, Lutz: "Kafka's Friend Max Brod. The Work of a Mediator." *GLL,* IV, No. 1 (Oct. 1950), 46-50.

Weltsch, Felix: "Freiheit und Schuld in Franz Kafkas Roman *Der Prozess.*" *Jüdischer Almanach auf das Jahr 5687* (Prague) (1926-1927), 115-121; "Religiöser Humor bei Franz Kafka," in Max Brod: *Franz Kafkas Glauben und Lehre.* Winterthur: Mondial/Munich: Desch; 1948, 155-192; "Der Bote des Königs" *Deutsch Rundschau* (Stuttgart), (1952), 527-531; "Kafkas Briefe an Milena." *DM,* V, No. 57 (1953), 311-317; "Kafkas Aphorismen." *NDH,* I, No. 4 (1954), 307-312; "Franz Kafkas Humor." *DM,* VI, No. 65 (1954), 520-526; "The Rise and Fall of the Jewish-German Symbiosis: The Case of F.K." *Leo Baeck Institute Yearbook* (London), (1956), 255-276; *Religion und Humor im Leben und Werk Franz Kafkas.* Berlin-Grunewald: F.A. Herbig, 1957, 95 pp.; "Franz Kafkas Geschichtsbewusstsein." *Deutsches Judentum.* Stuttgart: Deutsche Verlagstalt, 1963, 271-288.

Weltsch, Robert: "Franz Kafka's Home City." *Survey,* XXXVII (1961), 115-117.

Welzig, Werner: "Die 'universelle Thematik': der Romane F.Ks," in his *Der deutsche Roman im 20. Jahrhundert.* Stuttgart: Kröner, 1967, 226-239; ed. 1970, 281-290.

Wenzig, E.: "Das Mysterium der ungelösten Frage (Vergleich von Dostojewskis 'Grossinquisitor' und Ks. *Der Prozess.*" *Die Tat 20,* XII, No. 2 (1928/1929), 904-906.

Werfel, Franz: "Recollections." *KP,* 37.

Werner, Herbert: "Der Mensch in dieser Welt. Franz Kafkas *Der Prozess.*" *Die Stimme der Gemeinde* (Stuttgart), III, No. 1 (1951), 15-16; "Die Gottlosen haben keinen Frieden.' Zu dem Roman von Franz Kafka: *Das Schloss.*" *Die Stimme der Gemeinde* (Stuttgart), III, No. 8 (1951), 15; "Das Geheimmis Israels und die Dichtung Franz Kafkas." *Evangelische Theologie* (Bethel b. Bielefeld), XI, No. 12 (1951-1952), 533-548.

West, Rebecca: "Kafka and the Mystery of Bureaucracy." *Yale Review,* XLVIII (1957-1958), 15-35; and *H,* 109-117; *The Court and the Castle.* Yale University Press, 1957, 279-301, new ed. 1961.

White, John J.: "F.K's 'Das Urteil': An Interpretation." *DV,* XXXVIII (1964), 208-229; "Endings and Non-Endings in Kafka's Fiction." *TBL;* "Georg Bendemann's Friend." *PJ;* "'Blumfeld, an Elderly Bachelor'." *KD.*

White, John S.: "Psyche and Tuberculosis: The Libido Organization of Franz Kafka," in Warner Muensterberger and Sidney Axelrad (eds.): *The Psychoanalytic Study of Society.* N.Y.: International Universities Press, 1967.

White, William M.: "A Reexamination of Kafka's 'The Country Doctor' as Moral Allegory." *SSF,* III, No. 3 (1966), 345-347.

Wiegler, Paul: "Erinnerungen an Franz Kafka." *Aufbau* (Berlin), IV, No. 7 (1948), 608-609.

Wiese, Benno von: "Franz Kafka: 'Ein Hungerkünstler'" and Franz Kafka: "Die Verwandlung" in his *Die deutsche Novelle von Goethe bis Kafka.* Düsseldorf: Bagel, 1956, 325-342, (1962 ed., 319-345); "Franz Kafka: Die Selbstdeutung einer modernen dichterischen Existenz," in his *Zwischen Utopie und Wirklichkeit.* Düsseldorf: A. Bagel, 1963, 232-253; "Die Künstler und die moderne Gesselschaft." *Akz,* V, No. 2 (1958), 112-123. "Nachwort" to F.K.: *Der Heizer.* Frankfurt: Suhrkamp, 1975, 55-84.

Wildman, Eugene: "The Signal in the Flames: Ordeal as Game." *TriQ,* XI (1968), 145-162.

Wilhelm, Rigobert: "Das Religiöse in der Dichtung Franz Kafkas: Versuch einer Interpretation." *Hoch,* LVII, No. 4 (1965), 335-349.

Williams, Werner T.: *Elements in the Works of Franz Kafka as Analogue of his Inner Life.* University of Kentucky, 1972. DAI 32:5248A-49A (Ky.).

Wilson, A.K.: "'Null and Void': An Interpretation of the Significance of the Court in Franz Kafka's *Der Prozess. GLL,* XIV No. 3 (Apr. 1961), 165-169.

Wilson, Edmund: "A Dissenting Opinion on Kafka." *The New Yorker,* XXIII (Jul. 26, 1947), 58-64, rep. in his *Classics and Commercials.* N.Y.: Farrar, Straus & Co., 1950, 383-392, and in *GK,* 91-98.

Winkelman, John: "Kafka's 'Forschungen eines Hundes'." *Monatshefte,* LIX, No. 3 (Fall 1967), 204-216; "An

Interpretation of Kafka's *Das Schloss.*" *Monatshefte,* LXIV, No. 2 (Summer 1972), 115-131.

Winkler, R.O.C.: "Significance of Kafka." *Scrutiny* (Cambridge, England), VII, No. 3 (Dec. 1938), 354-360; "The Three Novels." KP, 192-198; "The Novels." *GK,* 45-51.

Witt, Mary Ann: *Prison Imagery in the Works of Franz Kafka and Albert Camus.* Harvard University, 1968, (typ dis); "Camus et Kafka." *Revue de Lettres Modernes,* III, No. 264-270 (1971), 71-86; "Confinement in *Die Verwandlung* and *Les séquestrés d'Altona.*" *CL,* XXIII, No. 1 (Winter 1971), 32-44.

Witte, Bernd: "Festellungen zu Walter Benjamin und Kafka." *NR,* LXXXIV (1973), 480-494.

Wolff, Kurt: "On F.K." *Twice a Year* (N.Y.), No. 8-9 (1942), 273-279; *Briefwechsel eines Verlegers 1911-1963.* Ed. by B. Zeller and E. Otten. Darmstadt, 1966, 24-60; *Autoren, Bücher, Abenteur. Betrachtungen und Erinnerungen eines Verlegers.* Berlin, 1965.

Wolkenfeld, Suzanne: "Christian Symbolism in Kafka's *The Metamorphosis.*" *SSF,* X (1973), 205-207.

Wöllner, Günter: *E.T.A. Hoffmann und Franz Kafka. Von der "fortgeführten Metapher" zum "sinnlichen Paradox".* Bern/Stuttgart, 1971 (Sprache und Dichtung, N.F. Bd. 20).

Wondratscheck, Wolf: "Weder Schrei noch Lächeln: Robert Walser und F.K." *TuK,* No. 12 (1965), 17-21.

Wood, Frank: "Hofmannsthal and Kafka: Two Motifs." *GQ,* XXXI, No. 2 (1958), 104-113.

Woodcock, George: "Kafka and Rex Warner." *Fo,* 59-65; *KP,* 108-116; and in his *The Writer and Politics.* London, 1948, 197-206.

Woodring, Carl L.: "Josephine the Singer, or The Mouse Folk'." *FKT,* 71-75.

Y

Yalom, Marilyn Koenick: *The Motif of the Trial in the Works of Franz Kafka and Albert Camus.* Johns Hopkins University, 1963 (typ dis); "Albert Camus and the Myth of the Trial." *MLQ,* XXV, No. 4 (1964), 434-450.

Z

Zampa, Giorgio: "Lettere inedite di Kafka a M. Bl." *Paragone* (Florence), 64 (1955), 18-41; *Rilke, Kafka, Mann. Letture e ritratti tedeschi.* Bari: De Donato, 1968; *"Der Prozess: romanzo e frammenti,"* in F.K.: *Il processo.* Milan: Adelphi, 1973.

Zangerle, Ignaz: "Die Bestimmung des Dichters." *Der Brenner* (Innsbruck), No. 16 (1946), 112-120, and with the title "Der Dichter und das Kreuz." *Das Goldene Tor* (Baden-Baden), III (1948), 413-426.

Zanoli, Anna: "Kafka e Pollak: Descrizione di un conflitto." *Paragone* (Florence), No. 248 (1970), 3-28.

Zatonsky, D.: "Kafka ohne Retusche." *KuL,* XII (1964) 804-824 and 939-955.

Zepp, Evelyn H.: *The Aesthetics of the Absurd Novel: Camus and Kafka.* Cornell University, 1973 (typ dis) DA34 (73/74) 7795A.

Zimmermann, Werner: *Deutsche Prosadichtungen der Gegenwart.* Düsseldorf: Pädagogischer Verlag Schwann, 1954, 1956, 1960, 1961, 174 pp. [Includes analyses of "Auf der Galerie," "Eine kaiserliche Botschaft," and Vor dem Gesetz"]; enlarged ed. and retitled *Deutsche Prosadichtungen unseres Jahrhunderts.* Dusseldorf: Schwann, 1966, 256 pp. [Includes analyses of "Das Urteil," 189-208; "Auf der Galerie," 209-215; "Eine kaiserliche Botschaft," 216-218; "Vor dem Gesetz," 219-227; and "Das Stadtwappen," 251-256]; new ed. in 2 vols., Dusseldorf: Schwann, 1969, [Adding "Der Nachbar," in Vol. II, 250-266].

Ziolkowski, Theodore: *Dimensions of the Modern Novel: German Texts and European Contexts.* Princeton University Press, 1969 [On *The Trial,* 37-67].

Zohn, Harry: "The Jewishness of F.K." *Jewish Heritage* (N.Y.), (Summer 1964), 44-50.

Zolla, Elemire: "F.K." *Letterature Moderne* (Milan), I (Dec. 1950), 495-507; "Le maschere e il volto di F.K." *Letterature Moderne* (Milan), V, No. 2 (1954), 151-159;

"Prefazione" to F.K.: *Confessioni e immagini*. Milan: Mondadori, 1960, (2nd. ed., 1964), 9-23.

Zyla, Wolodymyr: "F.K.: Writer for the Twentieth Century." *PCLS*, 165-172.

Zylberberg, Hélène: "Das tragische Ende der drei Schwestern Kafkas." *Wort und Tat*, No. 2 (1946/1947), 137; "La fin tragique des trois soeurs de Kafka." *Fontaine* (Paris), No. 48-49 (1946), 373-376.

III   Background and Biography
—A Recapitulation

An abbreviated list—full details in Section II.
Principal biographical sources, other than Kafka's
diaries and letters, are Brod and Wagenbach.

Bach, H.: "F.Ks. Leben."
Bahr, E.: "Kafka and the Prague Spring."
Bauer, J. & I. Pollak: *Kafka and Prague.*
Bauer, R.: "Kafka a la lumière de la religiosité juive."
Baudy, N.: "Entretiens avec Dora Dymant."
Baum, O.: "Recollections," *KP,* 25-31; "Der junge F.K."
Baumer, F.: *Franz Kafka.*
Baxandall, L.: "Kafka and Radical Perspective."
Beck, E.T.: *Kafka and the Yiddish Theater.*
Berence, F.: "Prague de Kafka."
Bergmann, S.H.: "Erinnerungen an F.K."
Bezzel, C.: *Kafka-Chronik.*
Binder, H.: "F.K. and the Weekly Paper *Selbstwehr;*" "Kafkas
    Hebräischstudien;" "Kafka und *Die Neue Rundschau;*"
    "Kafka und seine Schwester Ottla;" "Kafkas Briefscherze;"
    "Kafka und die Skulpturen;" and K. Wagenach₁ (eds):
    *Zeittafel (Chronological Table) in F.K.: Briefe an Ottla und
    die Familie.* Frankfurt: S. Fischer, 1974, 228-244; *Kafka-
    Kommentar,* 22-34 and 35-42.
Blei, F.: "F.K.;" Cf. P. Raabe: "F.K. und Franz Blei."

Bödeker, K.B.: *Frau und Familie im erzählerischen Werk F. Ks.*

Boeschenstein, H.: "Emil Utitz, der Philosoph aus dem Prager Kreis."

Born, J.: "F.K. und Felice Bauer;" "F.K. und seine Kritiker, 1912-1924;" "Vom 'Urteil' zum Prozess: Zu Kafkas Leben und Schaffen in den Jahren 1912-1914."

Brod, Max: *Franz Kafka. A Biography;* "Leben mit F.K.;" "Aus Ks. Freundekreis;" "Zusammen Arbeit mit F.K."; "The Jewishness of F.K.;" "Bemerkungen zu Lebensgeschichte"; *Der Prager Kreis; Über F.K.;* "F.Ks. Krankheit," *Therapeutische Bericht,* XXXIX (1967); "Kafka, Father and Son."

Buber, M.: "Kafka and Judaism;" *Briefwechsel aus sieben Jahrzehnten.*

Buber-Neumann, M.: *Mistress to Kafka: The Life and Death of Milena.*

Bullaty, S. & A. Lomeo: "Kafka's Prague."

Canetti, E.: *Kafka's Other Trial. The Letters to Felice.*

Cermak, J.: "En Bericht über umbekannte Kafka-Dokumente;" "Die tschechische Kultur und F.K."

Crawford, D.: *Franz Kafka: Man Out of Step.*

Dell'Agli, A.M.: "Kafka a Berlino: Raconto di un contresso."

Demetz, P.: *F.K. a Praha.*

Dietz, L.: "Kurt Wolffs Bücherei *Der Jüngste Tag;*" "F.K. und die Zweimonatsschrift *Hyperion;* "Die autorisierten Dichtungen Kafkas;" "Drucke F.Ks. bis 1924; "F.K.: Drucke zu seinen Lebzeiten."

Durant, W.A.: "Kafka."

Dymant, D.: "Ich habe F.K. geliebt;" Cf. interviews with N. Baudy, J.P. Hodin, and M. Robert.

Edschmid, Kasimir (ed): *Die doppelköpfige Nymphe. Aufsafätze über die Literatur und die Gegenwart.* Berlin, 1920, 121-122.

Edwards, B.: *The Extent and Development of Autobiographical Material in the Works of F.K.*

Ehrenstein, A.: "F.K."

Eisner, P.: *F.K. and Prague;* "F.Ks. *Prozess* und Prag."

Eisnerová, D.: "Bemerkungen."

Engerth, R.: *Im Schatten des Hradschin: Kafka und sein Kreis.*

Falke, R.: "Biographisch-literarische Hintergründe von Kafka's 'Urteil'."

Fastout, J.: "Kafka, solitaire ou solidaire?"

Feigl, F.: "Erinnerungen an F.K."

Fiedler, L.A.: "Kafka and the Myth of the Jew."

Flores, A.: "F.K." in S.J. Kunitz & H. Haycraft (eds.): *Twentieth Century Authors; F.K.: A Chronology and Bibliography: The Kafka Problem;* [& Homer Swander] (eds.): *Franz Kafka Today.*

Flores, K.: "Biographical Note."

Foltin, Lore B.: *Franz Werfel.* Stuttgart, 1972.

Foti, F.: "Kafka e altri amori *epistolari."*

Fowles, J.: "My Recollections of Kafka."

Frantzke, W.: "Der Liebespfeil in den Schläfen."

Franzen, E.: "Die Briefe Franz Kafkas."

Frey, H.: "Rudolf Steiner und Franz Kafka."

Frort, P.: "F.K. und das Prager Deutsch."

Frynta, E. & J. Lukas: *F.K. lebte in Prag; Kafka and Prague; Kafka et Prague.*

Fuchs, R.: "Social Awareness," *KP*, 247-250; "Reminiscenes of F.K."

Geritt, D.: "Brief Memories of F.K."

Glaser, F.B.: "The Case of F.K."

Glatzer, N.N. (ed.): *I am a Memory Come Alive.*

Gold, H. (ed.): *Max Brod. Ein Gedenbuch 1884-1968.*

Goldstücker, E.: "Zum Profil der Prager deutschen Dichtung um 1900;" "Über F.K. aus der Prager Perspektive;" "Grenzland zwischen Einsamkeit und Gemeinschaft;" "Die aufnahme F.Ks. in der Tschechoslowakei."

Greenberg, C.: "The Jewishness of F.K."

Grieser, D.: "Im Schloss für soziale Wohlfahrt."

Grossman, J.: "Kafka et Prague."

Gütling, A.: "Erinnerungen an F.K."

Haas, W.: "Um 1910 in Prag;" "Ricordo di F.K.;" "Prague in 1912;" *Die Literarischen Welt; Gestalten der Zeit.*

Hall, C.S. & R.E. Lind: *Dreams, Life, and Literature.*

Hardt, L.: "Recollections," *KP*, 32-36; "Erinnerung an F.K."

Hartung, R.: "Ein neues Kafka-Bild."

Hasselblatt, D.: *Zauber und Logik.*

Hatvani, P.: "Einige Bemerkungen."

Hebel, F.: "Max Brod: *F.K.: Eine Biographie."*

Hecht, M.B.: "Uncanniness, Yearning and F.K."

Heer, F.: "Josef Weinheber aus Wien."

Heller, E.: "Biographical Note" in his *F.K.,* xv-xx; "Kafka's True Will. An Introductory Essay" to F.K.: *Letters to Felice,* vii-xxiii, and "Notes", "Appendix," and "Chronology," 551-586; [and J. Beug] (eds.): *F.K.: Dichter über ihre Dichtungen.*

Hellmann, A.: "Erinnerungen an gemeinsame Kampfjahre."

Hering, G.F.: "F.Ks. *Tagebücher;*" "Kafka in drei Spiegeln."

Hermsdorf, K.: "Briefe des Versicherungsangstellten F.K.;" "Hinweis auf einen Aufsatz von F.K.;" *Kafka. Weltbild und Roman;* "Werfels und Kafkas Verhältnis zur tschechischen Literatur."

Hibberd, J.: *Kafka.*

Hinze, K.P.: "Neue Aspekte zum Kafka-Bild."

Hlavacova, J.: "F.Ks. Beziehungen zu Jicchak Löwy."

Hodin, J.P.: "Memories of F.K.;" "Erinnerungen an F.K.;" "Kafka und Prag," in his *Kafka und Goethe,* which contains also "Reminiscences" by Fritz Feigl and Dora Dymant.

Hoffman, F.J.: "Escape from Father," *KP,* 214-246.

Hoffmann, M.: "Dinah und der Dichter Kafka."

Hoffmann, W.: "Kafka und die jüdische Mystik."

Houska, L.: "F.K. und Prag."

Janouch, G.: "Erinnerungen an F.K.;" *Gespräche mit Kafka; Conversations with Kafka; Franz Kafka und sein Welt;* "Kafka in Stegliz."

Jens, W.: "Ein Jude namens Kafka;" *Un ebreo di nome Kafka.*

Jesenska, Milena: "F.K.;" "La malédiction des meilleures qualités;" "Milenas Nachruf auf Kafka."

Kafka, Frantizek: "F.Ks. Handschrift."

Kafka, Franz: *Diaries.* Vol. I. 1910-1913, Vol. II, 1914-1923; *Briefe 1902-1924; Brief an den Vater; Das Kafka-Buch; Letters to Milena; Letters to Felice; Briefe an Ottla und die Familie; Kafka par lui-même,* ed. by K. Wagenbach; *I am a Memory Come Alive,* ed. by N.N. Glatzer; *F.K.: Dichter über ihre Dichtungen,* ed. by E. Heller & J. Beug.

Kaiser, H.: *F.Ks. Inferno.*

Kautmann, F.: "Kafka et la Bohême."

Kayser, W. & H. Gronemeyer: *Max Brod.*

Klausing, H.: "Das Schicksal der Familie Kafkas."

Kreitner, L.B.: "Kafka as a Young Man."

Krejci, K.: "F.K. et Jakub Arbes."

Krolop, K.: "Herder-Blätter;" "Ein Manifest der 'Prager Schule';" "Hinweis auf eine verschollene Rundfrage;" "Zur Geschichte und Vorgeschichte der Prager deutschen Literat-

ur"; "Zu den Erinnerungen Anna Lichtensterns an F.K."
Kuhr, A.: "Neurotische Aspekte bei Heidegger und Kafka."
Kurzweil, B.B.: "F.K.: Jüdische Existenz ohne Glauben."

Levi, D.: "On Brod and Kafka."
Levi, M.: *Kafka and Anarchism.*
Levinsky, R.: "In Search of Kafka."

Mares, M.: "Wie ich F.K. kennenlernte."
Meissner, F.A.: "A Social Ecology of the German Jews in Prague."
Mounier, G.F.: *Étude psycho-pathologique sur l'écrivain Kafka.*

Nemeth, A.: *Kafka ou Le mystère juif.*
Neumeister, S.: *Der Dichter als Dandy.*

Osborne, C.: *Kafka*

Paoli, R.: L'amico di Kafka."
Pasley, M.: "F.K. Manuscripts;" "Rilke und Kafka;" [and K. Wagenbach]: "Datierung sämtlicher Texte F.Ks."
Pazi, M.: "F.K. und Ernst Weis;" *Max Brod,* 6-17.
Pick, O.: "F.K.;" "Zwanzig Jahre deutsche Schrifttum in Prag;" "Prager Dichter von Ferne gesehen: F.K." *Das Jüdische Prag.* Ein Sammelschrift. Prague: Verlag der Selbstwehr, 1917.
Pivasset, J.: *L'univers politique de Kafka.*
Politzer, H.: "Prague and the Origins of R.M. Rilke, F.K., and Franz Werfel;" (ed.): *Das Kafka-Buch.*
Preisner, R.: "F.K. and the Czechs."
Pulver, M.: "Spaziergang mit F.K."

Raabe, P.: "F.K. und Franz Blei;" "F.K. und der Expressionismus."
Rabi, W.: "Le juif de Prague;" "Kafka et la néo-Kabbale."
Ripellino, A.M.: *Praga Magica.*
Robert, M.: "Une figure de Whitechapel;" *Kafka;* "Lettres a Minze E."
Rohner, W.: *F.K.*

Spann, M.: "Die beiden Zettel Kafkas;" "The Minor Kafka Problem."
Stefani, G.: "F.K., impiegato delle Generali."
Steiner, M.: "The Facts about Kafka."

Stolzl, C.: *Kafkas böses Böhmen.*
Storch-Marien, O.: "Alchimistengässchen Nr. 22."

Terray, E.: "Einige Bemerkungen zu den *Herder-Blättern* und der Prager Avantgarde."
Thieberger, F.: "Erinnerungen an F.K."
Tramer, H.: "Prague, City of Three Peoples."
Trost, P.: "F.K. und das Prager Deutsch."
Turkov, M.: "F.Ks. Prag."

Urzidil, G.: "Notes on Kafka."
Urzidil, J.: "Personal Notes on F.K.;" "Recollections," *KP,* 20-24; "F.K. and Prague;" "Meetings with F.K.;" "Brand;" "Im Prag des Expressionismus," in P. Raabe: *Expressionismus.* Munich, 1965, 68-73; *There Goes Kafka;* "Der lebendige Anteil."
Utitz, E.: "Erinnerungen an F.K."

Wagenbach, K.: *F.K. Eine Biographie seiner Jugend (1883-1912); F.K. in Selbstzeugnissen; F.K. 1883-1924;* "Julie Wohryzek;" (ed.): *Kafka par lui-même.*
Weinberg, K.: "F.Ks. 'Erst Veröffentlichung.'"
Weltsch, F.: "The Rise and Fall of the Jewish-German Symbiosis;" *Religion und Humor im Leben und Werk F.Ks:* "F.Ks. Geschichtsbewusstsein."
Weltsch, R.: "Franz Kafka's Home City."
White, J.S.: "Psyche and Tuberculosis: The Libido Organization of F.K."
Wiegler, P.: "Erinnerungen an F.K."
Wolff, K.: "On F.K.;" *Autoren, Bücher, Abenteuer; Briefwechsel eines Verlegers.*

Zampa, G.: Lettere inedite di Kafka a M. Bl."
Zohn, H.: "The Jewishness of F.K."
Zolle, E.: "Le maschere e il volto di F.K."
Zylenberg, H.: "La fin tragique trois soeurs de Kafka."

IV Interpretations—A Recapitulation

Amerika and "The Stoker" (Der Heizer)* [1912].

* An asterisk indicates essays dealing particularly with "The Stoker. A Fragment," which became Chapter I of *Amerika*. Kafka originally entitled this novel "Der Verschollene" (Lost Without Trace); Max Brod retitled it *Amerika*.

Beck, E.T.: *Kafka and the Yiddish Theater*, 122-135.

Beicken, P.U.: *F.K.*, 251-261.

Benjamin, W.: "Le theatre d'Oklahoma."

Bergel, L.: "*Amerika:* Its Meaning, *FKT*, 117-125.

Bezzel, C.: *Natur bei Kafka*.

Borchardt, A.: *Kafkas zweites Gesicht*.

Borgese, G.A.: "In Amerika con Kafka."

* Born, J.: *KS*, 137-140.

Brod, M.: "Afterword" to F.K.: *Amerika*. N.Y., 1940, 298-299; 1946, 276-277.

David, C.: "L'Amérique de F.K."

Doss, K.: "Die Gestalt des Toren."

Emrich, W.: *F.K.: A Critical Study*, 276-315.

Foulkes, A.P.: *The Reluctant Pessimist*

Fürst, N.: *Die offenen Geheimtüren F.Ks.*, 53-71.

* Goldstücker, E.: "Kafka's 'Der Heizer'."

Goodman, P.: *Kafka's Prayer*, 188-196.

Gray, R.: *F.K.*, 67-82.

Greenberg, M.: "Kafka's *Amerika;*" *The Terror of Art,* 92-104.

Hermsdorf, K.: *F.Ks. Roman-fragment "Der Verschollene"; Kafka: Weltbild und Roman;* "Nachwort" to F.K.: *Amerika,* 307-317.

Hesse, H.: "Kafka."

Heuer, H.: *Die Amerikavision bei William Blake und F.K.*

Hillmann, H.: "Kafkas *Amerika:* Literatur als Problemlösungsspiel;" in tr., *KD.*

Hobson, I.: "Oklahoma, USA, and the Nature Theater." *KD.*

Jacobi, W.: "Ks Roman *Amerika* im Unterricht."

Jahn, W.: "Ks. Handschrift zum *Verschollenen;*" *Kafkas Roman "Der Verschollene."*

* Janouch, G.: *Conversations with Kafka,* 32-34 (1953 3d)

Kaiser, J.: "Glück bei Kafka."

* Klarman, A.D.: "F.Ks. 'Der Heizer'."

Klee, W.G.: *Die characterischen Motive,* 21-22.

Klinge, R.: "Mensch und Gesellschaft," 94-96.

Kobs, J.: *Kafka.*

Korst, M.R.: *Die Beziehung zwischen Held und Gegenwelt.*

Kuna, F.: *F.K.,* 64-98.

Loeffel, H.: "Das Raumerlebnis bei Kafka und Eichendorff."

Loose, G.: *F.K. und "Amerika."*

* Macklem, M.: "Kafka and the Myth of Tristan."

Malmsheimer, R.R.: "Kafka's 'Nature Theatre of Oklahoma'."

Mann, K.: "Preface" to F.K.: *Amerika; H,* 133-139.

Margeson, J.: "F.K."

Moseley, E.M.: "The American Dream..."

Musil, R.: *Tagebücher...,* pp. 687-688.

Nemeth, A.: *Kafka,* 140-145.

Nicholson, H.: *A Voyage to Wonderland.*

Northey, A.D.: "The Background of *Amerika." KD.*

Paci, E.: "Kafka e la Sfida del Teatro di Oklahoma."

Pascal, R.: "Dickens and Kafka;" *The German Novel,* 219-226.

* Pasley, M.: "Notes" to his ed. of F.K.: *Der Heizer* ... 13; *KS,* 62-63; "The Stoker," *KD*

Politzer, H.: *F.K. Parable and Paradox,* 116-162.

Pondrom, C.N.: "Purdy's *Malcolm* and Kafka's *Amerika.*"

Reinmann, P.: "Die gesellschaftliche Problematik..."

* Richter, H.: *F.K.,* 101-104.

* Rolleston, J.: Kafka's Narrative Theater, 18-31.

Ruf, U.: *F.K.: Das Dilemma der Sohne.*

Ruland, R.W.: "A View from Back Home: Kafka's *Amerika.*"

Schlant, E.: "Kafka's *Amerika.*"

Singer, C.S.: *Discovery of America by Accident.*

Sokel, W.H.: *F.K. Tragik und Ironie,* 311-329; "Zwischen Drohung und Errettung."

Sonnenfeld, M.: "Die Fragmente *Amerika* und *Der Prozess*..."

* Spector, R.D.: "Kafka's 'The Stoker' as a Short Story."

Spilka, M.: *Dickens and Kafka;* "*Amerika:* Its Genesis," *FKT,* 95-116; "Kafka and Dickens: The Country Sweetheart."

* Stern, G.: "Explication de Texte: 'Der Heizer'."

Stonier, G.W.: "Detaching Labels."

Tauber, H.: *F.K. An Interpretation of His Work,* 27-57.

Tedlock, E.W., Jr.: "Kafka's Imitation of *David Copperfield.*"

Thalmann, J.: *Wege zu Kafka. Eine Interpretation des Amerikaromans.*

Tilton, J.W.: "Kafka's *Amerika* as a Novel of Salvation."

Turner, A.: "Kafka's Two Worlds of Music."

Tyler, P.: "Kafka's and Chaplin's *Amerika;* "The Dream-*Amerika.*"

Uyttersprot, H.: "Zur Struktur von Kafkas Romanen; *Eine neue Ordnung der Werke Kafkas? Zur Struktur von "Der Prozess" und "Amerika;* "F.Ks. "Der Verschollene'."

Vasata, R.: "*Amerika* and Charles Dickens," *KP,* 134-139.

Walser, M.: *Beschreibung einer Form.*

Weinberg, H.A.: *The New Novel*..., pp. 1-13.

Winkler, R.O.C.: *KP*, 191-198.

Wöllner, G.: *E.T.A. Hoffmann und F.K.*

"Before the Law" (Vor dem Gesetz) *see The Trial.*

"Blumfeld, an Elderly Bachelor" (Blumfeld, ein älterer Junggeselle) [Feb-Apr. 1915].

Bergel, L.: "Blumfeld, an Elderly Bachelor," *KP*, 172-178.

Binder, H.: Kafka-Kommentar, 190-192.

Emrich, W.: *F.K. A Critical Study of his Writings*, 116-124.

Kassel, N.: *Das Groteske bei K*, 73-82.

Pasley, M.: *KS*, 65.

Richter, H.: *F.K.*, 174-175.

Tauber, H.: *F.K.: An Interpretation of his Works*, 122-123.

White, I.A. & J.J.: "Blumfeld." *KD.*

"The Bridge" (Die Brücke) [Dec. 1916].

Binder, H.: *Kafka-Kommentar*, 192-193.

Emrich, W.: *F.K. A Critical Study of his Writings*, 131-132.

Spahr, B.L.: "F.K.: The Bridge and the Abyss."

"The Bucket Rider" (Der Kübelreiter) [Winter 1916-1917]

Binder, H.: *Kafka-Kommentar*, 201-202.

Cusatelli, G.: *Critica e storia.*

Emrich, W.: *F.K. A Critical Study of his Writings*, 128-129.

Hahn, L.: "F.K.: 'Der Kübelreiter'."

Kraft, W.: *F.K.*, 30-35.

Richter, H.: *F.K.*, 133-136.

"The Burrow" (Der Bau) [Nov.-Dec. 1923].

Anders, G.: *F.K.*, 34-35.

Bangerter, L.A.: "'Der Bau': F.K's Final Punishment Tragedy."

Bänziger, H.: "'Der Bau'."

Baumer, F.: *Sieben Prosastücke*, 121-126.

Berger, L.: *KP*, 199-206.

Biemel, W.: *Philosophische Analysen...*, 66-140.

Binder, H.: *Kafka-Kommentar*, 301-322.

Blanchot, M.: "Le dehors, la nuit."

Bridgwater, P.: *Kafka and Nietzsche*, 139-142.

Burgum, E.B.: *KP,* 300-303.

Czermak, H.: *"The Metamorphosis* & Other Stories."

Emrich, W.: F.K. A Critical Study of his Writings, 206-224; "'Der Bau' und das Selbst des Menschen."

Fingerhut, K.H.: *Die Funktion der Tierfiguren...,* 189 ff.

Goodman, P.: *Kafka's Prayer,* 222-227, 259-260.

Henel, H.: "Kafka's 'Der Bau';" "Das ende Kafka's 'Der Bau'."

Hodin, J.P.: "Erinnerungen an F.K.," 92.

Jaeger, H.: "Heidegger's Existential Philosophy..."

Nagel, B.: *F.K.,* 275-317.

Pasley, M.: "Notes" to his ed. of F.K.: *"Der Heizer," "In der Strafkolonie," "Der Bau,"* 22-23.; "The Burrow," *KD*

Paucker, H.: "Der Einbruch des Absurden."

Politzer, H.: *F.K., Parable and Paradox,* 318-333; "Kafka im 'Bau'."

Rajan, B.: *Fo,* 9-10.

Richter, H.: *F.K.,* 272-276.

Sgorlon, C.: "Pagine de critica Kafkiana."

Sokel, W.H.: *F.K.: Tragik und Ironie,* 371-387.

Strauss, W.A.: "F.K.: Between the Paradise and the Labyrinth," 206-222.

Tauber, H.: *F.K. An Interpretation of his Works,* 211-213.

Thorlby, A.: *Kafka,* 47-51.

Walker, A.: "Allegory, a Light Conceit."

Weigand, H.J.: "F. Kafka's 'The Burrow';" *H,* 85-108.

"The Cares of a Family Man" (Die Sorge des Hausvaters) [Apr. 1917].

Backenköhler, G.: "Neues zum 'Sorgenkind, Odradek'."

Bansberg, D.: "Durch Lüge zur Wahrheit."

Bense, M.: *Die Theorie Kafkas,* 63-67.

Binder, H.: Kafka-Kommentar, 230-233.

Emrich, W.: "F.K.: 'Die Sorge des Hausvaters'"; *F.K. A Critical Study,* 102-116.

Heller, E.: *F.K.,* 20-21.

Hillmann, H.: "Das Sorgenkind Odradek."

Kraft, W.: *Wort und Gedanke,* 192 passim.

Nicolai, R.R.: "Diskussionsbeitrag zu Kafkas 'Die Sorge des Hausvaters'."

Pasley, M.: "Two Kafka Enigmas: 'Elf Sohne' and 'Die Sorge des Hausvaters';" "'Die Sorge des Hausvaters';" "Drei literarische Mystifikationen Kafkas;" *KS*, 67.

Richter, H.: *F.K.*, 148-149.

Stahl, A.: "Konfusion ohne Absicht?"

The Castle (Das Schloss) [1922].

In addition to full-length books devoted entirely to *The Castle* (Gray, Sheppard, Neumeyer), exhaustive analyses are to be found in major Kafka studies such as Sokel, Emrich, Politzer.

Adeane, L.: "The Hero Myth in Kafka's Writing."

Almasy, M.: "Diskussion in Kafkas Schloss."

Arega, L.: "L'Arpenteur."

Arendt, H.: *Sechs Essays*, 128-149; "The Jew as Pariah."

Baker, J.R.: *"The Castle:* A Problem in Structure."

Beck, E.T.: *Kafka and the Yiddish Theater*, 194-200.

Beicken, P.U.: *F.K.*, 328-338; *Perspektive und Sehweise...*

Binder, H.: *Motiv und Gestaltung bei F.K.*

Bernheimer, C.: "The Text as Suspension." *KD.*

Birch, J.: "Aspects of Narrative Prose Sentence Style;" *Dimension of Narrative Prose...*

Blanchot, M.: *La part du feu*, 80-91.

Bridgwater, P.: *Kafka und Nietzsche*, 90-103.

Braybrooke, N.: "Celestial Castles;" "The Geography of the Soul."

Brod, M.: "Additional Note" to F.K.: *The Castle*, N.Y.: Knopf, 1930 & 1941, 329-340; "The Homeless Stranger," *KP, 179-180; "The Castle;* Its Genesis," *FKT*, 161-164; *PFK*, 39-47.

Buber, M.: *Two Types of Faith*, 162-169.

Burgum, E.B.: "The Bankruptcy of Faith," *KP*, 298-318.

Chastel, A.: *"Le Chateau."*

Church, M.: *Time and Reality.*

Cohn, D.: "Castles and Anti-Castles;" "Kafka Enters the Castle."

Cohn, R.: "Watt in the Light of *The Castle.*"

Cantoni, R.: *Che cosa ha veramente detto Kafka,* 129-169.

Cook, A.: "Romance as Allegory."

Daniel-Rops [J.C.H. Pétiot]: "The Castle of Despair," *KP,* 184-191.

Emrich, W.: *F.K. A Critical Study,* 365-507.

Essner-Schaknys, G.: *Die epische Wirklichkeit . . .*

Fietz, L.: "Möglichkeiten und Grenzen . . ."

Fingerhut, K.H.: *Die Funktion der Tierfiguren . . . ,* 230-253.

Fleischmann, I.: "Auf dem Weg zum Schloss."

Foulkes, A.P.: *The Reluctant Pessimist,* 163-171.

Freedman, R.: "Kafka's Obscurity," 70-73.

Fürst, N.: *Die offenen Geheimtüren,* 16-35.

Goldstein, B.: *Key Motifs in F.K's "Der Prozess" and "Das Schloss".*

Goldstücker, E.: "Granzland zwischen Einsamkeit und Gemeinschaft . . ."

Goodman, P.: *Kafka's Prayer,* 185-227; "Plot Structure of *The Castle.*"

Gray, R.: *Kafka's Castle; F.K.,* 140-172.

Greenberg, M.: *Terror of Art,* 154-220.

Grieser, D.: "Im Schloss für soziale Wohlfahrt."

Hata, S.: "Bürokratie und Individuum."

Heller, E.: *F.K.,* 98-130.

Henrard, A.: "Une source espagnole au Chateau de Kafka."

Hermlin, S. and H. Mayer: *Ansichten über einige Bücher . . . ,* 158-163.

Hermsdorf, K.: "Nachwort" to his ed. of F.K.: *Erzählungen, Der Prozess Das Schloss*

Hilsbecher, W.: "Kafkas *Das Schloss.*"

Hora, J.: *"Le Chateau."*

Ita, J.M.: "Note on W. & E. Muir's translation of *Das Schloss;*" "Laye's *Radiance of the King* and Kafka's *Castle.*"

Jaeger, H.: "Heidegger's Existentialist Philosophy . . ."

Kern, E.: "Reflections on *The Castle . . .*"

Kisch, G.: Kafka-Forschung auf Irrwegen . . ."

Kobs, J.: *Kafka,* 239 ff.

Komplovszki, T.: "Kafka's Schloss und das Fortuna-Schloss de Comenius."

Korst, M.R.: *Die Beziehung zwische Held und Gegenwelt . . .*

Kudszus, W.: "Erzählhaltung . . ."; "Between Past and Future . . ."; "Erzählperspektive . . ."

Kuna, F.: *F.K.,* 136-172.

Livermore, A.L.: "Kafka and Stendhal's *De l'Amour.*"

Magny, C.E.: *KP, 85-89.*

Mann, T.: "Homage,"; Foreword to F.K.: *The Castle,* N.Y.: Knopf, 1941, v-xvi.

Margeson, J.: "F.K.", 36-39.

Martini, F.: "F.K.: *Das Schloss.*"

Muir, E.: "Introductory Note" to F.K.: *The Castle,* N.Y., 1930, v-xi.

Mueller, W.R.: "The Lonely Journey."

Nemeth, A.: *Kafka,* 123-139.

Neumeyer, P.F. (ed.): *Twentieth Century Interpretations of "The Castle."*

Nicholson, N.: *Man and Literature,* 163-168.

Olafson, F.A.: "Kafka and the Primacy of the Ethical."

Ong, W.J.: "Kafka's Castle in the West."

Parry, I.: *"The Castle."*

Pascal, R.: *The German Novel,* 233-244.

Pasley, M.: "Zur äusseren Gestalt des *Schloss*-Romans;" "Zur Entstehungeschichte;" "F.Ks. Mss."; *KS,* 71-72.

Pearce, D.: *"The Castle:* Kafka's Divine Comedy," *FKT,* 165-172.

Pfeiffer, J.: "La question de Chateaux."

Philippi, K.-P.: *Reflexion und Wirklichkeit . . .* 207-224.

Politzer, H.: *F.K., Parable and Paradox,* 218-281; "Das entfremdete Selbst."

Pongs, H.: "F.K.: *Das Schloss";* *F.K., Dichter des Labyrinths*

Ramm, K.: *Reduktion als Erzählprinzip,* 80-96.

Reed, E.E.: "Moral Polarity."

Rendi, A.: "Influssi letterari nel *Castello* di Kafka."

Richter, H.: *F.K.: Werk und Entwurf,* 252-272.

Robert M.: *L'Ancien et le nouveau; Kafka.*

Rohner, W.: *F.K.*

Rolleston, J.: *Kafka's Narrative Theater,* 112-129.

Roy, G.: *Kafka's "The Trial," "The Castle" and Other Works.*

Sandbank, S.: "Action as Self Mirror."

Saurat, D.: "A Note on *The Castle, KP,* 181-183.

Savage, D.S.: *KP,* 319-336.

Schoeps, H.J.: *KP,* 287-297.

Scott, N.A. Jr.: "F.K.: The Sense of Cosmic Exile."

Sebald, W.G.: "The Undiscovered Country: The Death Motif in Kafka's *Castle,*" "The Law of Ignominy," TBL. "The Death Motif." *KD.*

Sheppard, R.: *On Kafka's Castle.; "The Trial/The Castle" KD.*

Smith, Agnes W.: *"The Castle." The New Yorker,* (Sept. 20, 1930), 95-96.

Sokel, W.H.: *F.K. Tragik und Ironie;* 391 ff.

Steinberg, E.R.: "K. of *The Castle:* Ostensible Land-Surveyor;" *H,* 126-132.

Swander H.: "The Castle: K's Village," *FKT,* 173-192.

Tauber, H.: *F.K. An Interpretation of his Work,* 131-185.

Taylor, C.: *"The Castle." N.Y. Herald Tribune Books,* (Sept. 21, 1930), 7.

Thorlby, A.: *Kafka,* 68-83.

Uyttersprot, H.: "Zur Struktur von Kafkas Romanen."

Vivas, E.: *Creation and Discovery,* 36-39.

Wagenbach, K.: "Wo liegt Kafkas Schloss?" *KS,* 161-180.

Waidson, H.M.: *"Das Schloss."*

Walser, M.: *Beschreibung einer Form.*

Wasserstrom, W.: "In Gertrude's Closet."

Webster, P.D.: "A Critical Examination of F.K.'s *The Castle."*

Weinberg, H.: *The New Novel...,* 14-28.

Weinberg, K.: *Kafkas Dichtungen...*

Werner, H.: "'Die Gottlosen haben keinen Frieden'." ...

West, R.: *The Court and the Castle*, 279-305.

Winkelman, J.: "An Interpretation of Kafka's *Das Schloss.*"

Winkler, R.O.C.: *KP*, 192-198; "Significance of Kafka," 356-359.

"The City Coat of Arms" (Das Stadtwappen) [Sept. 1920].

Emrich, W.: *F.K. A Critical Study*, 229-230.

Ionesco, E.: "Dans les armes de la ville."

Zimmermann, W.: *Deutsche Prosadichtungen*, 251-256.

"A Common Confusion" (Eine alltägliche Verwirrung) [Oct. 21, 1917].

Arendt, H.: "F.K.: A Revaluation, 419-420; *Sechs Essays*, 128-149.

Trahan, E.: "'A Common Confusion'."

"The Conscription of Troops" (Die Truppenaushebung) [Oct. 1920].

Binder, H.: *Kafka-Kommentar*, 249.

Emrich, W.: *F.K. A Critical Study*, 257-268.

Ide, H.: "F.K.: 'Der Gruftwächter' und 'Die Truppenaushebung'."

Tauber, H.: *F.K.: An Interpretation of his Works*, 129-130.

"A Country Doctor" (Ein Landarzt) [Jan.-Feb. 1917].

Albrecht, E.A.: "Zur Entstehungsgeschichte von Kafka's 'Landarzt'."

Baumer, F.: *Sieben Prosastücke*, 109-115.

Beck, E.T.: *Kafka and the Yiddish Theater*, 172-175.

Beebe, M.: *Literary Symbolism*, 130-142.

Beicken, P.U.: *F.K.*, 293-302.

Binder, H.: *Motiv und Gestaltung*, 261, 335 ff.; *Kafka-Kommentar*, 208-217, 233-236.

Born, J.: *KS*, 158-159.

Bridgwater, P.: *Kafka und Nietzsche*, 111-115.

Busacca, B.: "A Country Doctor," *FKT*, 45-57.

Church, M.: "Kafka's 'A Country Doctor'."

Cohn, D.: "Kafka's Eternal Present: Narrative Tense in 'Ein Landarzt'."

Cooperman, S.: "Kafka's 'A Country Doctor'."

Czermak, H.: *"the Metamorphosis" & Other Stories,* 39-45.

Emrich, W.: *F.K. A Critical Study,* 151-161.

Fargues, A.M.: "Wirkungsgeschichte oder Übereinkunft am Nullpunkt der Literatur? Am Beispiel 'Ein Landarzt' von F.K. und 'Mite del dispensari' von Jordi Sarsanedes."

Fickert, K.J.: "Fatal Knowledge: Kafka's 'Ein Landarzt'."

Fingerhut, K-H.: *Die Funktion der Tierfiguren...,* 131-134.

Flach, B.: *Kafkas Erzählungen: Strukturanalyse und Interpretation,* 56 ff.

Friederich, R.H.: "The Dream Transference in Kafka's 'Ein Landarzt'."

Gardner, John and L. Dunlap: *The Forms of Fiction.* N.Y.: Random House, 1962, 68-73.

Goldstein, B.: "F.K.'s 'Ein Landarzt': A Study in Failure;" "A Study of the Wound."

Gray, R.: *F.K.,* 126-139.

Guth, H.P.: "Symbol and Contextual Restraint: Kafka's 'Country Doctor'."

Hardner, M.-L.: *Märchenmotive in der Dichtung F.Ks.*

Hatfield, H.: "Life as Nightmare: F.K.'s 'A Country Doctor'."

Heselhaus, C.: "Kafkas Erzählformen."

Kauf, R.: "'Verantwortung': The Theme of Kafka's *Landarzt* Cycle."

Kleinschmidt, G.: "'Ein Landarzt'."

Kraft, H.: *Kafka: Wirlichkeit und Perspektive.,* 50 ff.

Kurz, P.K.: "Doomed Existence. F.K's. Story: 'A Country Doctor'."

Lainoff, S.: "The Country Doctors of Kafka and Turgenev."

Lakin, M.: "Hofmannsthals *Reitergeschichte* und Kafkas 'Ein Landarzt'."

Lawson, R.H.: "Kafka's 'Ein Landarzt'."

Leiter, L.H.: "A Problem in Analysis: F.K.'s 'A Country Doctor'."

Leopold, K.: "F.K's Stories in the First Person."

Marson, E.L. and K. Leopold: "Kafka, Freud, and 'Ein Landarzt'."

Misselbeck, M.: "F.K.: 'Ein Landarzt'."

Motekat, H.: "F.Ks. 'Ein Landarzt'."

Müller, J.: "Erwägungen an dem Kafka-Text: 'Ein Landarzt'."

Musurillo, H.: "Healing Symbols in Kafka."

Peden, William: *Twenty-Nine Stories*. Boston: Houghton Mifflin, 1960, 196-198.

Politzer, H.: *F.K. Parable and Paradox*, 89-90, 345-348.

Ramm, K.: *Reduktion als Erzählprinzip bei Kafka*.

Richter, H.: *F.K. Werk und Entwurf*, 130-133.

Rösch, E.: "Getrübte Erkenntnis..."

Rubbini, C.: "F.K. e 'Il medico di campagna'."

Salinger, H.: "More Light on Kafka's 'Landarzt'."

Scherer, M.: "Das Versagen und die Gnade in Ks. Werk. Zu Ks. Erzählung 'Ein Landarzt'."

Schneeberger, I.: *Das Kunstmärchen...*, 17-46.

Schulze, H.: "Anwärter der Gnade."

Servotte, H.: "F.K.: 'Ein Landarzt'."

Sokel, W.H.: "On 'The Country Doctor'," *H*, 81-84; *F.K.*, 6-8; *F.K. Tragik und Ironie*, 251-281.

Struc, R.S.: "The Doctor's Predicament."

Tauber, H.: *F.K. An Interpretation of his Works*, 74-76.

Webster, P.D.: "A Critical Fantasy or Fugue."

White, W.M.: "A Re-examination of Kafka's 'The Country Doctor'"...

"Description of a Struggle" (Beschreibung eines Kampfes) [1904/1906 and Winter 1909-1910].

Arendt, H.: "The Jew as Pariah," 113-115.

Beck, E.T.: *Kafka and the Yiddish Theater*, 49-55.

Beicken, P.U.: *F.K. Eine kritische Einführung*, 226-234.

Binder, H.: *Motiv und Gestaltung...*, 376 ff.; *Kafka-Kommentar*, 44-57, 81-84.

Brod, M.: "Nachwort" to F.K.: *Beschreibung eines Kampfes*. Frankfurt: 1969, 341-356.

Dietz, L. (ed.): F.K.: *Beschreibung eines Kampfes. Die zwei Fassungen. Parallelausgabe nach den Handschriften*. Frankfurt: Fischer, 1969; "Zwei frühe Handschriften

Kafkas;" and "Kafkas Randstriche..."; and "Max Brods Hand in Kafkas Manuskripten der 'Beschreibung eines Kampfes'."

Emrich, W.: *F.K. A Critical Study*, 27 f., 87-88, 96 f., 112-113, 127-128, 506-507.

Greenberg, M.: *Terror of Art*, 28-32.

Groethuysen, B.: "Preface" to F.K.: *Description d'un combat*. Paris: Maeght, 1946.

Jens, I.: *Studien zur Entwicklung der expressionistischen Novelle*, 80-108.

Jens, W.: *Statt einer Literaturgeschichte*, 59-85.

Kassel, N.: *Das Groteske bei F.K.*, 42-57.

Kobs, J.: *Kafka*, 7-19.

Kowal, M.: *F.K.: Problems in Interpretation*, 134-184.

Kraft, H.: *Kafka. Wirklichkeit und Perspektive*, 24-27.

Middelhauve, F.: *Ich und Welt im Frühwerk F.Ks.*

Pasley, M.: *KS*, 58.

Platzer, H.: *A Study of the Relationship of Technique and Theme in the Shorter Works of Kafka*, 69-101.

Richter, H.: *F.K.*, 81-95.

Rolleston, J.: *Kafka's Narrative Theater*, 1-17.

Ryan, J.: "Die zwei Fassungen..."

Sanbank, S.: "The Unity of Kafka's 'Beschreibung eines Kampfes'."

Sokel, W.H.: *F.K. Tragic und Ironie*, 33-43.

Struc, R.S.: *Food, Air and Ground...* 18-40.

Tauber, H.: *F.K. An Interpretation of his Works*, 1-11.

Uematsu, K.: "Ein Problem vom Bewusstsein..."

Walser, M.: *Beschreibung einer Form*, 70 ff.

"A Dream" (Ein Traum) [Dec. 1914].

Binder, H.: *Kafka-Kommentar*, 182.

Kraft, W.: "Über dem Tod. Zu F.Ks. 'Ein Traum'."

"Eleven Sons" (Elf Söhne) [Mar. 1917].

Binder, H.: *Kafka-Kommentar*, 223-225.

David, C.: "Zu Ks. Erzählung 'Elf Söhne'."

Kraft, W.: "F.Ks. Erzählung 'Elf Söhne'."

Mitchell, B.: "Kafka's 'Elf Söhne': A New Look at the Puzzle."

Pasley, M.: "Two Kafka Enigmas: 'Elf Söhne' and 'Die Sorge des Hausvaters';" "Drei literarische Mystificationen."

Richter, H.: *F.K.*, 149-151.

"First Sorrow" (Erstes Lied) [Jan.-Feb. 1922].

Binder, H.: *Kafka-Kommentar*, 252-256.

Fürst, N.: *Die offenen Geheimtüren F.Ks.*, 77-80.

Richter, H.: *F.K.*, 237-239.

"The Giant Mole" (Der Riesenmaulwurf), the original title was Dorfschullehrer (The Village Schoolmaster) [Dec. 19, 1914-Jan. 6, 1915].

Anders, G.: *F.K.*, 93-95; "F.K.: Ritual without Religion," 568-569.

Binder, H.: *Kafka-Kommentar*, 186-190.

Emrich, W.: *F.K. A Critical Study*, 172-178.

Martini, F.: "Ein Manuskript F.Ks. 'Der Dorfschullehrer'."

Pasley, M.: *KS*, 65.

Rahv, P.: "Exegetical Notes."

Rolleston, J.: *Kafka's Narrative Theater*, 100-111.

Tauber, H.: *F.K.: An Introduction of his Works*, 199-201.

Vialatte, A.: "Note" [On Kafka: "Le terrier"].

"The Great Wall of China" (Beim Bau der chinesischen Mauer) [Mar. 1917].

Anders, G.: *Kafka-Pro und Contra*

Baumer, F.: *Sieben Prosastücke*, 115-121.

Beck, E.T.: *Kafka and the Yiddish Theater*, 190-192.

Beicken, P.U.: *F.K.*, 312-315.

Benjamin, W.: "F.K.: 'Beim Bau der chinesischen Mauer'."

Binder, H.: *Kafka-Kommentar*, 218-221.

Carrive, J.: "'La muraille de Chine'."

Collignon, J.: "Kafka's Humor," 55-61.

Emrich, W.: *F.K.: A Critical Study*, 225-229, 265-266.

Flach, B.: *Ks. Erzählungen.*

Gooden, C.: "The Great Wall of China."

Goodman, P.: "Kafka's Prayer, 235-240.

Greenberg, C.: *FKT,* 77-81.

Kracauer, S.: "Zu 'Beim Bau der chinesischen Mauer'."

Rahv, P.: "Exegetical Notes."

Ramm, K.: Reduktion als Erzählprinzip.

Richter, H.: *F.K.: Werk und Entwurf,* 223-225.

Rolleston, J.: *Kafka's Narrative Theater,* 109-111.

Sgorlon, C.: "Pagine di critica Kafkiana," 50-66.

Short, Raymond B. and Richard B. Sewall: *A Manual of Suggestions for Teachers Using "Short Stories for Study".* N.Y.: Holt, 1956, 42-45.

Spender, S.: *The Destructive Element,* 243-245.

Strauss, W.A.: "F.K.: Between Paradise and the Labyrinth," 209-212.

Tauber, H.: *F.K.: An Interpretation of his Works,* 123-129.

Weinberg, K.: *Ks. Dichtungen.*

"A Hunger Artist" *(Ein Hungerkünstler)* [Feb. 1922].

Anders, G.: *Kafka, Pro und Contra,* 96 ff.

Avery, G.C.: "Die Darstellung des Künstlers...."

Baumer, F.: *Sieben Prosastücke,* 126-133.

Beicken, P.U.: *F.K.,* 319-324; *Perspektive und Sehweise...*

Biemel, W.: *Philosophischen Analysen,* 38-65.

Binder, H.: *Kafka-Kommentar,* 257-261, 333-337; *Motiv und Gestaltung bei F.K.,* 194, 269 f., 299 f., 391.

Bridgwater, P.: *Kafka and Nietzsche,* 132-139.

Deinert, H.: "F.K.: Ein Hungerkünstler."

Dietz, L. "Kafkas lezte Publikation."

Edel, E.: "Zum Problem des Künstlers bei F.K."

Emrich, W.: *F.K., A Critical Study,* 180-200.

Falk, W.: *Leid und Verwandlung...,* 119 ff.

Fingerhut, K.H.: *Die Funktion der Tierfiguren...,* 292 ff.

Flach, B.: *Kafkas Erzählungen,* 95-120.

Foulkes, A.P.: *The Reluctant Pessimist,* 90-97.

Frey, E.: *F.Ks. Erzählstil...*

Fürst, N.: *Die offenen Geheimtüren F.Ks.,* 74-76.

Gray, R.: *F.K.,* 173-186.

Greenberg, M.: *Terror of Art,* 25-32.

Heilman, Robert B.: *Modern Short Stories.* N.Y.: Harcourt, Brace, 1950, 303-305.

Heller, E.: *F.K.,* 62-63.

Henel, I.: "Ein

Hermsdorf, K.: *Weltbild und Roman;* "Kunst und Künstler bei F.K."; "Nachwort" to F.K.: *Erzählungen.*

Hillmann, H.: *F.K.,* 68-112.

Kraft, H.: *Kafka: Wirklichkeit und Perspektive,* 60 ff.

Krotz, F.W.: "F.K.: Ein Hungerkünstler."

Michaelson, L.W.: "Kafka's 'Hunger Artist' and Baudelaire's 'Old Clown'."

Millett, Fred B.: *Reading Fiction.* N.Y.: Harper, 1950, 243-244.

Morrison, J.A.: *Kafka als Hungerkünstler.*

Moyer, P.: "Time and the Artist in Kafka and Hawthorne."

Nagel, B.: *F.K.,* 201-212.

Neumarkt, P.: "Kafka's 'A Hunger Artist': The Ego in Isolation."

Pasley, J.M.S.: "Asceticism and Cannibalism: Notes on an Unpublished Kafka Text."

Politzer, H.: *F.K., Parable and Paradox,* 303-308.

Pongs, H.: *F.K., Dichter des Labyrinths,* 86 ff.

Ramm, K.: *Reduktion als Erzählprinzip.*

Richter, H.: *F.K. Werk und Entwurf,* 242-251.

Robert, M.: *Kafka,* 190 ff.

Rubinstein, W.C.: "'A Hunger Artist'."

Sheppard, R.W.: "Kafka's 'Ein Hungerkünstler': A Reconsideration."

Sokel, W.H.: *F.K. Tragik und Ironie,* 501-531.

Spann, M.: "F.K.'s Leopard;" "Don't Hurt the Jackdaw."

Stallman, R.W.: "Kafka's Cage;" "The Hunger Artist;" "A Hunger Artist," *FKT,* 61-70.

Steinhauer, H.: "Hungering Artist or Artist in Hungering."

Tauber, H.: *F.K., An Interpretation of his Works,* 190-193.

Vigée, C.: "Les artistes de la faim."

Waidson, H.M.: "The Starvation-Artist and the Leopard."

Waldeck, P.B.: "Kafka's 'Die Verwandlung' and "Ein Hungerkünstler' as Influenced by Leopold von Sacher-Masoch."

Walter, S.: *Die Rolle der fuhrenden und schwellenden Elementen...*

Waterman, A.E.: "Kafka's 'The Hunger Artist'."

Weinberg, K.: *Kafkas Dichtungen*, 160, 182 ff.

Weltsch, F.: *Religion und Humour*, 79-83.

Wiese, B. von: "F.K.: 'Ein Hungerkünstler';" "Der Künstler und die moderne Gesellschaft."

"The Hunter Gracchus" (Der Jäger Gracchus) [Dec. 1916-Apr. 1917].

Beicken, P.U.: *F.K.*, 315-318.

Binder, H.: *Motiv und Gestaltung;* 171-185; *Kafka-Kommentar*, 193-201; Kafkas Schaffensweise und poetischer Topographie."

Born, J.: "Kafkas unermüdliche Rechner."

Bridgwater, P.: *Kafka and Nietzsche*, 123-126.

Emrich, W.: *F.K. A Critical Study*, 4-16, 44-49.

Fingerhut, F.H.: *Die Funktion der Tierfiguren...*, 60 ff.

Gordon, C.: "Notes on Hemingway and Kafka," GK, 75-83.

Kassel, N.: *Das Groteske bei F.K.*, 132-138.

Knieger, B.: "Kafka's 'The Hunter Gracchus'."

Kraft, W.: *F.K.*, 181-196.

Krock, M.: *Oberflächen- und Tiefenschicht im Werke Ks 'Der Jäger Gracchus' als Schlüsellfigur.*

Krusche, D.: "Die kommunikative Funktion der Deformation klassischer Motive 'Der Jäger Gracchus': Zur Problematik der Kafka-Interpretation;" "Kafka und Kafka-Deutung."

Nägele, R.: "Auf der Suche nach dem verlorenen Paradies. Versuch einer Interpretation zu Kafkas 'Der Jäger Gracchus'."

Neumann, G.: "Umkehrung und Ablenkung..."

Richter, H.: *F.K. Werk und Entwurf*, 232 ff.

Stierle, K.: "Mythos als 'bricolage'...., 463-467.

"An Imperial Message" (Eine kaiserliche Botschaft) [Mar.-Apr. 1917].

Hohof, C.: "Die Botschaft des Kaisers."

Mauer, O.: "Kommentar zu zwei Parabeln."

Mühlberger, J.: *F.K.: Die kaiserliche Botschaft.*

Politzer, H.: *F.K.: Parable and Paradox,* 86-87.

Richter, H.: *F.K.,* 146-148.

Schoeps, H.J.: *KP,* 294-296.

Schulze, H.: "Anwärter der Gnade."

Weiss, W.: "Dichtung und Grammatik," 235-256.

West, R.: *The Court and the Castle,* 301-305.

Zimmerman, W.: *Deutsche Prosadichtungen der Gegenwart,* 159-174 (1954 ed.), 216-218 (1966 ed.).

"In the Penal Colony" (In der Strafkolonie) [Oct. 15-18, 1914].

Adams, R.M.: *Strains of Discord,* 169-171.

Angus, D.: "The Existentialist and the Diabolical Machine."

Beck, E.T.: *Kafka and the Yiddish Theater,* 146-154.

Beicken, P.U.: *F.K.: Eine kritische Einführung,* 287-293.

Biemel, W.: *Philosophische Analysen...,* 1-37.

Binder, H.: *Motiv und Gestaltung,* 169 ff.; *Kafka-Kommentar,* 174-181.

Born, J.: *KS,* 151-157.

Bridgwater, P.: *Kafka and Nietzsche,* 104-111.

Brooks, Cleanth and Robert Penn Warren (eds.): *Understanding Fiction.* N.Y.: Appleton-Century-Crofts, 1960, 389-393.

Burns, W.: "Kafka and Alex Comfort: The Penal Colony Revisited;" and "'In the Penal Colony': Variations on a Theme by Octave Mirbeau."

Emrich, W.: *F.K.: A Critical Study,* 268-275.

Fickert, K.J.: "Kafka's 'In the Penal Colony';" and "A Literal Interpretation of 'In the Penal Colony'."

Fülleborn, U.: "Zum Verhältnis..."

Globus, G.C. and R.C. Pilliard: "Tausk's *Influencing Machine* and Kafka 'In the Penal Colony'."

Gray, R.: *F.K.,* 93-102.

Greenberg, M.: *Terror of Art,* 104-112.

Hall, James B. and J. Langland: *The Short Story*. N.Y.:Macmillan, 1956, 201-202.

Heller, E.: *F.K.,* 17-19, 25-26.

Henel, I.: "Kafkas 'In der Strafkolonie'."

Hofrichter, L.: "From Poe to Kafka," 411-417.

Jaffe, A.H. and V. Scott: "Analysis of 'In the Penal Colony'."

Kaiser, H.: *F.Ks. Inferno.*

Kassel, N.: *Das Groteske bei F.K.,* 102 ff.

Kramer, D.: "The Aesthetics of Theme: 'In the Penal Colony'."

Kuhr, A.: "Neurotische Aspekte..."

Kumar, S.: "F.Ks. 'In der Strafkolonie'."

Mendelsohn, L.R.: "Kafka's 'In the Penal Colony'."

Michel, K.: *Adalbert Stifter und die transzendente Welt,* 135-146.

Nagel, B.: *"Jud Süss* und *Strafkolonie;" F.K.,* 238-274.

Nemeth, A.: *Kafka,* 148-153.

Neumeyer, P.F.: "F.K., Sugar Baron."

Pasley, M.: "Notes" to his ed. F.K.: *Der Heizer, In der Strafkolonie, Der Bau.* Cambridge University Press, 1966, 14-22; *KS,* 65; "In the Penal Colony," *KD*

Politzer, H.: *F.K.: Parable and Paradox,* 98-115; *H,* 65-80.

Pongs, H.: *F.K.: Dichter des Labyrinths,* 55 ff.

Rehfeld, W.: *Das Motiv des Gerichtes...,* 173 f.

Richter, H.: *F.K. Werk und Entwurf,* 119-127.

Rolleston, J.: *Kafka's Narrative Theater,* 88-100.

Sacharoff, M.: "Pathological, Comic, and Tragic Elements in Kafka's 'In the Penal Colony'."

Schneeberger, I.: *Das Kunstmärchen....* 17-46.

Seidler, I.: *"Zauberberg* und *Strafkolonie."*

Sokel, W.H.: *F.K. Tragik und Ironie,* 118-121. 391 f.

Sonnenfeld, M.: "Eine Deutung der *Strafkolonie."*

Starobinski, J.: "Introduction" to his translation: F.K.: *La Colonie Pénitentiaire.* Paris: Egloff, 1945, 9-67.

Strauss, W.: "Albert Camus' Caligula."...

Street, J.B.: "Kafka through Freud: Totems and Taboos in 'In der Strafkolonie'."

Stumpf, W.: "F.K. Der Mensch und sein verlorenes Einst."

Tauber, H.: *F.K. An Interpretation of his Works,* 58-64.

Thomas, J.D.: "The Dark End of the Tunnel: Kafka's 'In the Penal Colony'."

Thorlby, A.: *Kafka: A Study,* 40-47.

Tucholsky, K: "'In der Strafkolonie'," *KS,* 154-156.

Wagenbach, K.: Notes and Supplementary Materials, in F.K.: *In der Strafkolonie.* Berlin: Wagenbachs Taschen-bücherei, 1975.

Warren, A.: "The Penal Colony," *KP,* 140-142.

Webster, P.D.: "F.K's 'In the Penal Colony'."

West, R.: *The Court and the Castle,* 30-32, 299-301.

"Investigations of a Dog" (Forschungen eines Hundes) [July 1922].

Binder, H.: *Kafka-Kommentar,* 261-297; "Kafkas Hebrä-ischstudien."

Czermak, H.: *"The Metamorphosis" & Other Stories,* 62-66.

Emrich, W.: *F.K. A Critical Study,* 201-211.

Fingerhut, K.H.: *Die Funktion der Tierfiguren.*

Furst, N.: *Die offenen Geheimturen F.Ks,* 9-15.

Goodman, P.: *Kafka's Prayer,* 231-235, 242-253.

Heller, E.: *F.K.,* 30-38.

Hillmann, H.: *F.K.,* 51-56.

Miller, J.H. Jr.: "F.K. and the Metaphysics of Alienation," 285-286.

Rahv, P.: "Exegetical Notes."

Richter, H.: *F.K.,* 272-285.

Sokel, W.H.: *F.K. Tragik und Ironie.*

Stumpf, W.: "Der Mensch und sein verlorenes Einst."

Tauber, H.: *F.K. An Interpretation of his Works,* 201-211.

Tiefenbrun, R.: *Moment of Torment,* 62-78.

Weinberg, K.: *Kafkas Dichtungen.*

Winkelman, J.: "Kafka's 'Forschungen eines Hundes'."

"Jackals and Arabs" (Schakale und Araber) [Jan. 1917].

Beck, E.T.: *Kafka and the Yiddish Theater,* 179-181.

Binder, H.: *Kafka-Kommentar*, 202-204.

Bridgwater, P.: *Kafka and Nietzsche*, 115-119.

Leibfried, E.: *Kritische Wissenschaft vom Text*, 337-342.

Richter, H.: *F.K.*, 141-143.

Rubinstein, W.C.: "Kafka's 'Jackals and Arabs'."

Sokel, W.H.: "Das Verhältnis der Erzählperspektive..."

Tauber, H.: *F.K. An Interpretation of his Works*, 69-70.

"Josephine the Singer, or the Mouse Folk" (Josefine, die Sängerin, oder Das Volk der Mäuse) [Mar. 1924].

Anders, G.: *F.K.*, 92-93.

Beck, E.T.: *Kafka and the Yiddish Theater*, 203-207.

Beicken, P.U.: *F.K.*, 325-327.

Biemel, W.: *Philosophische Analysen...*, 55 ff.

Binder, H.: "Kafka's Hebräischstudien," *Kafka-Kommentar*, 323-331.

Bridgwater, P.: *Kafka and Nietzsche*, 142-149.

Caspel. J. van: "Josephine und Jeremias."

Collins, H.P.: "Kafka's Views of Institutions and Traditions."

Edel, E.: "Zum Problem des Künstlers bei Kafka."

Emrich, W.: *F.K. A Critical Study*, 200-206.

Fingerhut, K.H.: *Die Funktion der Tierfiguren...*

Flach, B.: *Kafkas Erzählungen*, 95-120.

Fürst, N.: *Die offenen Geheimtüren...*, 73-74.

Gray, R.: *F.K.*, 173-186.

Hillmann, H.: *F.K.*

Nemeth, A.: *Kafka*, 164-168.

Politzer, H.: *F.K., Parable and Paradox*, 308-318.

Ramm, K.: *Reduktion als Erzählprinzip bei Kafka*, 141-145.

Richter, H.: *F.K.*, 246-251.

Rolleston, J.: *Kafka's Narrative Theater*, 130-139.

Sokel, W.H.: *F.K. Tragik und Ironie*, 501-531.

Tauber, H.: *F.K. An Interpretation of his Works*, 193-198.

Wiese, B. von: "Der Kunstler und die moderne Gesellschaft."

Woodring, C.L.: "Josephine the Singer," *FKT*, 71-75.

"The Judgment" (Das Urteil) [Sept. 22-23, 1912].

A number of essays is collected in the symposium *The Problem of "The Judgment"*, ed. by Angel Flores. Staten Island, N.Y.: Gordian Press, 1976.

Asher, J.A.: "Turning Points in Kafka's Stories."

Baumer, F.: *Sieben Prosastücke*, 101-109.

Beck, E.T.: *Kafka and the Yiddish Theater*, 70-121.

Beharriell, F.J.: "Kafka, Freud und 'Das Urteil'."

Beicken, P.U.: *F.K.*, 241-250; *Perspektive und Sehweise*, 409-465; "The Judgment," *PJ*.

Beissner, F.: "Kafka the Artist," *GK*, 15-31.

Benjamin, W.: *Über Literatur*, 154-156.

Beutner, B. *Die Bildsprache F.Ks.*, passim.

Binder, H.: *Motiv und Gestaltung*, 125-135, 340-396; *Kafka-Kommentar*, 123-152; "The Judgment," *PJ*.

Bödeker, K.B.: *Frau und Familie...*, 42-45.

Born, J.: *KS*, 149-151.

Corngold, S.: "The Judgment," *PJ*.

Czermak, H.: *"The Metamorphosis" & Other Stories*, 23-32.

Demmer, J.: *F.K., der Dichter der Selbstreflexion*.

Dietz, L.: "F.K.: Drucke zu seinen Lebzeiten;" "Drucke F.Ks. bis 1924;" "Die autorisierten Dichtungen Ks."

Doppler, A.: "Entfremdung und Familienstruktur," 75-91.

Edel, E.: "F.K.: 'Das Urteil'."

Ellis, J.M.: "Kafka: 'Das Urteil';" "The Judgment," *PJ*.

Falke, R.: "Biographisch-literarische Hintergründe von Ks. 'Urteil'."

Felheim, M.: "'The Judgment'."

Flores, K.: "F.K. and the Nameless Guilt;" "The Judgment," *FKT*, 5-24; "'La condena' de F.K.";"The Nameless Guilt," *PJ*.

Foulkes. A.P.: *The Reluctant Pessimist*, 100-106.

Gettman, Royal A. & Bruce Harkness: *Teacher's Manual for "A Book of Short Stories"*. N.Y.: Rinehart, 1955, 62-64.

Gibian, G.: "Dichtung und Wahrheit: Three Versions of Reality."

Gray, R.: *F.K.*, 57-66.

Greenberg, M.: "The Literature of Truth;" *The Terror of Art*, 47-68.

Haas, E.: "Differenzierende Interpretation..."

Heller, E.: *F.K.*, 1-13, 27-28; [& J. Beug:] *F.K.*, 19-30.

Ide, H.: "Existenzerhellung im Werke Ks." 100-103.

Kemper, H.G.: "Gestörte Kommunikation. F.K.: 'Das Urteil'."

Kobs, J.: *Kafka*, 301 ff., 342 ff.

Kraft, H.: *Kafka*, 39-44.

Kuna, F.: *F.K.*, 42 ff., 143 f.

Magny, C.E.: *KP*, 81-85.

Marson, E.L.: "F.Ks. 'Das Urteil'."

Memmi, G.: "Motivations inconscientes et formes dans 'Le verdict'."

Miyai, T.: "Motiv zu F.Ks. Erzählung 'Das Urteil'."

Murrill, V. & W.S. Marks: "Kafka's 'The Judgment' and *The Interpretation of Dreams.*"

Nagel, B.: *F.K.*, 172-200.

Neesen, P.: *Vom Louvrezirkel zum Prozess.*

Platzer, H.: "Kafka's 'Double figure..."

Politzer, H.: *F.K.: Parable & Paradox*, 53-65.

Pondrom, C.N.: "Coherence in K's 'The Judgment'."

Pongs, H.: *Im Umbruch der Zeit*, 81-85 (1952 ed.); *F.K.*, 50-55.

Rehfeld, W.: *Das Motiv des Gerichtes...*, 87-92.

Richter, H.: "Im Masstab der Klassik;" *F.K.*, 105-112.

Rolleston, J.: *Kafka's Narrative Theater*, 42-51.

Ruf, U.: *F.K.*, 11-51.

Ruhleder, K.H.: "F.K's 'Das Urteil': An Interpretation."

Russell, F.: *Three Studies...*, 55-57.

Ryan, L.: "Zum letzten Mal Psychologie!"

Sautermeister, G.: "Sozialpsychologische Textanalyse."

Schneeberger, I: *Das Kunstmärchen*, 17-46.

Scott, N.A. Jr.: *Rehearsals of Discomposure*, 35-36, 39-42.

Seidler, I.: "'Das Urteil'."

Sokel, W.H.: *F.K.,* 19-24; *F.K.: Tragik und Ironie,* 44-76; "The Judgment," *PJ.*

Steinberg, E.R.: "The Judgment in Kafka's 'The Judgment'."

Stern, J.P.: "F.K's 'Das Urteil'," also in *PJ.*

Szanto, G.H.: *Narrative Consciousness,* 15-68, 173-180.

Tauber, H.: *F.K.: An Interpretation of his Works,* 12-17.

Thalmann, J.: *Wege zu Kafka,* 52-55.

Thieberger, R.: *Le genre de la nouvelle.*

Thorlby, A.: *Kafka,* 28-34, also in *H,* 45-49.

Tiefenbrun, R.: *Moment of Torment,* 79-110.

Weber, A.: "'Das Urteil'."

Weinberg, K.: *Ks Dichtungen,* 318-350.

White, J.J.: "F.K's 'Das Urteil': An Interpretation;" "Georg Bendemann's Friend," *PJ.*

Zimmermann, W.: *Deutsche Prosadichtungen,* 1960 ed., 93-110; 1966 ed., 189-208.

"The Knock at the Manor Gate" (Der Schlag aus Hoftor) [Mar. 1917].

Binder, H.: *Kafka-Kommentar,* 222-223.

Mauer, O.: "Kommentar zu zwei Parabeln von F.K."

Reiss, H.S.: "Zwei Erzählungen F.Ks."

"A Little Fable (Kleine Fabel) [Nov.-Dec. 1920].

Binder, H.: *Kafka-Kommentar,* 252.

Schlingmann, C.: "Kleine Prosastücke"

"A Little Woman" (Eine kleine Frau) [Oct.-Nov. 1923].

Binder, H.: *Kafka-Kommentar,* 300-301.

Carrive, J.: "Un petit bout de femme."

Furst, N.: *Die offenen Geheimtüren F.Ks.,* 76-77.

Pfeiffer, J.: "F.K.: 'Eine kleine Frau'."

Richter, H.: *F.K.,* 239-242.

Tauber, H.: *F.K.: An Interpretation of his Works,* 189-190.

"The Married Couple" (Das Ehepaar) [1922].

Binder, H.: *Kafka-Kommentar,* 297.

Kraft, W.: "F.Ks. Erzählung 'Das Ehepaar';" *F.K.,* 133-138.

Scott, N.A. Jr.: *Rehearsals of Discomposure,* 27-28.

Thurston, J.: "The Married Couple," *FKT,* 83-91.

Ware, M.: "Catholic Ritual and the Meaning of F.K's. 'Das Ehepaar'."

"The Metamorphosis" (Die Verwandlung) [Nov. 17-Dec. 7, 1912].

A 103-page monograph by Schubiger is devoted entirely to "The Metamorphosis." *The Commentator's Despair* by Corngold summarizes and discusses more than 100 essays on this story.

Adams, R.M.: *Strains of Discord,* 168-179.

Adorno, T.W.: "Aufzeichnungen zu Kafka," also in English: "Notes on Kafka."

Albrecht, E.A.: "Kafka's Metamorphosis-Realiter."

Alves, J.R.: *Interpretaçao de Kafka,* 151-157.

Angress, R.K.: "Kafka and Sacher Masoch."

Angus, D.: "Kafka's 'Metamorphosis' and 'The Beauty and the Beast' Tale."

Baioni, G.: *Kafka,* 81-100.

Barnes, H.: "Myth and Human Experience."

Bauer, G.: "Nochmals..."

Beck, E.T.: *Kafka and the Yiddish Theater,* 135-146.

Beicken, P.U.: *F.K.: Eine kritische Einführung,* 261-272.

Beisnner, F.: *Der Erzähler F.K.,* 35-37; and *Kafka der Dichter,* 40-42.

Benjamin, W.: "F.K.: Zur zehnten Wiederkels seines Todestages"; also in English: "F.K.: On the Tenth Anniversary of his Death."

Bense, M.: *Die Theorie Kafkas,* 51-54.

Binder, H.: *Motiv und Gestaltung bei F.K.,* 357-369; *Kafka-Kommentar,* 152-172.

Binion, R.: "What the Metamorphosis Means."

Blengio Brito, R.: *Aproximación a Kafka,* 19-45.

Borges, J.L.: "Prefacio" to *La Metamorfosis.* Buenos Aires: Losada, 1938, 7-11.

Born, J.: *KS,* 140-149.

Bruck, M. von: "Versuch über Kafka."

Cervani, I.L.: *Considerazioni sulla "Verwandlung" di Kafka.*

Corngold, S.: Introduction to his critical ed. of F.K.: *Metamorphosis.* N.Y.: Bantam Books, 1972, XI-XXII; "Kafka's *Die Verwandlung:* Metamorphosis of the Metaphor;" (ed.): *The Commentators' Despair: The Interpretation of Kafka's "Metamorphosis."*

Daemmrich, H.S.: "The Internal Fairy Tale..."

Dalmau Castañón, W.: "El caso clínico de Kafka en *La Metamorfosis.*"

Dentan, M.: *Humour et création littéraire dans l'oeuvre de Kafka,* 11-16.

Dietz, L.: "F.K.: Drucke zu einen Lebzeiten."

Doppler, A.: "Entfremdung und Familienstruktur."

Edel, E.: "F.K.: *Die Verwandlung.* Eine Auslegung."

Erlich, V.: "Gogol and Kafka," 102-104.

Emrich, W.: *F.K. A Critical Study,* 132-148.

Fast, H.: *Literature and Reality,* 9-12.

Fingerhut, K.H.: *Die Funktion der Tierfiguren...,* 189-200.

Foulkes, A.P.: *The Reluctant Pessimist,* 107-111.

Freedman, R.: "Kafka's Obscurity..." 65-68.

Friedman, N.: "Kafka's *Metamorphosis:* A Literal Reading;" and "The Struggle of Vermin..."

Gaillard, J.M.: "Une mythologie du désespoir..."

Gibian, G.: "Dichtung und Wahrheit: Three Versions of Reality..."

Gilman, S.L.: "A View of Kafka's Treatment of Actuality in *Die Verwandlung.*"

Goldstein, B.: "A Study of the Wound in Stories by F.K.", 206-214.

Goodman, P.: "Preface" to F.K.: *The Metamorphosis.* N.Y.: Vanguard Press, 1946, 5-8.

Gray, R.: *F.K.,* 83-92.

Greenberg, M.: "Kafka's 'Metamorphosis' and Modern Spirituality," rep. in *Terror of Art,* 69-91; *H,* 50-64.

Gutmann, A.: "Der Mistkäfer."

Harder, M.L.: *Märchenmotive in der Dichtung F.Ks.*

Hasselblatt, D.: *Zauber und Logik,* 192-205.

Hasselblatt, U.: *Das Wesen des Volksmärchen...,* 191-198.

Hawkins, A.D.: "Fiction Chronicle." *The Criterion* (London), XVII (1938), 506-508.

Henel, I.: "Die Deutbarkeit von Kafkas Werken."

Heselhaus, C.: "Kafkas Erzählformen."

Holland, N.N.: "Realism and Unrealism: Kafka's 'Metamorphosis'."

Honig, E.: *Dark Conceit,* 63-68.

Hoover, M.L.: "Introduction" to her edition of *Die Verwandlung.* London: Methuen, 1962, i-vii.

Hosaka, M.: "Die erlebte Rede in 'Die Verwandlung'."

Kaiser, H.: *F.Ks. Inferno,* 53-61.

Kassel, N.: *Das Groteske bei F.K.,* 153-169.

Köhnke, K.: "Ks. guoter sündere: Zu der Erzählung 'Die Verwandlung'."

Kokis, S.: *F.K. e a expressao da realidade,* 62-70.

Konder, L.: *Kafka,* 9-12.

Kraft, W.: *F.K.: Durchdringung und Geheimnis.*

Krock, M.: "F.Ks. 'Die Verwandlung'."

Kuna, F.: *F.K.,* 49-63.

Lancelotti, M.A.: *Como leer a Kafka,* 18-36.

Landsberg, P.L.: "Kafka et *La Métamorphose;*" and "The Metamorphosis," KP, 122-133.

Lawson, R.H.: *"Ungeheueres Ungeziefer* in Kafka's *Die Verwandlung."*

Loeb, E.: "Bedeutungswandel der Metamorphose bei F.K. und E.T.A. Hoffmann: Ein Vergleich."

Ludwig, Richard and M.B. Perry (eds): *Nine Short Novels.* Boston: D.C. Heath, 1952, xlii-xlvii.

Luke, F.D.: "Kafka's 'Die Verwandlung';" and "'The Metamorphosis'," *FKT,* 25-44.

MacAndrew, M.E.: "A Splacknuck and a Dung-Beetle..."

Madden, W.A.: "A Myth of Mediation: Kafka's 'Metamorphosis'."

Margolis, J.: "Kafka vs. Eudaimonia and Duty."

Marion, D.: "'La Métamorphose'."

Martin, P.A.: "The Cockroach as an Identification..."

Moss, L.: "A Key to the Door Image in 'The Metamorphosis'."

Muller, R.: *KS*, 147-148.

Parry, I.: "Kafka and Gogol."

Pfeiffer, J.: "Über F.Ks. Novelle 'Die Verwandlung';" *GK*, 53-59; *Die dichterische Wirklichkeit*, 153-166.

Poggioli, R.: "Kafka and Dostoyevski," *KP*, 102-104.

Politzer, H.: *F.K.: Parable and Paradox*, 65-82.

Pongs, H.: "'Die Verwandlung' zwischen Ost und West."

Rahv, P.: "The Hero as Lonely Man."

Ramm, K.: *Reduktion als Erzählprinzip bei Kafka*, 90-102.

Reiss, H.S.: *F.K.*, 37-41.

Richter, F.K.: "'Verwandlungen' bei Kafka und Stehr..."

Richter, H.: *F.K.: Werk und Entwurf*, 112-119.

Rohner, W.: *F.K.*, 49-52.

Rolleston, J.: *Kafka's Narrative Theater*, 52-68.

Ruf, U.: *Das Dilemma der Sohne*.

Ruhleder, K.H.: "Die theologische Dreizeitenlehre in F.Ks. "Die Verwandlung'."

Sautermeister, G.: "Die sozialkritischer..."

Schlingmann, C.: "'Die Verwandlung': Eine Interpretation."

Schneeberger, I.: *Das Kunstmärchen...*, 17-46.

Schubiger, J.: *F.K.: "Die Verwandlung." Eine Interpretation*.

Schüddekopf, J.: "Rätzel der Faszination."

Schulze, H.: "Antwärter der Gnade."

Sokel, W.H.: "Kafka's 'Metamorphosis': Rebellion and Punishment;" *F.K.: Tragik und Ironie*, 77-103; *F.K.*, 19-22.

Sonnenfeld, M.: "Paralleles in [Goethe's] *Novelle* und *Verwandlung*."

Sparks, K.: "Drei schwarze Kaninchen...;" and "Kafka's *Metamorphosis:* On Banishing the Lodgers."

Spector, R.D.: "Kafka's Epiphanies."

Spilka, M.: "Kafka's Sources for *The Metamorphosis*."

Springer, M.D.: *"The Metamorphosis."*

Starobinski, J.: "Le rêve architecte."

Szanto, G.H.: *Narrative Consciousness...*, 15-68 and 173-180.

Tauber, H.: *F.K. An Interpretation of his Works,* 18-26.

Taylor, A.: "The Waking: The Theme of Kafka's *Metamorphosis.*"

Thalmann, J.: *Wege su Kafka,* 230-234.

Thorlby, A.: *Kafka,* 34-40.

Tiefenbrun, R.: *Moment of Torment,* 111-135.

Tindall, W.Y.: *The Literary Symbol,* 63-64.

Todorov, T.: *Einführung in die fantastische Literatur.*

Tomberg, F.: "Kafkas Tiere und die bürgerliche Gesellschaft."

Ulshöfer, R.: "Die Wirklichkeitsauffassung in der modernen Prosadichtung," 27-36.

Urzidil, J.: *There Goes Kafka,* 18-19, 82-96.

Volkening, E.: *"La Metamorfosis* de Kafka."

Waldeck, P.B.: "Kafka's 'Die Verwandlung' and 'Ein Hungerkünstler' as Influenced by Leopold von Sacher-Masoch."

Walzel, Oskar: "Logik im Wunderbaren," *KS,* 140-146.

Webster, P.D.: "F.K.'s 'Metamorphosis' as Death and Resurrection Fantasy."

Weinberg, K.: *Kafkas Dichtungen: Die Travestien des Mythos,* 235-317.

Wiese, B. von: "F.K.: 'Die Verwandlung'."

Witt, M.A.: "Confiment in *Der Verwandlung* and *Les séquestrés d'Altona.*"

Wolkenfeld, S.: "Christian Symbolism in Kafka's 'The Metamorphosis'."

Wöllner, G.: *E.T.A. Hoffman und Franz Kafka. Von der 'fortgeführten Metapher' zum 'sinnlichen Paradox'.*

"My Neighbor" (Der Nachbar) [Feb. 1917].

Binder, H.: *Kafka-Kommentar,* 216-218.

Hajek, S.: "F.K.: 'Der Nachbar'."

Kraft, W.: *F.K.,* 16-17.

Rutt, T.: "Betrachtung zu 'Der Nachbar'."

Zimmermann, W.: *Deutsche Prosadichtungen unseres Jahrhunderts,* Vol. II, 250-266.

"The Next Village" (Das nächste Dorf) [Jan.-Feb. 1917].

Binder, H.: *Kafka-Kommentar,* 213.

Lecomte, M.: "Le plus proche village."

Schlingmann, C.: "Kleine Prosastücke."

Tauber, H.: F.K. An Interpretation of his Works, 73-74.

"The New Advocate" (Der neue Advokat) [Jan. 1917].

Binder, H.: *Kafka-Kommentar,* 204-208.

Kassel, N.: *Das Groteske bei F.K.,* 138-144.

Kraft, W.: *F.K.,* 13-15.

Richter, H.: *F.K.,* 128-130.

"An Old Manuscript" (Ein altes Blatt) [Mar. 1917].

Beck, E.T.: *Kafka and the Yiddish Theater,* 192-193.

Binder, H.: Kafka-Kommentar, 221-222.

Bedwell, C.B.: "The Forces of Destruction in K's 'Ein altes Blatt'."

Bridgwater, P.: *Kafka and Nietzsche,* 119-121.

Kraft, W.: *Wort und Gedanke,* 129-131.

Lynskey, Winifred: *Reading Modern Fiction.* N.Y.: Scribner's, 1957, 320-322.

Metzger, M. and E.: "F.Ks. 'Ein altes Blatt' im Deutschunterricht."

Richter, H.: *F.K.,* 137-139.

Rogers, J.A.: "Kafka's 'An Old Manuscript'."

"On Parables" (Von den Gleichnissen) [1922-1923].

Allemann, B.: "Kafka: 'Von den Gleichnissen'."

Arntzen, H.: "F.K.: 'Von den Gleichnissen'."

Beicken, P.U.: *F.K.: Eine kritische Einführung,* 168-172.

Binder, H.: *Kafka-Kommentar,* 299.

Brandsetter, A.: "Zum Gleichnirreden der Dichter..."

Brettschneider, W.: *Die moderne deutsche Parabel.*

Emrich, W.: *F.K.: A Critical Study,* 108-109.

Fülleborn, U.: "Zum Verhältnis..."

Kerkhoff, E.: "Noch einmal: F.K.'s 'Von den Gleichnissen'."

Kloocke, K.: "Zwei späte Erzählungen Kafkas."

Kraft, W.: *F.K.,* 11-13.

Philippi, K.P.: "Parabolisches Erzählen..."

Richter, H.: *F.K.: Werk und Entwurf,* 220 ff.

Strohschneider-Kohrs, I.: "Erzähllogik und Verstehensprozess in Kafkas Gleichnis 'Von den Gleichnissen'."

"The Problem of Our Laws" (Zur Frage der Gesetze) [Oct. 1920].

Beck, E.T.: *Kafka and the Yiddish Theater,* 192-193.

Binder, H.: *Kafka-Kommentar,* 248-249.

Emrich, W.: *F.K.: A Critical Study,* 249-253.

Hebel, F.: "Kafka: 'Zur Frage der Gesetze' und Kleist..."

Richter, H.: *F.K.,* 221-223.

Spittler, E.: "F.Ks. 'Gesetz' unter dem Aspekt des Atems."

"A Report to an Academy" (Ein Bericht für eine Akademie) [Apr. 1917].

Beck, E.T.: *Kafka and the Yiddish Theater,* 181-188.

Beicken, P.U.: *F.K. Eine kritische Einführung,* 307-312.

Binder, H.: *Motiv und Gestaltung,* 161-166.; *Kafka-Kommentar,* 225-230.

Bridgwater, P.: *Kafka and Nietzsche,* 127-131.

Czermak, H.: *"The Metamorphosis & Other Stories,* 66-69.

Emrich, W.: *F.K. A Critical Study,* 148-151.

Fingerhut, K.H.: *Die Funktion der Tierfiguren...,* 144 ff., 251-254.

Foulkes, A.P.: "Kafka's Cage Image;" *The Reluctant Pessimist,* 81 ff.

Gump, M.: "From Ape to Man and from Man to Ape."

Jarv, H.: *Varaktigare an koppar,* 205-274.

Kaiser, H.: *F. Ks. Inferno.*

Kassel, N.: *Das groteske bei F.K.,* 144-153.

Kauf, R.: "Once Again: Kafka's 'A Report to an Academy'."

Leopold, K.: "F.K's Stories in the First Person," 59-61.

Loeb, E.: "Bedeutungswandel der Metamorphose..."

Lortz, H.: "F.K.: 'Ein Bericht für eine Akademie'."

Magny, C.E.: *KP,* 89-92.

Michael, W.: "The Human Simian."

Neumann, G.: "'Ein Bericht für eine Akademie'."...

Neumeyer, P.F.: "F.K., Sugar Baron."

Philippi, K.P.: *Reflexion und Wirklichkeit*, 116-147.

Politzer, H.: *F.K. Parable and Paradox*, 91-92.

Richter, H.: *F.K. Werk und Entwurf*, 155-159.

Rubinstein, W.C.: "A Report to an Academy" *FKT*, 55-60.

Schulz-Behrend, G.: "Kafka's 'Ein Bericht für eine Akademie': An Interpretation."

Sokel, W.H.: *F.K. Tragik und Ironie*, 330-355.

Struc, R.S.: "Zwei Erzählungen . . ."

Stuart, D.: "Kafka's 'A Report to an Academy'."

Weinstein, L.: "Kafka's Ape."

Wöllner, G.: *E.T.A. Hoffmann und F.K. . . .*, 138 ff.

"The Silence of the Sirens" (Das Schweigen der Sirenen) [Oct. 23, 1917].

Binder, H.: *Motiv und Gestaltung; Kafka-Kommentar*, 238.

Born, J.: "Ks. unermüdliche Rechner."

Emrich, W.: "Die Bilderwelt F.Ks." *Akz*, (Apr. 1960), 190 ff.

Foulkes, A.P.: "An Interpretation of Kafka's 'Das Schweigen der Sirenen."

Kassel, N.: *Das Groteske bei F.K.*, 132-138.

Krusche, D.: *Kafka und Kafka-Deutung*.

Naumann, D.: "Kafkas Auslegungen."

Neumann, G.: "Umkehrung und Ablenkung."

Politzer, H.: "'Das Schweigen der Sirenen'."

Urzidil, J.: "Das Reich des Unerreichbaren."

Weinberg, K.: *Kafkas Dichtungen*, 37 ff.

"The Stoker" *see Amerika*.

"The Test" (Die Prüfung) [Nov. 1920].

Binder, H.: *Kafka-Kommentar*, 250.

Kloocke, K.: "Zwei späte Erzählungen Kafkas."

Reiss, H.S.: "Zwei Erzälungen F.Ks."

Renner, I.: "F.K.: 'Die Prüfung'."

The Trial (Der Prozess) [Jul.-Dec. 1914] and "Before the Law" (Vor dem Gesetz)* [Dec. 1914].

Besides dissertations (Langguth, Seidler, Smith, Yalom), full-length books on *The Trial* include Frey, Gentile, Glickson, Jaffee, Marson, Neesen, Rhein, and Rolleston.

* An asterisk indicates essays dealing particularly with "Before the Law," a parable which Kafka published separately and later included in his short-story collection *The Country Doctor*. It also appears as part of *The Trial* (in Chapter IX).

Adolf, H.: "From *Everyman* ..."

Adorno, T.W.: "Notes on Kafka."

Anders, G.: *F.K.*, 32-35 passim.

Allemann, B.: "Kafka: *Der Prozess.*"

Anderson, B.: "F.K.'s *The Trial.*"

Arendt, H.: "F.K.: A Revaluation."

Arntzen, H.: "F.K.: *Der Prozess.*"

Aschka, F.: "Vergleich mit Kafkas *Prozess.*"

* Baumer, F.: *Sieben Prosastücke*, 89-97.

Beck, E.T.: *Kafka and the Yiddish Theater*, 154-171.

* Binder, H.: *Kafka-Kommentar*, 183-186.

Beicken, P.U.: *F.K.*, 273-286.

Benjamin, W.: "F.K. On the 10th Anniversary of his Death."

Bezzel, C.: *Natur bei Kafka*, 87-92.

Blanchot, M.: *La part du feu*, 9-19; "Reading Kafka," *JRT*.

* Born, J.: "Kafka's Parable 'Before the Law'."

Bridgwater, P.: *Kafka and Nietzsche*, 67-90.

Brod, M.: "Postscripts" to F.K.: *The Trial*. N.Y.: Knopf, 1957 (definitive ed.), 326-338.

Bryant, J.H.: "The Delusion of Hope: F.K.'s *The Trial.*"

Buber, M.: *Schuld und Schuldgefühle*, 50-68.

Butler, E.M.: "The Element of Time ..."

Camus, A.: "Hope and Absurdity." *KP*, 251-261.

Canetti, E.: *Kafka's Other Trial*.

Church, M.: "Time and Reality in K's *The Trial* and *The Castle;* "Dostoievsky's *Crime and Punishment* and K's *The Trial; Time and Reality.*

Claudel, P.: *"Le Procès* de K. ou le drame de la justice."

Cohen, S.: "Kafka's K. and Joseph K."

Collins, R.G.: "Kafka's Special Methods of Thinking."

Corngold, S.: "The Question of Law, the Question of Writing," *JRT*.

Cournot, M.: "Avant-critique du *Procès*."

Dauvin, R.: "The Trial: Its Meaning." *FKT,* 145-160.

* Deinert, H.: "Kafka's Parable 'Before the Law'."

Dev, A.: "Joseph K. and Jean-Baptiste Clamence."

* Diller, E.: "Theonomous Homiletics "Vor dem Gesetz';"
"'Heteronomy' versus 'Autonomy'."

Dyson, A.E.: "Trial by Enigma."

Eisner, P.: "F.Ks. *Prozess* und Prag."

Emmel, H.: *Das Gericht . . .,* 7-21.

Emrich, W.: *F.K.: A Critical Study . . .,* 316-364; "The Role
of Women," *JRT.*

Feuerlicht, I.: "Kafka's Chaplain;" "Kafka's Joseph K.:"
"Discussions and Contradictions in Kafka's *Trial.*"

Fickert, K.J.: "The Window Metaphor in Kafka's *Trial.*"

Fort, K.: "The Function of Style in F.K's *The Trial.*"

* Foulkes, A.P.: *The Reluctant Pessimist,* 157-163.

Frey, G.: *Der Raum und die Figuren . . ., F.Ks. Roman "Der
Prozess".*

Fromm, E.: The Forgotten Language, 249-263; (213-224,
1952 ed.).

Fürst, N.: *Die offenen Geheimtüren F.Ks.,* 36-52.

* Gaier, U.: "'Vor dem Gesetz'."

Gentile, F.S.: *Kafka, processo alla giustizia.*

Glickson, J.M.: *"Le Procès": Kafka. Analyse critique.*

Göhler, H.: "F.Ks. Prozess."

Goldstein, B.: *Key Motifs in F.K's "Der Prozess" and "Das
Schloss".*

Goodman, P.: *Kafka's Prayer,* 147-182.

Gray, R.: *Franz Kafka,* 103-125.

Greenberg, M.: *Terror of Art,* 113-153.

Groethuysen, B.: "The Endless Layrinth," *KP,* 376-390.

Grossvogel, D.I.: "Kafka: *The Trial.*"

Guadagnino, L.M.: "La giustizia di Kafka."

Guignard, R.: "Les romans de Kafka."

Gunwaldsen, K.M.: "The Plot of Kafka's *The Trial.*

Haas, W.: "Kafkas letztes Werk."

Hamburger, K.: "Erzählformen des modernes Romans," 16-
19.

Handler, G.: "A Textual Omission...;" "A Note on the Structure of Kafka's *Der Prozess.*"

Heger, R.: *Der osterreichische Roman*... Part 1, 49-85; Part II, 50-58.

Heinz, H.: "Herman Melville's Erzählung 'Bartleby' in Vergleich zu F.Ks. Roman *Der Prozess.*"

Heller, Erich: *Franz Kafka,* 71-97; "The Imagery of Guilt," *JRT.*

* Henel, I.: "Die Türhüterlegende und ihre Bedeutung für Ks. *Prozess.*" tr. as "The Legend of the Doorkeeper," *JRT.*

Hermsdorf, K.: "Nachwort" to his ed. of F.K.: *Erzählungen, Der Prozess, Das Schloss,* 775-820.

Hoffman, F.J.: "Kafka's *The Trial:* The Assailant as Landscape."

* Hoffmann, W.: "Kafkas Legende 'Vor dem Gesetz'."

Ide, H.: "F.Ks. *Der Prozess:* Interpretation des ersten Kapitels."

Isermann, G.: *Unser Leben, unser Prozess.*

Jaffe, A.H.: *The Process of Kafka's Trial.*

Kartiganer, D.M.: "Job and Joseph K."

Kavanagh, T.M.: "Kafka's *The Trial:* The Semiotics of the Absurd;" also in *JRT.*

Kelly, J.: *"The Trial* and the Theology of Crisis."

Klee, W.G.: *Die characteristischen Motive...*"

Kobs, J.: *Kafka.*

Köhnke, K.: "Das Gericht und die Helfer."

Korst, M.R.: *Die Beziehung zwischen Held und Gegenwelt...*

Kraft, H.: *Kafka: Wirklichkeit und Perspektive.*

Krieger, M.: *The Tragic Vision,* 114-144.

Kudszus, W.: "Erzählhaltung...;" "Between Past and Future;" "Erzählperspektive..."

Kuepper, K.J.: "Gesture and Posture as Elemental Symbolism..." also in *JRT.*

Kuhn, I.: "The Metamorphosis of *The Trial.*"

Kuna, F.: *F.K.,* 99-135.

Lachmann, E.: "Das Türhütergleichnis in Kafkas *Prozess.*"

Ladendorf, H.: "Kafka und die Kunstgeschichte."

Lamprecht, H.: "Muhe und Kunst des Anfangs..."

Langguth, C.W.: *Narrative Perspecitve and Consciousness in F.K's "Trial".*

Leopold, K.: "Breaks in Perspective in F.K's *Der Prozess."*

Lesser, S.O.: "The Source of Guilt and the Sense of Guilt..."

Levi, M.: "K.: An Exploration of the Names of Kafka's Central Characters."

Lindsay, J.M.: "Kohlhaas and K.: Two Men in Search of Justice."

Livermore, A.L.: "Kafka and Stendhal's *De l'Amour."*

Macklem, M.: "Kafka and the Myth of Tristan."

Marache, M.: "L'Image fonctionnelle dans *Le Procès..."*

Marson, E.L.: "Justice and the Obsesses Character...;" "Die *Prozess*-Ausgaben;" *An Analytical Interpretation of F.K.'s "Der Prozess;" Kafka's "Trial".*

Mellen, J.: "Joseph K. and the Law."

Miller, N.: "Erlebte und verschleierte Rede."

Mueller, W.R.: "The Theme of Judgment: F.K.'s *The Trial."*

Mühlberger, J.: *F.K.*

Nagel, B.: *F.K.* 213-237.

Neesen, P.: *Vom Louvrezirkel zum "Prozess": F.K. und die Psychologie Franz Brentanos.*

Nemeth, A.: *K,* 76-122.

Nicholson, N.: *Man and Literature,* 168-177.

Noble, C.A.M.: "Kafkas Männer ohne Eigenschaften."

Pascal, R.: *The German Novel,* 226-233.

Pasley, M.: "Two Literary Sources of Kafka's *Der Prozess.*

Politzer, H.: *F.K., Parable and Paradox,* 163-217; "The Puzzle of K's Prosecuting Attorney."

Pondrom, C.N.: "Kafka and Phenomenology: Joseph K's Search for Information."

Pongs, H.: *F.K.: Dichter des Labyrinths.*

Purdy, S.B.: "Religion and Death in Kafka's *Der Prozess;"* * "A Talmudic Analogy to Kafka's 'Vor dem Gesetz'."

Rahv, P.: "The Hero as Lonely Man," 68-73; "Death of Ivan Ilyich and Joseph K." *Image and Idea,* 121-139 (1957 ed.).

Rasmussen, S.: "Uudgrundelighedens offer..."

Reed, E.E.: "Moral Polarity..."; "F.K.: Possession and Being."

Rehfeld, W.: *Das Motiv des Gerichtes...*

Rhein, P.H.: *The Urge to Live...*

Richter, H.: *F.K. Werk und Entwurf;* 139-141; 190-217; "Entwurf und Fragment: Zur Interpretation von Kafkas *Prozess."*

Rohner, W.: *F.K.*

Rolleston, J.: *Kafka's Narrative Theater,* 69-87; (ed.): *Kafka's The Trial.*

Rommerskirch, E.: "Prozess gegen Gott."

* Rosteutscher, J.: "Ks Parable 'Vor dem Gesetz' als Anti-märchen."

Roy, G.: *Kafka's "The Trial," "The Castle" and Other Works.*

Ruhleder, K.H.: "Biblische Parallelen in F.Ks. *Der Prozess."*

St. Leon, R.: "Religious Motives in Kafka's *Der Prozess."*

Schillemeit, J.: "Welt im Werk F.Ks."; "Zum Wirklichkeits-problem der Kafka-Interpretation."

Schoeps, H.J.: "The Tragedy of Faithlessness," *KP,* 287-297; "Theologische Motive in der Dichtung F.Ks;" *Gestalten an der Zeitwende,* 54-76.

Scott, N.A. Jr.: *Rehearsals of Discomposure,* 56-64.

Seidler, M.: *Strukturanalysen der Romane "Der Prozess" and "Das Schloss..."*

Serrano Plaja, A.: "Kafka y la segunda consulta al Doctor Negro."

Singer, C.S.: "Kafka and *The Trial:* The Examined Life."

Slochower, H.: "Secular Crucifixion," 109-114; *FKM,* 14-19.

Smith, D.E.: *The Use of Gesture...*

Sokel, W.H.: *F.K.: Tragik und Ironie,* 356-370; "Das Verhältnis..." "The Programme of K's Court." *TBL;* "The Opaqueness of *The Trial." JRT.*

Sonnenfeld, M.: "Die Fragmente *Amerika* und *Der Prozess* als Bildungromane."

Spaini, A.: *"The Trial," KP,* 143-150.

Spiro, S.J.: "Verdict—Guilty! A Study of *The Trial."*

* Spittler, E.: "F.Ks. 'Gesetz' unter dem Aspekt des Atems."

Staroste, W.: *Raum und Realität...*, 123-155.

Steinberg, M.W.: "F.K.: The Achievement of Certitude."

Stelzmann, R.A.: "Kafka's *The Trial* and Hesse's *Steppenwolf.*"

Stern, J.P.: "F.K.: The Labyrinth of Guilt;" "The Law of the Trial," *TBL.*

Strauss, W.A.: "Albert Camus's *Caligula.*"

Storz, G.: *"Der Prozess;"* "Über den 'Monologue intérieur'."

Strelka, J.: *Kafka, Musil, Broch...*

Szamek, P. & Others: *"The Trial."*

Szanto, G.H.: *Narrative Consciousness...*

Tauber, H.: *F.K. An Interpretation of his Works,* 77-120.

Thorlby, A. *Kafka, A Study,* 52-68.

Tucholsky, K.: *"Der Prozess."*

Usmiani, R.: "Twentieth Century Man..."

Uyttersprot, H.: "Zur Struktur von Ks. *Der Prozess;"* and "Zur Struktur von Ks. Romanen;" "The Trial: Its Structure," *FKT,* 127-144.

Vallette, R.M.: *Der Prozess* and *Le Procès...*"

Vialatte, A.: *L'Histoire secrète du "Procès";* "Introduction" to F.K.: *Le Procès.*

Volkmann-Schluck, K.H.: "Bewusstein und Dasein in Ks. *Prozess."*

Waismann, F.: "A Philosopher Looks at Kafka," 177-186.

Waldmeir, J.J.: "Anti-Semitism as an Issue in the Trial of K's Joseph K."

Walser, M.: *Beschreibung einer Form,* 91-95, 98-104, 116-127.

Wasserstrom, W.: "In Gertrude's Chest," 256-259.

Webster, P.D.: "Arrested Individuation;" *Dies Irae;* also in *H,* 118-125.

Weinberg, K.: *Ks. Dichtungen. Die Travestien des Mythos.*

Weitzmann, S.: *Studie über Kafka,* 37-130.

Wenzig, E.: "Das Mysterium..."

Wilson, A.K.: "'Null and Void': An Interpretation of the Significance of the Court in F.K.'s *Der Prozess."*

Winkler, R.O.C.: *KP,* 192-198.

Witt, M.A.: "Camus et Kafka."

Yalom, M.K.: *The Motif of the Trial in the Works of F.K. and Albert Camus;* "Albert Camus and the Myth of the Trial."

* Zimmermann, W.: *Deutsche Prosadichtungen,* 169-174, (1966 ed., 219-227).

Ziolkowski, T.: *Dimensions of the Modern Novel,* 37-67.

"Up in the Gallery" (Auf der Galerie) [Jan.-Feb. 1917].

Baumer, F.: *Sieben Prosastücke,* 97-101.

Beicken, P.U.: *F.K., Eine kritische Einführung,* 302-306.

Binder, H.: *Kafka-Kommentar,* 212.

Beicken, P.U.: *F.K., Eine kritische Einführung,* 302-306.

Emrich, W.: *F.K. A Critical Study,* 31-32 passim.

Foulkes, A.P.: "'Auf der Galerie': Some Remarks Concerning Kafka's Concept and Portrayal of Reality."

Glaser, H.: "F.K.: 'Auf der Galerie'."

Klempt, H.: "Die Deutung des Lebens in dichterischer Gestaltung."

Kobs, J.: *Kafka,* 81-93.

Kraft, H.: *Kafka.*

Margetts, J.: "Satzsyntaktisches Spiel mit der Sprache: Zu F.Ks. 'Auf der Galerie'."

Mast, G.: "Ein Beispiel moderner Erzählkunst..."

Philippi, K.P.: *Reflexion und Wirklichkeit,* 51-57.

Richter, H.: *F.K.,* 136-139.

Sokel, W.H.: "Das Verhältnis der Erzählperspektive..."

Spahr, B.L.: "Kafka's 'Auf der Galerie': A Stylistic Analysis."

Stamer, U.: "Sprachstruktur und Wirklichkeit in Kafkas Erzählung 'Auf der Galerie'."

Zimmermann, W.: *Deutsche Prosadichtungen der Gegenwart,* 159-174 (1954 and 1956 eds.), 209-215 (1966 ed.).

"A Visit to a Mine" (Ein Besuch im Bergwerk) [Jan.-Feb. 1917].

Binder, H.: *Kafka-Kommentar,* 212-213.

Kraft, W.: *F.K.,* 47-49.

Pasley, M.: "F.K.: 'Ein Besuch im Bergwerk';" "Drei literarische Mystifikationen Kafkas."

"The Warden of the Tomb" (Der Gruftwächter) [Dec. 1916].

Beckmann, Heinz: "F.Ks. 'Gruftwächter'" *Rheinische Merkur* (Coblenz/Cologne), V, No. 47 (1950), 8.

Ide, H.: "F.K.: 'Der Grufwächter' und 'Die Truppenaushebung'."

Krüger, H.P.: "F.Ks. Dramenfragment 'Der Gruftwächter'."

"Wedding Preparations in the Country" (Hochzeitsvorbereitungen auf dem Lande) [1907].

Binder, H.: *Kafka-Kommentar,* 62-67.

Emrich, W.: *F.K. A Critical Study,* 40-41, 132-134.

Greenberg, M.: *The Terror of Art,* 33-38.

Middelhauve, F.: *Ich und Welt im Fruhwerk Franz Kafkas.*

Rohner, W.: "'Hochzeitsvorbereitungen auf dem Lande'."

Abbreviations

AG	Acta Germanica (Capetown)
AI	The American Imago (Wayne State University, Detroit)
AION-SG	Annali Istituto Universitario Orientale (Naples)—Sezione Germanica
Akz	Akzente: Zeitschrift für Literatur (Munich)
ALit	Acta Litteraria Academiae Scientiarum Hungarica (Budapest)
AUMLA	AUMLA: A Journal of Literary Criticism, Philology and Linguistics (Australian Universities Language and Literature Association, University of North Queensland).
BA	Books Abroad (University of Oklahoma)
CdS	Cahiers du Sud (Marseilles)
CE	College English (National Council of Teachers of English, Urbana, Ill.)
CL	Comparative Literature (University of Oregon, Eugene, Oregon)
CLS	Comparative Literature Studies (University of Illinois, Urbana, Ill.)
Cent Rev	Centennial Review (Michigan State College)
Civitas	Civitas: Monatschrift für Politik und Kultur (Zurich)
CLAJ	College Language Association Journal (Morgan State College, Baltimore)
Coloquio	Coloquio—Letras (Lisbon)

Criticism	Criticism (Wayne State University, Detroit)
Critique	Critique (Paris)
CS	The Complete Stories [of F.K.]. Ed. by Nahum N. Glatzer. N.Y.: Schocken Books, 1971, 486 pp.
CuH	Cuadernos Hispanoamericanos (Madrid)
D1	The Diaries of F.K. 1910-1913. Ed. by Max Brod. Tr. by Joseph Kresh, N.Y.: Schocken, 1948, 345 pp.
D2	The Diaries of F.K. 1914-1923. Ed. by Max Brod. Tr. by Martin Greenberg & H. Aredņt. N.Y.: Schocken, 1949, 343 pp.
DA	Dissertation Abstracts [now DAI].
DAI	Dissertation Abstracts International (Ann Arbor, Mich.)
DF	Dearest Father, Stories and Other Writings [by F.K.]. Tr. by Ernst Kaiser and Eithne Wilkins. N.Y.: Schocken, 1954, 409 pp.
Die F	Die Fähre (Munich)
dis	dissertation
DM	Der Monat (Munich/Berlin/Frankfurt)
DS	Description of a Struggle [by F.K.]. Tr. by Tania and James Stern. N.Y.: Schocken, 1958
DU	Der Deutschunterricht (Stuttgart)
DUA	Deutschunterricht für Auslander (Munich)
DV	Deutsche Vierteljahresschrift für Literaturwissenschaft und Geistesgeschichte (Stuttgart)
ed	edited
EG	Etudes Germaniques. Revue trimestrelle de la Société des Etudes Germanique (Lyons/Paris)
Euphorion	Euphorion (Heidelberg)
Europe	Europe (Paris)
Explicator	Explicator (Virginia Commonwealth University, Richmond, Va.)
FK	Franz Kafka
FKM	Franz Kafka Miscellany. N.Y.: Twice a Year Press, 1940, 99 pp. (enlarged and revised 1946, 120 pp.)
FKT	Franz Kafka Today. Ed. by Angel Flores and

	Homer Swander. University of Wisconsin Press, 1958, 290 pp.; N.Y.: Gordian Press, 1976.
Fo	Focus One. Ed. by B. Rajan and Andrew Pearse. London: Dennis Dobson, 1945, 144 pp.
Genre	Genre (University of Illinois at Chicago).
GK	Ronald Gray (ed.): Kafka. A Collection of Critical Essays. Englewood Cliffs, N.J.: Prentice-Hall, 1962, 182 pp.
GLL	German Life and Letters (Oxford)
GN	Germanic Notes (Lexington, Ky.)
GP	Germanistica Pragensia (Prague)
GQ	German Quarterly (American Association of Teachers of German, Philadelphia, Pa.)
GR	The Germanic Review (Columbia University, N.Y.)
GRM	Germanisch-Romanische Monatsschrift (Heidelberg)
GW	The Great Wall of China. Stories and Reflections [by F.K.]. Tr. by Willa and Edwin Muir. N.Y.: Schocken, 1946, 315 pp.
H	Leo Hamalian (ed.): Franz Kafka. A Collection of Criticism. N.Y.: McGraw-Hill, 1974, 151 pp.
Hoch	Hochland (Munich)
JDSG	Jahrbuch der deutschen Schiller-Gesellschaft (Stuttgart)
JEGP	Journal of English and German Philology (University of Illinois, Urbana)
JRT	James Rolleston (ed.): *Kafka's "The Trial"*. Englewood Cliffs, N.J.: Prentice-Hall, 1976.
JWB	Jahrbuch der Wittheit zu Bremen (Bremen/ Hanover)
KD	Angel Flores (ed.): *The Kafka Debate*. N.Y.: Gordian Press, 1976
Kenyon	Kenyon Review (Gambier, Ohio)
KFLQ	Kentucky Foreign Language Quarterly (University of Kentucky, Lexington, Ky.) [now *KRom Q*]
KP	Angel Flores (ed.): *The Kafka Problem*. N.Y.:

	New Directions, 1946; N.Y.: Octagon Press, 1963; N.Y.: Gordian Press, 1975, 503 pp.
KS	Kafka-Symposion. Ed. by Jürgen Born, Malcolm Pasley, Paul Raabe and Klaus Wagenbach. Berlin: Verlag Klaus Wagenbach, 1965, 189 pp.
KuL	Kunst und Literatur (Berlin)
LuK	Literatur und Kritik (Vienna/Salzburg)
M	Metamorphosis and Other Stories [by F.K.]. Penguin Books, 1961, 1963, 1964, 1965, etc., 218 pp.
MAL	Modern Austrian Literary Journal of International Arthur Schnitzler Research (University of California at Riverside)
MdF	Mercure de France (Paris)
Merkur	Merkur: Deutsches Zeitschrift für europäisches Denken (Stuttgart).
MFS	Modern Fiction Studies (Purdue University, Lafayette, Ind.)
MLJ	Modern Language Journal (National Federation of Modern Language Teachers Association, Buffalo, N.Y.)
MLN	Modern Language Notes (Johns Hopkins University, Baltimore, Md.)
MLQ	Modern Language Quarterly (University of Washington, Seattle, Wash.)
MLR	Modern Language Review (King's College, London)
Monatshefte	Monatshefte für deutschen Unterricht, deutsche Sprache und Literatur (University of Wisconsin, Madison, Wisc.)
Morg	Der Morgen (Berlin)
Mosaic	Mosaic: A Journal of Comparative Study of Literature and Ideas (University of Manitoba, Winnipeg, Canada)
MR	Massachusetts Review (University of Massachusetts, Amherst)
NDH	Neue Deutsche Hefte (Berlin)

NDL	Neue Deutsche Literatur (Berlin/Weimar)
Neophilologus	Neophilologus (Groningen, Netherland)
Novel	Novel: A Forum on Fiction (Brown University, Providence, R.I.)
NR	Die Neue Rundschau (Berlin)
NRF	Nouvelle Revue Française (Paris)
NSR	Neue Schweizer Rundschau (Zurich)
OGS	Oxford German Studies (Oxford University)
P	Parables and Paradoxes [by F.K.]. Ed. by Nahum N. Glatzer. Tr. by Willa and Edwin Muir, and Clement Greenberg. N.Y.: Schocken, 1961 (7th printing 1970)
Part	Partisan Review (N.Y.)
PC	The Penal Colony. Stories and Short Pieces [by F.K.] Tr. by Willa and Edwin Muir. N.Y.: Schocken, 1948, 1949, etc. 320 pp.
PCLS	Proceedings of the Comparative Literature Symposium. Vol. IV Franz Kafka: His Place in World Literature. Lubbock: Texas: Texas Technological University, 1971, 174 pp.
PFK	H. Politzer (ed.): *Franz Kafka: Wege der Forschung*. Darmstadt: Wissenschaft Buchgesellschaft, 1973, 560 pp.
PJ	Angel Flores (ed.): *The Problem of "The Judgment,"* N.Y.: Gordian Press, 1976
PLL	Papers on Language and Literature (Southern Illinois University, Edwardsville, Ill.)
PMLA	Publications of the Modern Language Association of America (N.Y. and Menasha, Wis.)
pp	pages
PP	Philologica Pragensia (Academy of Sciences, Prague)
PPr	Pädagogische Provinz (Frankfurt)
PR	Franz Kafka aus Prager Sicht 1963. Prague: Verlag der Tschechoslowakischen Akademie der Wissenschaften, 1965, 305 pp.
PsR	Psychoanalytic Review (N.Y.)

QRL	Quarterly Review of Literature (Princeton, N.J.) [Vol. 2, No. 3, 1945]
rep	reprinted
rev	revised
RLC	Revue de Littérature Comparée (Paris)
RLMC	Rivista di Letterature Moderne e Comparate (Florence)
RLV	Revue de Langues Vivantes/Tijdschrift voor Levende Talen Brussels, Belgium)
RS	Research Studies (Washington State University)
Seminar	Seminar: A Journal of Germanic Studies (Victoria College, Toronto, and Newcastle University, New South Wales)
SG	Studi Germanici (Istituto Italiano di Studi Germanici, Rome)
SN	Studia Neophilologica: A Journal of Germanic and Romance Philology (Stockholm, Sweden)
SR	Schweizer Rundschau (Zurich)
SS	Selected Short Stories of Franz Kafka. Tr. by Willa and Edwin Muir. N.Y.: The Modern Library, 1952, 328 pp.
SSF	Studies in Short Fiction (Newberry College, S.C.)
SuF	Sinn und Form. Beiträge zur Literatur (Berlin, East Germany)
Sur	Sur (Buenos Aires)
SW1	Shorter Works. Vol. I [By F.K.]. Tr. and ed. by Malcolm Pasley. London: Secker & Warburg, 1974, 196 pp.
Sym	Symposium (Syracuse University, N.Y.)
SZ	Stimmen der Zeit (Freiburg)
TBL	Trial by Language. New Essays in Kafka Criticism. Ed. by Franz Kuna. London: Elek, 1976 [title changed to On Kafka. Semi-Centenary Perspectives.]
TCL	Twentieth Century Literature (Hofstra University, Hempstead, N.Y.)

Th	Thought. Fordham University Quarterly (N.Y.)
TM	Temps Modernes (Paris)
tr	translated
TR	Table Ronde (Paris)
TriQ	Tri-Quarterly (Northwestern University, Evanston, Ill.)
Triv	Trivium (Zurich)
TuK	Text und Kritik: Zeitschrift für Literatur (Munich)
typ dis	typewritten dissertation
Univ	Universitas (Stuttgart)
Wand	Die Wandlung (Heidelberg)
WB	Weimarer Beiträge (Weimar)
WoW	Wort und Wahrheit (Freiburg)
WSCL	Wisconsin Studies in Comparative Literature (University of Wisconsin, Madison, Wisc.)
WuW	Welt und Wort (Tübingen, Bad Wörishofen)
WW	Wirkendes Wort (Dusseldorf)
WZ	Wort in der Zeit (Vienna)
YFS	Yale French Studies (Yale University)
ZDP	Zeitschrift für Deutsche Philologie (Berlin)
ZRG	Zeitschrift für Religions- und Geistesgeschichte (Cologne)